ReFocus: The Films of João Pedro Rodrigues and
João Rui Guerra da Mata

ReFocus: The International Directors Series

Series Editors: Robert Singer, Stefanie Van de Peer, and Gary D. Rhodes

Board of advisors:
Lizelle Bisschoff (Glasgow University)
Stephanie Hemelryck Donald (University of Lincoln)
Anna Misiak (Falmouth University)
Des O'Rawe (Queen's University Belfast)

ReFocus is a series of contemporary methodological and theoretical approaches to the interdisciplinary analyses and interpretations of international film directors, from the celebrated to the ignored, in direct relationship to their respective culture—its myths, values, and historical precepts—and the broader parameters of international film history and theory.

Titles in the series include:

edinburghuniversitypress.com/series/refocint

ReFocus:
The Films of João Pedro Rodrigues and João Rui Guerra da Mata

Edited by José Duarte and Filipa Rosário

Edinburgh University Press is one of the leading university presses in the UK. We publish academic books and journals in our selected subject areas across the humanities and social sciences, combining cutting-edge scholarship with high editorial and production values to produce academic works of lasting importance. For more information visit our website: edinburghuniversitypress.com

Edinburgh University Press Ltd
The Tun—Holyrood Road
12 (2f) Jackson's Entry
Edinburgh EH8 8PJ

Typeset in 11/13 Ehrhardt MT by
IDSUK (DataConnection) Ltd, and
printed and bound by CPI Group (UK) Ltd,
Croydon, CR0 4YY

A CIP record for this book is available from the British Library

ISBN 978 1 4744 6080 4 (hardback)
ISBN 978 1 4744 6082 8 (webready PDF)
ISBN 978 1 4744 6083 5 (epub)

Contents

Figures

Notes on Contributors

Julián Daniel Gutiérrez Albilla is Professor of Spanish and Portuguese and Comparative Literature at the University of Southern California. His research focuses on feminist and queer theory in Iberian and Latin American cinema. He has co-edited a volume with Parvati Nair dedicated to Spanish and Latin American women filmmakers, and another volume with Rob Stone on Luis Buñuel. His first book focused on the Spanish and Mexican cinema of Luis Buñuel. He is the author of *Aesthetics, Ethics, and Trauma in the Cinema of Pedro Almodóvar* (Edinburgh University Press, 2017). Gutiérrez Albilla translated Bracha Ettinger's feminist psychoanalytic work into Spanish for GEDISA, an academic press in Barcelona. He is currently working on a monograph on the (re)presentation of fragility: vulnerable bodies and subjectivities in Iberian performance art and cinema, which includes a chapter on mourning, finitude, and aging in *To Die Like a Man*.

Fran Benavente is Associate Professor of Audiovisual Communication at Pompeu Fabra University (Spain), where he teaches History of Audiovisual Genres, and Theory and Analysis of TV Fiction. He is also a lecturer for the Master's degree program in Contemporary Film and Audiovisual Studies. As a film and television critic, he has been a member of several magazine editorial boards. He is the author of the book *El héroe trágico del western. El género y sus límites* (*The tragic hero in westerns. Genre and its limits*, 2017) and co-editor of the book *Poéticas del gesto en el cine europeo contemporáneo* (*Poetics of gesture in contemporary European cinema*, 2013). Benavente is part of UPF's CINEMA research group. He has also been published in numerous academic journals and movie magazines and has collaborated in a considerable number of books on cinema and serial fiction. His latest research is focused on the study of political structure of images and representation strategies of history in contemporary cinema, most specifically in European and Spanish cinema; on the analysis of the imagery and aesthetic trends in Contemporary Portuguese Cinema; and on the study of tendencies and innovations of contemporary television fiction.

José Bértolo holds a PhD from the University of Lisbon in a joint program with KU Leuven and the University of Bologna, and he is a researcher at the University of Lisbon Center for Comparative Studies. He is the author of *Imagens em Fuga: Os Fantasmas de François Truffaut* (*Images on the Run: The Ghosts of François Truffaut*, 2016), *Sobreimpressões: Leituras de Filmes* (*Superimpositions: Film Readings*, 2019), and *Espectros do Cinema: Manoel de Oliveira e João Pedro Rodrigues* (*Specters of Cinema: Manoel de Oliveira and João Pedro Rodrigues*, 2020), and co-editor of *A Escrita do Cinema: Ensaios* (2015), *Morte e Espectralidade nas Artes e na Literatura* (*Death and Spectrality in Art and Literature*, with F. Guerreiro, 2019), and *Imitações da Vida: Cinema Clássico Americano* (*Imitations of Life: Classical Hollywood Film*, with C. Rowland and F. Guerreiro, 2020).

Carlos Alberto Carrilho lives and works in Lisbon. He studied Economics (UNL-FE), Drawing and Painting (Ar.Co) and Visual Arts (Maumaus). Currently, he is taking his Master's degree in Cinema at FCSH-UN. Since 2008, he has worked with Maumaus as Head of Administration and Artistic Direction Assistant of the International Residency Program and of the Lumiar Cité exhibition space, organizing and producing publications, lectures, seminars, films, artistic residencies and exhibitions, including: Gabriel Abrantes, Judith Barry, Manthia Diawara, Loretta Fahrenholz, Harun Farocki, David Hammons, Renée Green, Florian Hecker, Sarat Maharaj, Allan Sekula, and Albert Serra. Between 2015 and 2019 he was a founding member and programmer of the cinema collective White Noise. Carrilho has participated in lectures, discussions and publications about cinema. Since 2016, he has been a regular collaborator of the cinema website *À pala de Walsh*.

António Fernando Cascais is Professor of Communication Sciences at the NOVA University of Lisbon, Portugal. He was coordinator of the R&D projects *Models and Practices of Science Communication in Portugal* (2004–9) and *History of the Visual Culture of Medicine in Portugal* (2009–13). He edited issues 38 ("Mediation of Knowledge"), 33 ("Body, Technology, Subjectivities"), and 19 ("Michel Foucault. An Analytics of Experience") of the *Journal of Communication and Languages*. He was also the editor of *Hospital Miguel Bombarda 1968* (2016), *Olhares sobre a Cultura Visual da Medicina em Portugal* (2014), *Queer Film and Culture. Queer Lisboa International Queer Film* (2014), *Lei, Segurança, Disciplina. Trinta anos depois de Vigiar e punir de Michel Foucault*

(2009), *Indisciplinar a teoria* (2004), and *A SIDA por um fio* (1997). He has published over 200 essays on the Mediation of Knowledge, Philosophy of Technology and the Body, Foucauldian Studies and Queer Studies, and the Visual Culture of Medicine, Biopolitics and Bioethics.

Olivier Cheval is a visual artist, filmmaker, and film teacher. He is the author of *Le Partage de la douleur. Une Impolitique du film* (2018). He writes regularly on cinema, art, literature, and politics for French reviews and currently teaches plastic art at the University of Paris VIII.

Caterina Cucinotta holds a degree and a Master's in Artistic Studies in Italy (Palermo and Bologna), and a PhD in Film Studies (2015) from NOVA University of Lisbon. Since 2017, she has been an integrated researcher at the Institute of Contemporary History (IHC) of the same university, developing a post-doctorate project on "Costumes and Space Texture: Design and Art in the last 50 years of Portuguese Cinema" with an FCT (Fundação para a Ciência e a Tecnologia) grant. In 2018 she published the book *Viagem ao Cinema através do seu Vestuário* (*Journey into cinema through its costumes*). Since 2010, she has published texts in scientific journals in Portugal and abroad on the connections between fashion and clothes on films, with particular attention to the Portuguese context and its problematics. She has also co-edited a special issue of *ANIKI* dedicated to "Materiality in Portuguese Cinema: aesthetics, practices and techniques" (2021).

José Duarte teaches cinema at the School of Arts and Humanities (University of Lisbon). He is a researcher at ULICES (University of Lisbon Centre for English Studies) and his essays have been published in several international journals. He co-edited the volume *Cinematic Narratives: Transatlantic Perspectives* (2017) and, with Timothy Corrigan, *The Global Road Movie: Alternative Journeys Around the World* (2018).

Rita Gomes Ferrão lives and works in Lisbon. She holds a degree in Painting from the Faculty of Fine Arts (FBAUL-UL) and a Postgraduate Studies and Diploma of Advanced Studies in History of Contemporary Art (FCSH-UNL). Currently, she is a PhD candidate and collaborator Researcher at the Art History Institute (IHA-FCSH-UNL). As an artist, she has participated in several national and international exhibitions, since the beginning of the 1990s and worked as assistant of the Belgian artist Françoise Schein, between 1996 and 1999. As a researcher, Ferrão has collaborated on several books, being the author of *Querubim Lapa: Primeira Obra Cerâmica 1954–1974* (2015), *Hansi Staël: Cerâmica, Modernidade e Tradição* (2014), and of numerous articles and essays on design, film, and contemporary art. As a curator, she has been responsible for several exhibitions of modern and contemporary art, design, and ceramics held at Portuguese museums and galleries.

Andrija Filipović is Associate Professor at the Faculty of Media and Communications, Singidunum University in Belgrade, Serbia. He is the author of *Conditio ahumana: Immanence and ahuman in the Anthropocene* (2019), and monographs on Gilles Deleuze (2015) and Brian Massumi (2016). His work has appeared in *Sexualities, Contemporary Social Science, Journal of Homosexuality, NORMA: International Journal for Masculinity Studies, Philosophy and Society*, and a number of edited volumes. His research interests include environmental humanities, contemporary continental philosophy and aesthetics, and queer theory. He is Executive Editor of *AM: Journal of Art and Media Studies*.

Hyemin Kim (they/them) holds a PhD in Comparative Literature from SUNY Buffalo with a specialization in avant-garde poetics and continental philosophy. Their current research centers around non/human mythopoetics and queer aesthetics in twentieth- and twenty-first-century artists' literature, books, and cinema. In that direction, their writings have appeared in *Millennium Film Journal*, Black Mountain College Museum and Arts Center, *Desistfilm*, and *Full Stop*, among others. They are currently writing a book on the intersection of poetry and cinema. Hyemin Kim currently teaches in the English Department at Baruch, CUNY.

Filipa Rosário is a Research Fellow at the Center for Comparative Studies, University of Lisbon (CEC-UL), where she teaches Portuguese Cinema and Film Analysis. She is the President of AIM—The Association of the Moving Image Researchers (Portugal) and the coordinator of THELEME, CEC-UL's Interart and Intermedia Studies Group. Rosário is the principal investigator of the research cluster "Cinema and the World—Studies in Space and Cinema" (CEC-UL) and the author of *O Trabalho do Actor no Cinema de John Cassavetes* (2017). She co-edited the book *New Approaches to Cinematic Spaces* (2019).

Glòria Salvadó-Corretger is Associate Professor of Audiovisual Communication Studies at Pompeu Fabra University in Barcelona (Spain). Her PhD is in Audiovisual Communication, specializing in Contemporary Portuguese Cinema. She is a member of the university's CINEMA research group, as well as a lecturer for the Audiovisual Communication undergraduate degree program and the Contemporary Film and Audiovisual Studies Master's degree program. Her published work includes contributions to academic journals and collaborative books, both national and international, on subjects such as Portuguese contemporary cinema, European and Spanish cinema, TV fiction, new forms of serial fiction and on the works of Joaquín Jordà. She is the author of the book *Espectres del cinema portugués contemporani* (*Spectres of contemporary Portuguese cinema*, 2012), and co-editor of *Poéticas del gesto en el cine europeo contemporáneo* (*Poetics of gesture in contemporary European cinema*, 2013). Her latest research is focused on the aesthetic tendencies and history of Portuguese, Spanish, and European cinema; and on trends, imagery, aesthetics and new formats of contemporary television, particularly in its serial fiction forms.

Juan Antonio Suárez is a Professor in English Studies at the University of Murcia. He is the author of *Bike Boys, Drag Queens, and Superstars* (1997), *Pop Modernism* (2007) and *Jim Jarmusch* (2007) and the co-editor of *Culture, Space, and Power: Blurred Lines* (2015), *The Spatial Politics of Contemporary Fiction* (2017) and *Reimaginar la disidencia sexual en la España de los 70* (2019). Recent essays have appeared in *Grey Room*, *Screen*, *L'Atalante*, *The Journal of Cinema and Media Studies*, and in edited collections such as *The Modernist World* (eds Ross and Lindgren, 2015) and *The Music and Sound of Experimental Cinema* (eds Rogers and Barham, 2017). He is currently completing the book *Experimental Film and Queer Materiality*.

Acknowledgments

The Films of João Pedro Rodrigues and João Rui Guerra da Mata stemmed from our will to contribute to the international reception of both directors' film and art works, by focusing on the thematic, stylistic, aesthetic, theoretical, and conceptual recurrences and discourses their works animate. These have inspired us deeply. We would like to thank João Pedro Rodrigues and João Rui Guerra da Mata for the generosity, kindness, and grace they have granted us at every stage of this volume's development.

We are very grateful to Robert Singer, Stefanie Van de Peer, and Gary Rhodes, the ReFocus series editors, whose enthusiasm and endorsement since the very beginning of this project were truly encouraging, while literally making us smile in every email exchange. We would also like to thank Gillian Leslie at Edinburgh University Press for her continuous support. We are very thankful to the contributors to this book—an amazing group of scholars— who have always promptly delivered, even when the COVID-19 pandemic put our plans temporarily on hold.

Thank you to Sofia Mira Ferreira and Margarida Louro, of the Center for Comparative Studies of the University of Lisbon, for their never-failing assistance, as well as their problem-solving agility. We also thank Rhian Atkin for the volume's linguistic review and Marta Lisboa for its index. We are grateful to Leonor Noivo for allowing us to use her photograph on the cover of the book.

On a more personal note, José Duarte and Filipa Rosário would also like to thank to Ana Bela Morais and Mariana Liz, for their friendship and support at key moments, and in-between them.

This work is financed by national funds through the FCT—Fundação para a Ciência e a Tecnologia, I.P.—under the project UIDB/00509/2020.

Introduction: Nonconformities and Unconventional, Unreal Liberties—The Cinema of João Pedro Rodrigues and João Rui Guerra da Mata

José Duarte and Filipa Rosário

In April 2020, during the six-week lockdown imposed by the Portuguese government at the beginning of the COVID-19 pandemic, João Pedro Rodrigues shot *Turdus merula Linnaeus, 1758*,[1] a fourteen-minute-long film documenting the first days of a new-born common blackbird. The film opens with images of the birds' eggs placed in a cup-shaped nest that had been built by the breeding parents in a privet hedge in front of Rodrigues and Guerra da Mata's apartment in Lisbon. It is a sequence of fixed shots covering the first weeks, gestures, and actions of the naked and blind chick, punctuated by black cards giving date information. The last date to be presented—25 April—introduces footage of a grown chick, quite large, in its hatching nest, followed by images of the same nest in its now unoccupied state. The common blackbird flew the nest on the same day that, forty-six years before, a military coup in Lisbon had deposed the dictatorial *Estado Novo* (New State) regime, putting an end to the Portuguese colonial wars in Africa and enabling a democratic Portugal to emerge in Europe.

The soundtrack of the film includes direct sounds from the directors' domestic space (passages of dialogue, noises, diegetic music playing tracks from the French director Guy Gilles's films), as well as non-diegetic Portuguese music. More specifically, we hear the two songs that in 1974 secretly signaled the start of the coup to the rebel military officers who enacted it: Paulo de Carvalho's "E Depois do Adeus," and "Grândola, Vila Morena," which was written and performed by the influential political singer-songwriter José Afonso. During the spring lockdown, at 3pm on 25 April 2020, "Grândola, Vila Morena" was played on loudspeakers and in homes across Lisbon, in a celebratory, symbolic gesture performed by those who, due to the pandemic, could not commemorate the historical landmark on the streets as they usually would. The last scene of *Turdus merula Linnaeus, 1758* mixes ornithological documentary with historical momentum in a home movie that has cinephile and queer melodramatic resonances, and which simultaneously reflects on the pandemic-related condition of self-isolation. Like the bird, Portugal broke free in 1974 to move towards democracy, and like the bird, we hope soon to be free of the confinement caused by the COVID-19 virus. In this film, the prosaic meets the extraordinary through narrative economy, and its subversive power stems also from the genre-defying logic of the movie: such is the rule of the game in the films of João Pedro Rodrigues and João Rui Guerra da Mata.

All sorts of transits—gender, geographical, existential, genre—govern the creative universe of the award-winning partnership between director João Pedro Rodrigues (b. 1966) and art director and director João Rui Guerra da Mata (b. 1966).[2] Together, they have collaborated on five feature films: *O Fantasma* (*Phantom*, 2000), *Odete* (*Two Drifters*, 2005), *Morrer Como um Homem* (*To Die Like a Man*, 2009), *A Última Vez Que Vi Macau* (*The Last Time I Saw Macao*, 2012), and *O Ornitólogo* (*The Ornithologist*, 2016). The majority of these films were directed by Rodrigues with art direction by Guerra da Mata, except for *The Last Time I Saw Macao*, which was co-directed by the pair. Their partnership extends to all of the other film and art projects that they have produced individually, such as short films (documentary, experimental, and fiction films),[3] as well as to several works and installations for museums and galleries. For instance, they each acted in the other's short film (Rodrigues's *Parabéns!* [*Happy Birthday!*, 1997] cast Guerra da Mata, while Guerra da Mata's *O Que Arde Cura* [*As the Flames Rose*, 2012] cast Rodrigues), and they have been writers, cinematographers, and/or editors of the films that they have co-directed (*China, China*, 2007; *Alvorada Vermelha* [*Red Dawn*, 2011]; *The Last Time I Saw Macao*; *Mahjong*, 2013, and *Iec Long*, 2015).

THE "SMALL CINEMA" OF RODRIGUES AND GUERRA DA MATA

The filmic and artistic production of Rodrigues and Guerra da Mata is the result of a creative partnership lasting more than twenty years, in which Rodrigues mainly directs and Guerra da Mata is predominantly in charge of the art direction of the films. *ReFocus: The Films of João Pedro Rodrigues and João Rui Guerra da Mata* envisions the pair as artists whose authorship can be traced in the thematic and stylistic consistency of their films, which ultimately express both of their individual personalities in a collectively produced art form. Moreover, their worldviews, affinities, and sensibilities imbue their body of work with a thematic, formal, and narrative unity that is appreciated internationally. *Phantom* premiered in the Official Competition at the 2000 Venice International Film Festival, while Rodrigues's short film *Happy Birthday!* had received a Special Mention from the jury of the same festival in 1997. *To Die Like a Man* premiered at the 2009 Cannes Film Festival as part of the official selection for *Un Certain Regard*, having also won the Best Feature Film category at the 2010 BAFICI—Buenos Aires International Festival of Independent Cinema. *The Ornithologist* was awarded the Golden Leopard for Best Direction at the 2016 Locarno Film Festival, while Guerra da Mata's *As the Flames Rose* was the recipient of the Pardi di Domani at the 2012 edition of the same festival.

Rodrigues and Guerra da Mata's films continue to be screened internationally, with retrospectives taking place worldwide. In 2013, the film critic Shinsuke Ohdera organized an itinerant retrospective of Rodrigues's works in Kawasaki, Tokyo, and Osaka (Japan). Two years later, in 2015, Rodrigues and Guerra da Mata's films were presented at the BAMcinématek in New York City and at the Harvard Film Archive (Cambridge, MA); and, in 2016, the Centre Pompidou (Paris, France) honored Rodrigues with a complete retrospective and an exhibition of installations. In the following year, the Instituto Moreira Salles in Rio de Janeiro (Brazil) also organized a retrospective on Rodrigues, as did the MALBA—Latin American Art Museum of Buenos Aires (Argentina) in 2018.[4]

Film festivals, art-house theaters, and cinephile audiences have long appreciated Rodrigues and Guerra da Mata's oeuvre. Together with the works of Pedro Costa and Miguel Gomes, among others, this positive reception has placed contemporary Portuguese cinema on the international stage, despite the country's industrial and cultural marginality in global terms,[5] as well as its ever-constrained national film industry.[6] In her discussion of Portugal's status in international film coproductions, Mariana Liz points out that:

> Struggle, survival and resistance are key terms for the study of contemporary Portuguese film. They are also central to the definition of 'cinema of the small nations'—a particular productive framework to understand contemporary Portuguese cinema. [. . .] Portugal follows most of the criteria Mette Hjort and Duncan Petrie (2007) list as characterizing "small nations", including having a limited geographical area (92,391 km²), population (c. 10 million inhabitants) and internal market; low GDP; and limited influence in the world, which leads it to seek partnerships with other nations—within Europe, as a member of the European Union (EU), and globally, with former colonies in Africa, Asia and Latin America. [. . .]
>
> To examine Portugal's cinema through the "small nation" lens is to assume that producing films in Portugal is not only about making the most of the opportunities that arise from structural limitations, but also

about engaging in consistent resistance to cultural homogeneity. Being the cinema of a small nation has consequences for the form and content of contemporary Portuguese film.[7]

Contemporary Portuguese cinema is low-budget, artisanal, transnational, cosmopolitan, and sophisticated; it is "one of the richest and most distinctive film cultures in the world," argues Dennis Lim.[8] The ways in which filmmakers combine documentary with fiction in a poetic, intellectual, and groundbreaking way, while remaining conscious of the neoliberal world order and of Portugal's own symbolic place within it, has granted this national cinema a distinct, albeit heterogeneous, global appeal, and has won it international critical recognition.[9]

This volume questions issues of spatiality, marginality, and intertextuality, and examines the films, artistic practices, and labors that have placed Rodrigues and Guerra da Mata's idiosyncratic films within the cinema world-system. A key contribution to this achievement is the way in which the works of Rodrigues and Guerra da Mata, more or less assertively, address questions such as globalization, national and transnational identities, cosmopolitanism, diaspora, and postcolonialism from the perspective of a peripheral "small nation," condensing in those questions three distinct operative forces: queerness, spatial thought, and cinephilia.

QUEERNESS, SPATIAL THOUGHT, AND CINEPHILIA

Rodrigues and Guerra da Mata's films are about queer ways of being in the world. They create queer worlds, yet their characters "are developed as individuals instead of intending to be a staple representation of groups/ categories,"[10] and "they do not constitute a collective entity (or identity)."[11] This analysis by Antônio M. da Silva of Rodrigues's *Phantom, Two Drifters*, and *To Die Like a Man* may be applied more broadly to both filmmakers' individual and collective works, and may in turn explain why their films are more likely to be screened in world cinema venues than in LGBTQ+ film festivals. In this respect, the international reception of Rodrigues and Guerra da Mata is comparable to that of the Thai director Apichatpong Weerasethakul, who "is regarded as gay, and his artistic practice is understood as queer. However, he has been embraced in the West by mainstream critics and proponents of art cinema as an international auteur."[12] Our intention in this book is precisely to present Rodrigues and Guerra da Mata as international *auteurs*, through an examination of the structuring forces of their oeuvre that include, but are not limited to, queerness, spatial thought, and cinephilia.

The (anti-)heroes of Rodrigues and Guerra da Mata's feature films are postclassic, marginal, lonely characters whose queer individualized subjectivities deepen the peripheral essence of their trajectories all the more. Their stories are anchored in the narrative structure of classic cinema. *Phantom* tells the story of a gay night-time garbage collector who withdraws from conventional existence and is transformed into a creature who dresses in black latex, is moved by sexual desire, and lives in a dumpster on the outskirts of Lisbon, Portugal. In *Two Drifters*, Odete becomes the dead gay man with whom she has been obsessed, while *To Die Like a Man* focuses on the final months of a dying, sixty-year-old drag performer who cancels her sex change operation in order to die as she was born, like a man. *The Last Time I Saw Macao* is the neo-noir story of the journey of a former inhabitant of that city, who encounters contemporary Macao as a rearranged, dystopian—even if realistically portrayed—city. Finally, in *The Ornithologist*, a birdwatcher dies in the wilderness and is reincarnated as St. Anthony of Padua.

The films deal with topics such as the (eroticized male) body,[13] identity, life, and death. These topics and realms are combined in the filmmakers' oeuvre to such an extent that all of the worlds portrayed in it in some way resonate with concepts such as nonconformity, the unconventional, unreal liberties, transference, and transcendence. The dramatic and melodramatic contours of the characters' lives and experiences code these ideas in such a way as to generate the in-between places and thresholds where characters are located. Consequently, their identities are defined by these in-between states—the "neither," as Rachel ten Haaf[14] terms it—that are originated by transfiguration and metamorphosis, as well as by the mystery surrounding those states. A transformative drive towards a territory located elsewhere, beyond, resides in their queer, cinephile, spatial film-world; this is Rodrigues and Guerra da Mata's film trope *par excellence*. Nonetheless, Rodrigues states that "place is where the dramatic idea of the scene is born,"[15] and indeed, he has filmed in Lisbon,[16] Macao, and, more recently, the wilderness.

On a textual level, the structuring forces of Rodrigues and Guerra da Mata's work stem from the mysterious, even if familiar, spaces and places that their films map. They build a fantasy-themed but realistic diegetic universe where characters, animals, and even space itself can be transmuted. It is a world in which cinephilia and self-reflexivity operate: iconic (transnational) filmic references are incorporated within the characters' identities and experiences, as well as in the settings of the films, their atmospheres and, ultimately, the concepts and political perspectives that they present. For instance, in *Two Drifters*, Olivier Père acknowledges that:

[i]ndeed, the filmmaker draws on a heterogeneous range of references. He continually shifts between an almost Bressonian rigour (using mod-

els more than actors) and the flamboyant lyricism of Douglas Sirk's melodramas, the sober fantasy of Jacques Tourneur and the dreamlike, operatic baroque of Werner Schroeter's films. [. . .] *Odete* is part of a particular tradition of fantasy-melodrama in which love triumphs over death, lovers love beyond the grave, beyond the borders of dream and reality, life and death. One cannot help but think of *The Ghost and Mrs. Muir, Peter Ibbetson, Portrait of Jennie*.

The shadow of *Vertigo* is also felt hovering throughout João Pedro Rodrigues' film, which is suffused with an atmosphere of morbid fetishism. The film might well be entitled "d'entre les morts," as was the French novel by Boileau and Narcejac that inspired the Hitchcock masterpiece.[17]

The Last Time I Saw Macao also invokes film history with a neo-noir atmosphere that can be considered a postmodern rewriting of Josef von Sternberg and Nicholas Ray's *Macao* (1952), while at the same time it is a film that explores a postcolonial discourse on the former Portuguese colony. Iván Villarmea Álvarez suggests that the film is based on the confrontation between Macao's colonial past and postcolonial present. This contradiction is inhabited by Guerra da Mata's character: a displaced subject who can only recognize familiar places through memory.[18] Haden Guest concurs, noting that the directors "turn to film genres not as postmodern citation, but as lenses through which to reimagine Macao and its history, openly pointing to cinema itself as crucial to the exoticization and, ultimately, colonization of the Far East as a cultural imaginary."[19]

By creating their own autonomous thematic and theoretical frameworks, these two distinctly cinephile tropes make Rodrigues and Guerra da Mata's narratives conceptually more complex. Nonetheless, at the centers of these narratives lie the unceasing, plot-commanding, operative, and transformative force that all their works have in common, and which forms a vibrant, tragic universe in which life/presence cannot be separated, nor distinguished, from death/absence.

THE FILMS OF JOÃO PEDRO RODRIGUES AND JOÃO RUI GUERRA DA MATA

ReFocus: The Films of João Pedro Rodrigues and João Rui Guerra da Mata is the first scholarly volume to be published internationally to examine the themes outlined above. The analytical and theoretical approaches of the various chapters contained herein depart from the texts and contexts of the films, and as a whole, the volume significantly expands what is currently a very restricted field of scholarship on these two transnational Portuguese filmmakers.

While some scholarly attention has been given to Rodrigues and Guerra da Mata in Portuguese, French, and English, the small body of criticism available is disproportionate to the importance and magnitude of the directors' body of work and its reception. Nonetheless, the following studies have had a noteworthy impact. *Le jardin des Fauves: Conversations avec Antoine Barraud* (2016) presents João Pedro Rodrigues's thoughts and opinions on his films. *De Casa em Casa—Sobre um Encontro entre Etnografia e Cinema* (2011) by Filomena Silvano, gives an interesting account of the films *Esta É a Minha Casa* (*This Is My Home*, 1997) and *Viagem à Expo* (*Journey to Expo*, 1998)—with the author accompanying Rodrigues and Guerra da Mata in the making of the films. Finally, José Bértolo's book, which derives from his PhD thesis and is entitled *Espectros do Cinema: Manoel de Oliveira e João Pedro Rodrigues* (2020), is partially dedicated to Rodrigues and Guerra da Mata and provides a comparative study that analyzes the work of the two Portuguese filmmakers.

Apart from these volumes, a limited number of scholarly articles that focus exclusively on Rodrigues and Guerra da Mata's feature and short films have been published in English, such as: Antônio da Silva, "The Portuguese Queer Screen: Gender Possibilities in João Pedro Rodrigues' Cinematic Production" (2014); Jimmy Weaver, "Ghosts of Macau: *The Last Time I Saw Macao*'s haunting transnational performance" (2016) and "Sirens and Flames: The Short Films of João Pedro Rodrigues & João Rui Guerra da Mata" (2019); John Mercer, "The Love That Dare Not Speak Its Name: *O Fantasma* and Erotomania" (2017), which was published in the collection *Tainted Love: Screening Sexual Perversion*; and Rachel ten Haaf, "Exploring the Neither in João Pedro Rodrigues and João Rui Guerra da Mata's *A última vez que vi Macau*" (2017). While all of these publications attest to the importance given to the directors by critics, film festivals, or curators, they somehow restrict the possibilities of fully understanding and experiencing their films. Although it is not the purpose of this introduction to present an exhaustive list of all of the studies on Rodrigues and Guerra da Mata, those mentioned here comprise a valuable contribution to the growing scholarly interest in the work of these directors in particular, and in Portuguese cinema in general.

In this sense, and taking into account the purpose of the *ReFocus* series, this edited collection presents a focused, interdisciplinary, multi-authored study that aims at positioning these two international directors at the center, rather than at the margins of cinematic discourse. Moreover, by tackling and offering an overview of all of Rodrigues and Guerra da Mata's works, we aim to provide a critical historical portrait that represents the different aspects of the directors' work that, concomitantly, built their worldview. As such, the volume refreshes and deepens scholarly discussion of these contemporary directors.

This book is comprised of ten chapters dedicated to the study of Rodrigues and Guerra da Mata's works, from feature films to short films to art installations, and an interview investigating the cinematic world of these directors.

These texts are presented in four interrelated parts. Part 1—"Queer (Dis) Placements, Exquisite Bodies"—opens with Fran Benavente's and Glòria Salvadó-Corretger's "Sculpting the Body, Sculpting History." These authors offer a comprehensive view of the body in short and medium-length films such as *O Corpo de Afonso* (*The King's Body*, 2012) and *China, China*, as well as in installations. Their study illuminates our understanding of the importance of the body throughout Rodrigues and Guerra da Mata's work, and particularly in *The Ornithologist*. The authors connect several of directors' films via the body, which they use as a starting point for a deeper consideration of cinema and ultimately history. This approach is especially relevant when we consider Rodrigues's affirmation in an interview that all of his films reflect how he "lived in the world at the time [he] made them."[20]

The importance of the body is likewise central to Olivier Cheval's chapter, "The Injury: On *Pathosformel* in João Pedro Rodrigues's Work." Cheval takes as his point of departure the films that comprise what he defines as "The Trilogy of the Flesh"—*Phantom*, *Two Drifters*, and *To Die Like a Man*. He applies Aby Warburg's concept of *pathosformel* in order to understand how these three films and *The Ornithologist* all stem from the same trope: a kiss on a wound. Through this approach, Cheval explores how the trope of the kiss figures as a representation of the unique way in which queer bodies meet the Christian utopia of a single flesh.

In Chapter 3, "Love is Stronger than Death: João Pedro Rodrigues's *Two Drifters* and the Ghost(s) of Manoel de Oliveira," José Bértolo delves into the aesthetic cinematic relationship between three films by the great Portuguese master and João Pedro Rodrigues's *Two Drifters*. Bértolo's comparative analysis completes and complements the findings of the two previous chapters with regard to the significance of cinema as a medium for the creation and transformation of reality and, consequently, of the characters that inhabit the cinematic world. As such, the ghost(s) (stories) to which the chapter title refers to express "cinema's deeply unstable nature," while at the same time they allude to the real/unreal corporeal dimension of Odete, the protagonist of *Two Drifters*.

In addition to the (queer) body, cinema and the cinematic landscape are other crucial dimensions of the directors' work. The spaces and places that they occupy are essential to the characterization of Rodrigues and Guerra da Mata's characters. These spaces and places also provide a means of understanding what drives them to direct these films and tell these specific stories, which are not only personal and national, but also universal and transnational.

As filmmakers, Rodrigues and Guerra da Mata belong to a generation that has focused the majority of its films on national themes. At the same time, these directors elevate the films to a different level, as Tiago Baptista has stated.[21] Mariana Liz explains further: "The generation of filmmakers coming to prominence in this decade portrays people in Portugal not as Portuguese people, but as people; stories taking place in Portugal are featured on screen not as Portuguese stories, but as stories."[22] In her explanation of some of the new features of contemporary cinema, Liz also mentions that Portuguese cinema is connected increasingly with other cultures and (national) cinemas.

Location and dialogue between spaces, whether they are real, unreal, or cinematic, is key to understanding Rodrigues and Guerra da Mata's films. The five chapters presented in Part 2—"Cinematic Landscapes and Territories"—therefore focus on the exploration and representation of the spaces and places of the directors' films. Andrija Filipović, "Phantoms, Drifters, and Desiring Saints: Landscapes, Soundscapes, and Becoming-queer in the Films of João Pedro Rodrigues and João Rui Guerra da Mata," António Fernando Cascais, "Queer Metamorphoses and Displacements in the Cinema of João Pedro Rodrigues and João Rui Guerra da Mata" and Hyemin Kim, "Neo-Baroque Landscapes: João Pedro Rodrigues's Docu-fiction and Ecosophical Kinships in *The Ornithologist*" form an (involuntary) trilogy of chapters on space and becoming.

In Chapter 4, Andrija Filipović analyzes the specific image of becoming-queer that is presented in Rodrigues and Guerra da Mata's films. His analysis of both landscape and soundscape in the directors' work is founded on the theories of Agamben and Deleuze and Guattari. Filipović demonstrates how characters' bodies are opened up to specific environments that go beyond the "traditional division between human and non-human," thus questioning any kind of "linear, stable, world." In this respect, his reading is consistent with the chapters in the first part of this volume.

António Fernando Cascais's chapter also focuses on the idea of becoming, and especially on the concept of metamorphosis. He follows a line of inquiry that examines identity changes against the spatial background of the films *Phantom*, *To Die Like a Man*, *Two Drifters*, and *The Ornithologist*, in order to reveal how characters and their bodies undergo drastic transformations precisely because of the (corporeal) relation with the surrounding space.

Like Filipović and Cascais's studies, Hyemin Kim's chapter examines the landscape-centered ethno-fiction that characterizes *The Ornithologist*. The author's investigation seeks to understand the many symbolic layers of which the film is composed: whether Kim is discussing fiction and documentary, or the natural and the human, this author points towards ecosophical kinships that contribute to an understanding of the world beyond traditional views. Indeed, Alvalade, the Bairro Alto, Lisbon, Macao, and the wilderness are all places of "desire and despair,"[23] but they are mostly places of transformation, and they allow or contribute to the (in)visibility of the characters who inhabit them.

Chapter 7 is also dedicated to the importance of landscape and territories, and pertinently focuses on the filmic/real territories that represent the possibility of presence and absence, continuity and rupture, or memory and void. In "Failure, Erasure, and Oblivion in João Pedro Rodrigues and João Rui Guerra da Mata's Asian Trilogy: *Red Dawn, The Last Time I Saw Macao,* and *Iec Long,*" Juan Antonio Suárez explores the films comprising the "Asian Trilogy" through an examination of how failure and elision can produce "alternative paths of desire and cognition." His focus on these less widely studied films paves the way for further research on the work of Rodrigues and Guerra da Mata.

In "Space and Memory: The Window as Freeze-frame," Carlos Alberto Carrilho and Rita Gomes Ferrão provide an analytical connection with Part I of this volume, and construct a bridge to the ideas developed in Part 3. The chapter develops the discussion of the relationship between cinema and the city, and explores the specific case of Portugal and of Rodrigues and Guerra da Mata's personal and professional trajectories during the cultural transformation that has taken place since the end of the dictatorship in 1974. This chapter deepens our understanding of the directors' experience, and makes a vital contribution to this volume as it "seeks to decipher the domestic and urban territories that exist off-screen in Rodrigues and Guerra da Mata's works."

The majority of the authors in this volume discuss the corporeality of Rodrigues and Guerra da Mata's films, and the final two chapters share a close affinity with the preceding sections. "Artistic Practices" examines the material profilmic elements that compose and code the directors' auteurist universe. Caterina Cucinotta deals specifically with scenery and props, costume, make-up, and objects in her chapter, "New Frontiers in Art Direction: João Guerra da Mata's Contribution to Portuguese Cinema as a Case Study." She explores Guerra da Mata's importance as an art director for the feature films directed by Rodrigues. In her study, not only does Cucinotta acknowledge the creative force of the duo, but she also recognizes and underlines the significance of the material environments that exist in the films.

Similarly, Filipa Rosário goes beyond purely filmic creations in her chapter, "Other Landscapes: On the Expanded Cinema of João Pedro Rodrigues and João Rui Guerra da Mata." This final chapter considers the works that the directors have developed for galleries, and the "white cube." The chapter analyzes the materials that are intimately connected with the directors' oeuvre, such as the video installations of the casting for *Phantom.* In the process, Rosário's work returns us to the very beginning of our discussion, to *Turdus merula Linnaeus, 1758,* and to the playful, defiant condition not only of the films directed by Rodrigues and Guerra da Mata, but also to the other works that the directors have made, created, or curated. In this respect, Rosário's work brings us full circle, referring us back to Chapter 1.

This volume does not seek to view or present the two directors' work as a whole. Indeed, Rodrigues himself has advised that such an approach should be avoided:

I don't like to see my body of work as a whole; I think each film is different. But there are connections, of course: while my first feature was about a lonely garbage collector, and it focused on one actor, *The Ornithologist* is also about a lonely figure and his adventures in nature. I think there is a cycle that's been more or less closed now, from *O Fantasma* to *The Ornithologist*, which both concentrate on one figure, one actor.[24]

However, the book does seek to locate the visual, aesthetic, and thematic entanglements that are created by the duo, and which operate at different levels. It recognizes the directors' prominence within the Portuguese context, and it also acknowledges how they are influenced by other, classic, international directors such as Douglas Sirk or Pedro Almodóvar. It also takes account of how Rodrigues and Guerra da Mata are aligned with other contemporary filmmakers such as Gregg Araki or Apichatpong Weerasethakul. The volume ends, therefore, with Julián Daniel Gutiérrez Albilla's interview with the directors, in which all of these issues are discussed. Over the course of this long conversation, which derived from a series of encounters between the interviewer and the directors, Gutiérrez Albilla enables us to better understand their significance in an increasingly complex world. This interview completes the volume and provides evidence of the directors' openness to dialogue. Furthermore, it reveals how Rodrigues and Guerra da Mata's work cannot be reduced to a single vision and, thus, both the interview, and the volume as a whole, provide a timely testimony as to the singularity and importance of Portuguese cinema and of these (and other) Portuguese directors on the international stage.

PART I

Queer (Dis)Placements, Exquisite Bodies

CHAPTER I

Sculpting the Body, Sculpting History

Fran Benavente and Glòria Salvadó-Corretger

FLESH AND MONUMENT

The body is one of the key motifs in the work of João Pedro Rodrigues. The director problematizes the body by considering its meaning in liminal terms and in relation to the need to mold it. Furthermore, the body in Rodrigues's films is a complex issue: it may be disguised, combined, transformed, or sculpturally chiseled. It is a plural, hybrid, multiple, or split body; a chiasmus. It is a body that is present or absent, visible or invisible, inhabited by the ghost of history. It is an animal body and a spiritual body.

Moreover, in Rodrigues's work, the body is an open, bordering entity. It is a space for negotiation and change that draws out the idea of identity. Yet this identity, trapped in a dialectic between permanence and variation, is not only an individual character's identity, or a gender identity, because the body also operates as a place for questioning a collective identity. As such, national identity is examined through a history that evokes notions of colonialism and modernity (in a country that is heavily defined by the Catholic tradition). Finally, the body in Rodrigues's films is also the body of cinema and of cinematic history.

One of our principal aims in this chapter is to make sense of João Pedro Rodrigues's work through an investigation of his side projects: his short or medium-length films, his collaborations with João Rui Guerra da Mata, and his audiovisual installations. A good starting point in this sense is *O Corpo de Afonso* (*The King's Body*, 2012), or, more specifically, the reading of this film that was offered by the filmmakers themselves at the installation *Identidade Nacional (Príncipe Real)* [*National Identity (Príncipe Real)*]. The installation was exhibited in 2019 at the Reservatório da Patriarcal (an exhibition space located under the Príncipe Real gardens in Lisbon) on the occasion of the Biennial of Contemporary Arts (BoCA). It is not unusual for Rodrigues to adapt his work to an exhibition format. In a way, this device of migration requires the delivery of not only a new presentation of the images, but also a reinterpretation of those images as they are placed in contact with other materials. The installation was described as a "descent into the roots that recontextualizes the bodies that the filmmakers have been filming over the years."[1] In it, images from *The King's Body* were juxtaposed with objects and photographs taken mainly from the feature film *Morrer Como um Homem* (*To Die Like a Man*, 2009). What interests us here is the fact that the filmmakers bring these two films into dialogue around the concept of national identity and that this process involves the idea of recontextualizing the body. Thus, sculpting the body becomes a way of sculpting history.[2]

In *To Die Like a Man*, the body of Tónia is the body of conflict. The film opens with images of a military operation on a dark night, specifically, the image of a young soldier putting camouflage paint on his face. The notion of the mask as something malleable, and as a revealer of the body in the darkness, is combined with the conflictive tone that defines the film. In the malleable flesh, and in the logic of the tactile, Rodrigues plays with the interstices between the visible and the invisible. It is thus a film about a war that is waged in the body and spirit of Tónia, who is battling against time, disease, and the definitive sex change operation. The war imagery at the beginning of the film thus delves into the concepts of gender and genre: the questioning of gender identity and the conflict that arises in relation to Tónia's sexuality; and also the emergence of the homosexual relationship, and thus of queerness as a transformation of the horizon of expectations of the war film tradition. On the other hand, when positioned within the concept of "national identity," the war scene naturally evokes the military operations of the colonial era. This allusion triggers the open and conflictive relationship between the individual body and the national body within the body of the film. The main dialectic is thus established between an insistent resurgence of the past and the possibility of a different future, and that issue is projected onto history and onto time.

These concepts are articulated in conflictive terms on the body of the protagonist. They bring into play the ideas of legacy and transmission into the future, which are embodied in the figures of Rosário (Tónia's demanding, dependent lover) and Tónia's son. Both of these relationships are also conflictive and turbulent. The notions of the eternal, the permanent, and that which returns or persists, are associated with tradition and with a particular idea of essence. Tónia is an "unidentified" body; she is both male and female. Hers is a sculptural body in a process of transformation, linked to becoming (the passage of time) but subject to and determined by a tradition, the Catholic faith. That faith represents the essential element that resists change, along with the ghost of war that opens the film. Army and religion have been two of the pillars that traditionally have forged Portuguese identity. Both were key elements in the articulation of national identity under the fascist regime of Salazar, who was the prime minister of Portugal from 1932 to 1968. The question therefore appears to be how to become something new. In what sense does the metamorphosis of the appearance, the transformation of the body, represent a real change of identity?

This dialectic between the eternal or permanent, and what is potentially multiple and unstable or transformable, is played out on the battlefield of the body. It takes us back to *The King's Body*, and it also resounds forcefully in another of João Pedro Rodrigues's short films, which is almost experimental in nature: *Manhã de Santo António* (*Morning of Saint Anthony's Day*, 2012). In both of these films, the question is posited through the motif of the statue that is erected against a new cinematic body and created as a cinematic aggregation of bodies that are constructed as an image sculpted by cinema.

In *The King's Body*, the body of Portugal's first monarch and emblem of national history, D. Afonso Henriques, is problematized as an absent body. It represents pure virtuality or essence for the construction of a particular identity, and the question explored here is how to bring that essence into the present in a real body. Or rather, how to embody something that has been established as an eternal essence, as an idea, as a cornerstone. Based on this premise, the film is presented as the shooting of a casting session to find an actor to play Afonso I. As such, acting out history means bringing a body back to life in order to observe that body in the dialectic between transformation on contact with the present and transformation on contact with the permanence of history. In different ways and through editing or superimposition, this *dispositif* film sets in opposition the sculptural depictions that establish the "eternal" myth and the potential cinematic recreation of those depictions in the multiple bodies of those auditioning to play the king. Consequently, the camera lingers over the flesh of these sculptural, physical, nearly always muscular bodies, as well as over the stories of the candidates, all of whom are Galicians and all of whom, in one way or another, are victims of the economic crisis. In this way, Rodrigues and Guerra da Mata transform a commemoration that pays tribute to Guimarães—the town that is considered to be the "cradle" of Portuguese culture—into a conflictive questioning of being and becoming: it is an interrogation of identity in a turbulent present that is marked by the permanence of the past. From the monumental statue to the real body, the filmmakers film the bodies against a green screen. They are flattened against the chroma backdrop onto which images related to the Lusitanian king are projected. The result is the appearance of a new, multiple, and complex image-body that is echoed in the numerous stories of young Galicians who translate into words the personal stories that are written on their bodies and in their circumstances (all of which are related to the economic crisis). This story resounds powerfully in a country like Portugal, which was one of the most severely affected by the global recession.[3]

The sculpture, or rather monument, is a central motif again in *Morning of Saint Anthony's Day*. Rodrigues draws once more on an eternal myth; this time it is the myth of the patron saint of Lisbon. However, he also draws on tradition: the custom of lovers laying potted bush basil beneath the statue of St. Anthony on 13 June, as a token of their love. The objective here is to transform—or rather to oppose—this custom with a body that resists and pluralizes the eternalizing gaze in order to bring history or tradition into the present. The filmmaker thus effects a genuine "return" based on the image of the living dead, the body that comes back to life. The collective body of youth comes back home after the nocturnal festivities. This is a choreographed, almost musical film in which the figures are depicted according to the code of the zombie film genre: in the crowd of young people, individuals stagger, fall, or vomit. They walk stiffly or drag themselves through the empty city, in a scene typical of a zombie movie.

The filmmaker builds from tradition and from the reality of the bodies and spaces to transfigure those bodies and spaces in a cinematic movement that is propelled by the musical and fantastic genres, which in turn push beyond reality to effectuate the emergence of the "Other." The wandering bodies of the young people are articulated in a precise choreography of movements and postures that are marked by a musically designed soundtrack of ambient noises. They are shown mostly from high angles, as though from the central, immutable, and watchful gaze of the statue of Saint Anthony, which seems to be sanctioning these bodies returned from the dead that point to another possible national identity. The resistance of the "new" body of youth to the vigilant regime of the eternal gaze is confirmed in the denouement of *Morning of Saint Anthony's Day*, when one of the youths hurls a flowerpot at the statue's face in a dying gesture of revolt. The vacant gaze of the monument remains impervious to the man's body, which is shown fallen before another young man comes to pick him up in a gesture that replicates the *Pietà* motif. The image is an expression of solidarity that is characteristic of those who are brought together only to confront a self-sufficient authority in its atemporal power (the massive statue with the cross). Then, a carnation (the flower that symbolically is associated with Portugal's revolution of 25 April 1974[4]) is blown by the wind until, in the final shot, we see a note tied to it that bears a verse from a poem by Fernando Pessoa: "At the dance where everyone dances/There are some who don't dance, just stare./Better not to go to the dance/Than to be there without being there."[5] Published in 1934, this poem is part of a group of popular poems written under the Portuguese poet's own name, and its presence relates the ending of the film to the image of the Portuguese people, thus positioning this film in the conflictive dimension of "national identity." After all, was the Carnation Revolution not an attempt at collective transformation of the national body in opposition to the hard and immutable tradition that had been held up as an emblem of the national spirit by Salazar's dictatorship, and which is embodied in the monuments of the Catholic saint and the warrior king? The melancholy note that Rodrigues offers in this ending brings the historical reading of his films in line with that of other Portuguese filmmakers of his time, such as Pedro Costa or Miguel Gomes, particularly in relation to the perceived failure or utopia of the Carnation Revolution and the confusion that is caused by such paradoxical points of view.

The problematic relationship of body and identity translates the forms of history into ways of depicting the body and its relationship with space. From this perspective, it is worth noting the "figurative economy" of the films analyzed so far, after the analytical method proposed by Nicole Brenez.[6] In terms of the formal properties of the shot, *The King's Body* positions the screen-body (an updated image-body) in opposition to the volumetric form of a sculptural regime that cloaks the void or mystery of the real body of the historical figure. The flesh of the real body, constructed in the diversity of bodies of the "people," contrasts with the stony texture of the statue, which is singular and self-sufficient in its authoritarian presence. The collective, diverse, and secularized invocation responds to the unitary transcendence of the messianic figure. The technical method of signaling the reappropriation of the eternal body in the new bodies thus involves developing that eternal body in the contrast between figure and background, whether on the chroma screen or in the editing. It is also developed through the embodiment of the historical narrative in the different voices of the candidates, and the confrontation of the mythical epic tale with the everyday epic stories of the men who form the different embodiments of Afonso.

In *Morning of Saint Anthony's Day*, as noted above, the motif of the statue returns in opposition to a diverse, collective body that constitutes an image of "the people": this is a fragmentary body articulated in musical choreography and marching under the sanctioning gaze that ultimately provokes its collapse. In the case of both films, the situation depicts a people trying to articulate a transformation and to become something different in relation to both the ideologemes established by tradition, and the return or permanence of history.

Rodrigues and Guerra da Mata use their short films and installations as a laboratory or testing ground. They apply the results of their experiments fully in lengthier works such as *O Ornitólogo* (*The Ornithologist*, 2016). This feature film condenses and multiplies the impact of the dialectic between the national myth of St. Anthony of Padua (the same Anthony whose statue gazes upon bodies and space in *Morning of Saint Anthony's Day*) and the transformative potential of cinema as a creative tool. *The Ornithologist*, like all of the works analyzed so far, maps out a trajectory of metamorphoses: an identity change from Fernando into António and from the actor Paul Hamy into João Pedro Rodrigues, a shift from the material body into the spiritual body, and a movement from vision into touch. Nonetheless, rather than a linear transformation, this film depicts a multiplication of potentialities and an "opening up" of the body. It is a kind of generalized unfolding that shifts the fixed identity (Fernando's, but also the mythical story of St. Anthony's life) into multiple variations or episodes comprising a multiple, cumulative body (St. Anthony, St. James, St. Thomas, Jesus, the tortured body, and the body in ecstasy).

In this context, two elements in particular are worth highlighting. The first relates to the conflictive, reversible, and hybrid system of the gaze. Responding to the ornithologist's gaze is the gaze of the observed and observing animal body, to which we will return in relation to the animal body represented in the duo's so-called "Asian films." Also corresponding to this playing with gazes is the dialectic between the vertical gaze that signals the transcendent or spiritual axis (from below to above) or the watchful, sanctioning regime, and the horizontal gaze that underscores sensuality and contact with nature. As in the case of *Morning of Saint Anthony's Day*, overhead and high-angle shots abound, and these are suggestive of a superior or watchful gaze. They are the mark of an "other" presence: the spiritual gaze of a godlike figure who is simultaneously a forest spirit or animal (dove, eagle, griffin, or vulture). In this "insular" film, the linguistic communications of the isolated main character are generally unsuccessful, abortive, or labored. The sensual relationship involves reducing the gap between bodies from the far-off gaze to touch (sex, fighting, the deeper incision into a preexisting wound). This ultimately articulates the axes of the gaze in a kind of copulative circuit (as signaled by the final song by António Variações) that brings together all of the characters, journeys, and trajectories in a "happy ending that is no longer happy."[7]

The other main element of *The Ornithologist* is the idea of the body being brought back to life. Like the zombies in *Morning of Saint Anthony's Day*, in the later film too there is an array of figurative representations of resurrection or rebirth: Fernando is resuscitated by the Chinese pilgrims; the white dove recovers the power of flight after the inexplicable healing of its broken wing; and Jesus's body returns as Thomas, his twin brother. Everything folds back and returns in a complex dialectic of transformation that recalls the traditional fantastic figures of the double and the threshold between life and death, which are articulated in the liminal realms between day and night.

LIMINAL CINEMA AND BODIES BETWEEN IMAGES

We will now look at the figurative work on the body and the appearance of history in the filmmakers' "Asian films." These films are a pivotal point in the collaborations between João Pedro Rodrigues and João Rui Guerra da Mata. The cycle of films, which so far cover the period from 2007 (*China, China*) to 2015 (*Iec Long*), is set mainly between Lisbon and Macao. In them, the directors examine from a postcolonial perspective the clash between Portuguese and Chinese cultures, between East and West. This clash makes these films interesting for their exploration of the conflictive relationships between body and history in relation to the notion of identity. The following analysis is informed by some of the ideas proposed by Homi K. Bhabha in *The Location of Culture*.

Of particular interest here is the notion of the boundary or borderline as a central trope of our times, which Bhabha discusses at the beginning of his book. This trope determines every level of the poetics shared by Rodrigues and Guerra da Mata in these films, as it does all of their other collaborations. Indeed, and as Heidegger points out in the epigraph that Bhabha uses in the introduction to his book, a boundary is that from which "something begins its presencing."[8] One could say that the position on the boundary is a new horizon from which to consider matters, especially "identity." That same position allows something to be "made to appear" and, consequently, to be brought into the image. As such, the perspective from the boundary defines what a cinematic representation of substance should endeavor to achieve.

What is this boundary, borderline, or "in-between" in the films of João Pedro Rodrigues and João Rui Guerra da Mata? One of the particular features of the "Asian films" is their way of articulating a presence/absence dialectic in the representation of bodies. This is especially evident in *A Última Vez Que Vi Macau* (*The Last Time I Saw Macao*, 2012), which to some extent constitutes the central piece of a mosaic of films that function as a single whole. In this film, the protagonist, João Rui Guerra da Mata himself, is a voice with no visible body. Candy (Cindy Crash), his transsexual friend who asks him for help, appears only at the beginning of the film, performing a musical number that evokes Jane Russell in *Macao* (Nicholas Ray and Josef von Sternberg, 1952). She is then reduced to a voice on the phone, before finally disappearing altogether. In this way, there is a shift from a system of representation of bodies to this liminal system between the absence of the body and the effects of the presence or the trace in the image. This is a metonymic system, where objects and fragments replace the representation of the body.

In this sense, the body is what appears upon its very disappearance, or rather, what begins to establish its presence on the boundary of its unrepresentability. This idea can take various forms: the high-heeled shoe that appears throughout the "Asian films," the boundary between night and daybreak, or the passage from darkness to light. For example, in the film *Alvorada Vermelha* (*Red Dawn*, 2011), we see the shoe without an owner, the collective body of the market workers, and the mutilated, fragmented bodies of animals; or at the beginning of *China, China* the female protagonist's body appears in those liminal territories that we describe above.

On the boundary or borderline complex figures appear, which are articulated between difference and identity, and between past and present. Candy's musical number at the beginning of *The Last Time I Saw Macao* (in which João Rui Guerra da Mata returns to his former home for the first time since its decolonization) is perhaps the moment that best encapsulates the film: it presents Candy affirming her presence; she is performing shortly before her disappearance in the story (first only the voice remains, then the mobile phone, then only the shoe and the wig). She is a hybrid, composite, aggregated, and liminal body: male-female, present-past (a blend of Candy and Jane Russell, the actress she is mimicking), animal-human (between human and tiger), and Chinese-Portuguese.

A crossover, mixed body opens up the story to all kinds of conflict and doubt in relation to identity and to an examination of transformation (change) and permanence. As Bhabha postulates, "these 'in-between' spaces provide a terrain for elaborating strategies of selfhood—singular or communal—that initiate new signs of identity, and innovative sites of collaboration, and contestation, in the act of defining society itself."[9] Through the liminal body, the conflict of (the filmmakers') self-identity is explored and projected onto a collective or "national" identity. Herein lies the political component of these liminal approaches to representation, which link the filmography of Rodrigues and Guerra da Mata to the work of other filmmakers who have also addressed the problem of national identity and history through bodies in conflictive metamorphoses, such as Rainer Werner Fassbinder or Pedro Almodóvar (both of whom are notable for their queer displacement of cinema's traditional figures).

The interstice thus becomes a space for creativity and negotiation: it is a place of difference for examining identity. Although one can locate this foundational element in all of Rodrigues's films, its expression is self-conscious and operative within the "Asian films." The interstitial dividing line brings out an image that is composed of dialectics and conflict. For instance, the "Asian films" use a documentary framework that is transfigured by fiction, and for which genre-based plots serve as the vehicle.

The initial idea for *The Last Time I Saw Macao* was to return to the familiar places of Guerra da Mata's childhood and to film the city of Macao in the present from the perspective of memory. However, the filmmakers felt the need to move beyond this superficial, documentary view to explore an "inhabited" city through the eyes of genre fiction. The noir plot structure turns the story into an investigation that is aimed at revealing something hidden and shedding light on a dark, complex, and labyrinthine space. At the same time, it invokes the adventurous exoticism of film history through its referencing of *Macao*, and thus turns the development of a possible crime story into a clash with "otherness," in an alienation of the past and a negation of any possibility of an exotic or tourist perspective. The noir style signals the structure of the film and its use of voice-over, nocturnal settings, dead-end alleyways, criminal conspiracies, and the depiction of a rather despairing outlook. There is nothing at the end of the road beyond the confirmation of difference and the impossibility of entering this web of dark secrets. The noir style is an instrument of penetration or transfiguration of reality that enables the filmmakers to dodge the clichés, instead sliding over them.

We recognize the same conceptual mechanism in *Mahjong* (2013), which presents an exact reflection of its predecessor, *The Last Time I Saw Macao*. In the later film, the action is transferred from Macao to the industrial district of Varziela, the biggest Chinatown in Portugal. João Rui Guerra da Mata is the protagonist (once again, his voice predominates). He plays an investigator looking into some mysterious fires and searching for a missing woman (a double of Candy). The film is structured as an ambiguous nocturnal quest that once again brings out the mysteries and complexities of the Chinese community.

The female character, a femme fatale, is elusive and evanescent (a shoe and a mannequin metonymically stand in for her), and the game of mahjong is offered as a symbol of mysterious movement, an inscrutable code with an indecipherable meaning in this universe. In both cases, the splitting of voices and gazes is particularly interesting. This splitting provides a narrative style that multiplies their possibilities of being "in-between." *The Last Time I Saw Macao* splits the narrative between Guerra da Mata's voice and Rodrigues's, which occasionally intervenes. The former stands in for the childhood memories that propel the movement of the investigation. The latter, Rodrigues, is the voice of cinema entering unfamiliar territory through the mixture of contemporary images and stories that invoke fiction, memory, and the past. The observer-investigator João Rui Guerra da Mata is observed and watched by the members of the sect of man-dogs.

In *Mahjong*, the gazes are also split in two. Guerra da Mata investigates, while Rodrigues watches and pursues the pursuer. In the end, these gazes come together in a duel that has a fatal denouement. As we have shown, this system of circulation, exchange, and confrontation of gaze is what ultimately reveals a glimpse of the two filmmakers in the body of Fernando, the protagonist of *The Ornithologist*. Added to film noir and adventurous exoticism (the narrative vehicle and critical iconography) is a fantastic dimension that invokes the power of cinema to conjure up what lies beyond the visible in the image. The form of the fantastic, as Jean-Louis Leutrat suggests, is that of cinema itself operating between appearance and disappearance, precisely in the "in-between," on the threshold. The in-between is the place of frozen time and of the appearance of specters. Behind the visible image, another virtual, invisible but no less present image takes shape,[10] and that shape is like the body of a ghost.

We can project this space between times and the presence of the ghost into the prism of history in the postcolonial context. For example, in *Iec Long* the device is similar: documentary-style images show a fireworks celebration in the present, and these are followed by the exploration of the ruins of a pyrotechnics factory (for much of the twentieth century, fireworks were Macao's biggest industry), which will soon be turned into a tourist attraction. The fireworks materialize a particular visible and sonic expression that heralds the passage from night into day. The contrast is highlighted between the dark night and the bursts of light, and between the curtains of smoke and the explosions tearing through them. The festival, the commemoration, and the ritual evoke the past within the present time.

Similarly, in the empty ruins of *Iec Long*, the ghost of the "people"—the exploited factory workers—emerges in the archive images. The bodies in the photographs inhabit time in a suspended space. Particularly interesting here is the insistent presence of photographs of specter-children, which expose the phantoms of child exploitation and the misery of colonialism that call out insistently from the ruins. In this way, with the phantasmal network of bodies appearing in the "in-between," the filmmakers construct a politics of the image that reveals the history behind the ruins in order to uncover the identity of the space's inhabitants before globalizing tourism buries that memory.

Iec Long is also the setting for the second scene in *The Last Time I Saw Macao*, after Candy's performance. The scene is of a war game, and once again, the dimension of war or violence determines the relationship between bodies and space. The fireworks that take up the whole first part of the short film are also seen at the end of *The Last Time I Saw Macao*. Just as the past returns with its specters projected onto history, this ending underscores the apocalyptic tone that runs throughout the film. Positioned between the return of the past and the threat of a catastrophic future, the film concludes with fireworks in an experimental ending that points to dissolution in death and the return to the primitive (represented by the forest of the beginning) as a means of escaping the cycles of progress and of historical destruction.

As indicated by Françoise Proust, "[T]ime is prophetic and spectral."[11] The key concepts seem to be death or disintegration as a fact, the persistence of specters, and metamorphosis or transformation as an expression of desire and resistance against the inertia of the disaster. This is also what happens in *The Ornithologist*. Fernando's body rises up out of the water, as determined by the shadow of death, to resist in a transformation that shifts and rewrites the catastrophe as a profound, immersive contact with nature: with the animal world and the return to the primal (practically to the savage or the primitive). In this sense, Jean-Louis Leutrat writes:

> We are thus faced with the "between" time par excellence, located between the "already seen" and the "not yet." This moment, which painting has

such a hard time showing, can be represented easily in cinema, and this ease is what it must try to retain in order to capture the power contained in the instant, the movement of displacement held by the bodily presence, the imminence of arrival and the trace of disappearance, with the aim of rendering a vibration visible.[12]

For Rodrigues and Guerra da Mata, the fantastic and its cyclically recurring temporality operate as a way to conceive history and its bodies. This is the same temporality, between what has already gone and what is not yet seen, that underpins *The Last Time I Saw Macao*.

It is also worth highlighting the allusion to painting, which Rodrigues admits is always his first point of reference and inspiration.[13] His intensive exploration of the desiring and tortured body draws on its depiction in classical painting (the threshold between torment and ecstasy in Italian art, for example), and it is transfigured by the cinematic mode, and particularly by the addition of movement in time. All of this is very clear in *The Ornithologist*, in which the protagonist's body is portrayed as the materialization of the dialectic between spirit and flesh. João Gabriel's painting for the publicity poster works simultaneously as inspiration and as an introduction to this way of filming the body. The same painting appears in an earlier short piece that was filmed during Rodrigues's residency in Le Fresnoy for the retrospective of his work that was organized by the Centre Pompidou in Paris.

Où En Êtes-Vous, João Pedro Rodrigues? (*Where Do You Stand Now, João Pedro Rodrigues?*, 2017) is a kind of self-portrait that contextualizes the aforementioned painting in a series of motifs that the filmmaker presents as the substance of his filmography. At the beginning of this short film, Rodrigues offers his own torso (a fragmented body as in classical sculpture) to the camera while he asks himself where he is. He then explores João Gabriel's painting, which is the portrait of a body unleashed to sensation. Here, the body is shown stripped of its original representation in a realization of the conversion between religious sentiment and pictorial atheism, in the sense described by Deleuze.[14]

This confrontation evokes António's and Tónia's bodies within the filmmaker's own body, which is shown immediately afterwards as a reflection in a window. It is evanescent against the forest outside. In a voice-over narration, the filmmaker reads fragments from *The Birth-Mark* (1846), Nathaniel Hawthorne's story in which the facial blemish supplants the perfection of the body and transforms it. The blemish is what needs to be touched: it is an affluence of blood that serves as a hybrid of the mark of sensual sin and the ideal dimension of the perfect body. The series culminates with domestic images of monarch butterflies on their migratory route. The filmmaker claims that he wants to capture movement in order to film shapes in transformation. Here, the very substance of João Pedro Rodrigues's body of work is revealed: cinema is that which brings movement into a dialectic with immobility, and the discontinuity that lurks in the shadows of a film. Desire, movement, and metamorphosis are the tools that cinema can make use of in this sense.

CONCLUSION

Catherine Malabou refers to plasticity as "the excess of the future over the future."[15] It is precisely the potential of plasticity in cinema, in every sense, that Rodrigues and Guerra da Mata experiment with in their films. This capacity for transformation and for changing the past appears as a process of disrupting and opening up systems, and particularly systems of personal, gender (queer displacement), and national identities. It is here, in this affirmation of plasticity, that we believe the figurative and political potential of these films is encoded, in full harmony with the work of other contemporary Portuguese filmmakers.

> Most of the time, lives follow their routes like rivers. Occasionally they break out of their course, without any geological factor or underground feature being able to explain such a swelling or overflowing. The suddenly abnormal and deviant shape of these lives possesses an explosive plasticity.[16]

Malabou's observation seems to define the structure of *The Ornithologist* from the moment of the accident that diverts Fernando's body and gaze from the course of the river and throws him into a series of situations that will shape his transformation. It is perhaps even more definitive of the structure of *O Fantasma* (*Phantom*, 2000), in which Sérgio's transformation, his becoming-other, is encoded both in the animal and in his latex skin. The latex is a plastic coating whose sheen begins to present another body on the borderline of the night. It is an explosive and overflowing "plastic construction" that combines a horizon of negativity (almost of dissolution) and of regression. It is a becoming-animal as a response to the prospect of destruction. Against death, and against disappearance, the balancing entry of the potential of plasticity is asserted as the "possible."

"Destruction has its sculptor's chisel," says Catherine Malabou, and she goes on:

> Organic matter is like the sculptor's clay or marble. It produces its waste and its residue. But these organic remains are absolutely necessary to complete the living form that finally appears, obviously, at the price of their disappearance. Again, this type of destruction does not contradict

positive plasticity, but rather constitutes its condition. It serves the definition and the power of the form achieved. In its way, it composes the force of living. Both in psychoanalysis and in neurology, cerebral and psychological plasticity find the best balance between the capacity for change and the ability to remain the same, between the future and memory, between receiving and giving shape.[17]

Sculptural metaphors move on the threshold and construct plasticity on the threshold that overflows, in the territory of the hybrid and of variations or aggregations. In this way, the work of figurative representation on the body becomes a political task. From the literary works of writers from Ovid to Kafka, and the reinterpretations of such works in cinema, the question revolves around the possibility of a change of nature. Transformation of being is a response to the disorder of the present and presents a prospect for the future. "What can the body do?" asked Spinoza. A body can transform, split, and multiply, and in this way, it constitutes a form of escape, for the body begins "presencing," as defined by Heidegger and cited by Homi Bhabha, at the border of its disappearance.[18]

CHAPTER 2

The Injury: On *Pathosformel* in João Pedro Rodrigues's Work

Olivier Cheval

CHRISTIAN IMAGERY

The great "trilogy of flesh" by João Pedro Rodrigues is composed of *O Fantasma* (*Phantom*, 2000), *Odete* (*Two Drifters*, 2005), and *Morrer Como um Homem* (*To Die Like a Man*, 2009). These three feature films seek the dividing line that separates the great vital power from our animal-becoming, our imperceptible-becoming, our transgender-becoming, and from the deadly logic that presides over definitive transformations. The characters in these films are caught between a vital energy and a death drive, between the creative power of the invention of their body and the schizophrenic danger of having really become someone other than themselves.

This dividing line meets another one. There are always at least two movies coexisting within each of the first three feature films by the Lisbon filmmaker. On the one hand, there is a Christian drama of the flesh that is without solution when it is faced with the incommensurability of its desire. This is the drama of a soul that is too incarnated for its quest for the absolute, crushed by the absence of a horizon between a sky filled with heavy clouds and a land covered with the thick mud of the world. At the same time, the influences of the rigidity of Dreyer and Bresson, and of Baroque religious painting, are palpable. On the other hand, however, this great Christian drama of a European auteur is always diminished by the intrusion of imagery that is foreign to the solemnity of this film genre. Rodrigues describes the romantic destiny of a Deleuzean *devenir-mineur* to which he gives all his belief until his film becomes as minor as his character. The singularity of his cinematographic gesture is to link the physical transformation of the main character to the mutation of the films, which come to be contaminated by minor genres such as pornographic film, fantasy film, melodrama, B or Z-series, S&M, the Gothic, and popular religious imagery.

This ambivalence in terms of genre culminates in *To Die Like a Man*, where the mutant body of Tónia causes the mutation of the psychological drama into a fairy tale. This happens during a picaresque and burlesque episode in a chimerical forest where a giant moon suddenly turns the night a purple color. However, the shift occurs at an even deeper level in terms of Rodrigues's figurative work with Catholic imagery. The film portrays Tónia ironically, as a devotee surrounded by kitsch icons and small statuettes of the Virgin in snowglobes purchased in Fátima. Her faith is at the root of the moral dilemma of vaginoplasty, which Tónia considers to be a sacrilege. However, there is something deeper than the superstitious mind of Tónia: there is a holy dimension which comes from the figurative wager on making Tónia into a new Virgin and her lover, the aptly named Rosário, into a new Christ. The scene where Tónia, in a red stage dress, finds Rosário one evening after the cabaret recalls a *Pietà* in the style of Caravaggio: he is lying on the asphalt, overdosing, with his pale body highlighted by the moonlight.

The reenactment of the pictorial tenebrist genre, naturalized to a contemporary fictional setting, is a classic feature of the European auteur drama: it has precursors in Pudovkin's *Mat* (*The Mother*, 1926), Rossellini's *Paisà* (*Paisan*, 1946) and *Roma città aperta* (*Rome, Open City*, 1947), and Parajanov's *Tini zabutykh predkiv* (*Shadows of Forgotten Ancestors*, 1964). Rodrigues's film also sits alongside more contemporary variations on this theme, such as the *The Godfather III* (Coppola, 1990), *Bringing Out the Dead* (Scorsese, 1999), *Mat i syn* (*Mother and Son*, 1997) by Sokurov, *Batalla en el Cielo* (*Battle in Heaven*, 2005) by Reygadas, or the aptly named *Pietà* (2012) by Kim Ki-duk. Nonetheless, the trope finds a new political significance in Rodrigues's work, where it has the function of representing the disturbing similarity between a minority genre and the canon, and between a social form of abnormality and a moral and aesthetic norm: it equates the two carnal dramas by affirming the equal dignity of the sufferings of a trans woman and those of the Virgin, in order to reveal the nobility of bodies and destinies that society in general, and the Church in particular, have designated as ignoble or monstrous.

However, the sublime gesture of the film is that it goes beyond this iconological solemnity to imbue Tónia, on the day of her burial, with the grace of finally being the Virgin that she wants to be: a Virgin of cabaret; a cheap icon-type Virgin like those sold as souvenirs in holy places. Dressed in her most beautiful red and blue stage costume, the ghost of Tónia towers above the funeral caskets singing a fado; at the same time, on the ground, her body, dressed in a man's suit, is buried next to the grave of her lover. This last shot is a *tableau vivant* inspired by "The Assumption of Titian," as Rodrigues confessed to me.[1] The composition is at once absolutely sublime and absolutely camp, beyond any measure and good taste; it is a drag show that exceeds the limits of the stage and of death to invade the world with her pathetic song. The emotional impact of the shot is increased by the fact that Tónia is not shown on stage during the entire movie. Prior to the release of *To Die Like a Man*, the earlier film, *Phantom*, had freed an S&M fetishist from the backrooms into a world which has become a giant, nocturnal, and apocalyptic discharge, a heavenly hell for the masochist. Rodrigues is a realist, Bressonian, and "Bazinian" filmmaker who is also a camp *imagier*. His singular work extracts sexual or corporal performances from their small theater to place them on the infinite stage of the world.

Even so, Rodrigues's queer work is not an apology for performance, nor is it the dramatic equivalent of Gregg Araki's queer comedies or Bruce LaBruce's "pornoqueer."[2] His work is about sexual anxiety, which seeks that which resists our becoming, that which is forgotten, and that which is preserved in our transformations. Indeed, bodies do not escape so easily from the models offered by the Christian tradition—from the anthropology of a body modeled on God and made flesh by Christ.[3] For instance, in *Two Drifters* the heroine is like Tónia: a new Virgin. Her nervous pregnancy begins on a stormy night, when a violent wind comes to open her window: it spreads the curtains and performs an immaculate conception. Odete dreams of motherhood and mourning; she wants to be a Madonna with child and a Mater Dolorosa. It is the failure of this project and the deflation of her pregnancy that lead her to disguise herself as a man.

A FORMULA OF PATHOS

The kiss on the wound is a trope that runs throughout Rodrigues's work, from his first short film of 1997, *Parabéns!* (*Happy Birthday!*). This motif is located at the intersection between the vital energy and the death drive of the characters, and between Christian solemnity and queer erotic imagery. It is the sign of the resistance of the Christian flesh to transgender mutations. The queer body is the utopia of a bodily singularity that engenders itself as unique. The Christian flesh is the utopia of a salvation that redeems the sins of our bodies (created in the image of God but failing to equal the image of Christ) thanks to their dissolution in a great single flesh that is indistinct and glorious. On the one hand, there is the promise of distinctive otherness; on the other, the promise of equalizing absorption. Therefore, I argue that in each film, the kiss on the wound is the accident that interrupts a queer process of making the individual distinctive by provoking the encounter with others.

Georges Didi-Huberman has identified a "formula of pathos" that runs through Christian imaginary, from the incredulity of St. Thomas to the bloody kiss of a prostitute who calls herself God in *Madame Edwarda* by Georges Bataille. He also explores the kiss of Catherine of Siena on the stigma of the rib of Christ when he appeared to her, and the kiss of St. Francis to the leper.[4] The author traces the literary lineage of this ancient gesture as a violent and pathetic trope that moves through Western history from the gospels to an erotic novella of the twentieth century, through hagiographic narrative and mystical treatise. Rodrigues's cinema reappropriates this Christian "formula of pathos" by bringing to it a fantastic strangeness, often through the inclusion of Gothic and popular imagery of blood pacts or vampirism. These kisses, which appear in his films as intense, figurative events that undermine the usual regime of representation, acquire a new status in his latest feature film, *O Ornitólogo* (*The Ornithologist*, 2016). In this film, the kiss is multiplied: it is parodied (the kiss of over-equipped Chinese pilgrims) and it is deliberately blasphemous (the close-up of the finger that penetrates Thomas's wound in an aesthetic porn parody of a gore movie). This film appears as an extension of Rodrigues's cinema in which his figurative obsession, which works covertly throughout his cinema, moves beyond it to become the object of a game of representation and a proliferation of images. Yet at the same time, it also allows us to return to and reread all of the bloody kisses of his cinema, which are less overt in the earlier films.

In *Happy Birthday!*, after a night of love, the kiss is seemingly harmless: a boy who imitates a mad dog kisses the finger of his distant and distracted lover—who has cut himself with a kitchen knife—as if with this gesture the boy wanted to heal him. However, the act has a particularly threatening dimension in the era of AIDS, which killed many people in the homosexual community. In *Phantom*, a colleague bites Sérgio's lip when he tries to steal a kiss from her, drawing blood: the kiss is no longer soothing here, but bruising, and it marks the animal union of these two wild creatures at the same time as it shows their human enmity. The kiss in this instance represents contamination—a vampiric contagion—which is exactly how "the propagation of the animal populating of the human being" functions, as described by Deleuze and Guattari.[5]

In *Two Drifters*, there are two kisses: the last kiss of Rui to Pedro before Pedro spits out his blood, in a male and gory *Pietà*; and that of Odete, who kisses the corpse of Pedro on the lips during the funeral vigil before stealing his engagement ring in her mouth, in a kind of post-mortem, digital blowjob. The rings exchanged by Rui and Pedro were the symbol of a marriage between men that was still impossible at the time. Kissing the dead and stealing the ring are the two gestures by which Odete creeps into their pact as the ceremonial symbol of the vampirization of the soul of the dead. At the end of the movie, disguised as Pedro, she caresses Rui's scar, which came from the wound that he made on his arm while trying to commit suicide. This gesture is the inversion of the *Pietà* of the first sequence: thanks to a disguise, it is now the dead man who comforts the living. This inversion, subversion, and distortion of the image of the *Pietà* anticipates one of the most beautiful shots of the later work, *To Die Like a Man:* Tónia's kiss on the wound of Jenny, her rival in the cabaret.

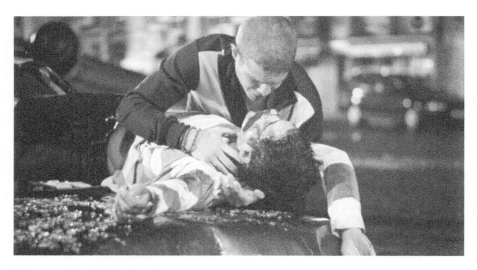

Figure 2.1 *Two Drifters* (2005)

TÓNIA'S KISS

The scene takes place in the dressing rooms of the drag show cabaret where Tónia works, on the night of Rosário's birthday, after he has disappeared. The reflection of a body without a face appears in the large mirror in front of which Tónia is putting on her make-up. It is the muscular body of one of the cabaret performers disguised as a sadomasochist master. After a close-up showing the foot of one of Tónia's colleagues, who is donning a high heel, the stripper who has been summoned to look for Rosário passes his masked head between the curtains to peer into the main performance room of the cabaret, which remains invisible to the viewer. However, backstage of the show is already a scene: it is a specular universe made up of fetishes and idols, reflections and projections; it is the place of a pure phantasmatic visibility, of a phantasmagoria of disembodied body-images. The immense mirrors redouble the specular becoming of bodies that are made-up, disguised, and transformed into clichés, or, what is more, into pure simulacra: they become dummy images of what they will never be (queens, virgins). The fetishes surrounding Tónia—erotic posters and religious icons—confirm the same artificiality of the image: they are representations of idealized bodies, unattainable models of femininity, or fantasies of virility. They share the same idolatry. The same love of the image which forbids everything is beneath the visible body (the flesh), and everything is beyond the visible world (the withdrawal, the distance, the invisible face of the divine).

Jenny is Tónia's rival on stage. She is younger, more beautiful, and above all, surgically enhanced. Jenny provokes Tónia by laughing at Rosário's departure before asking her to help zip up her dress. The two women are separated in the shot by a wall that forms a long mirror. Tónia joins Jenny on the other side of the mirror, where she is waiting for her with her back turned. Tónia's large body hides Jenny's back, and when Tónia hurts her with the zipper, we hear a cry of pain. An editing glitch shows Tónia already squatting, now to the left of Jenny's body. She kisses Jenny's wound and turns her face to the camera with her mouth full of blood. In addition to causing spatial confusion, the editing glitch takes only a few seconds to jump the action forward a notch and upset the image, in a move that is similar to that of the zip that gets stuck. From this scene onwards, time seems to be suspended and Tónia's face and Jenny's body remain motionless, as though they are posing. The montage of these two shots signals that there is more going on in this wound than an accident at work. Tónia kisses Jenny, whom she has just wounded and whom she hates, in a gesture that has no logic for the fiction of the character. Her insistent gaze in our direction, although it is not quite a direct gaze into the camera, indicates the importance of the image—and indeed, the shot was used as the image for the film's publicity poster.

The physical and moral violence of the vaginoplasty that Tónia must endure is concealed by the scientific neutrality of the medical discourse in the film's opening credits, while the accompanying image shows a doctor's hands modeling the operation with an origami figure. That same violence resurfaces here by detour, sliding, and displacement, imbuing it with a figurative logic.

Figure 2.2 *To Die Like a Man* (2009)

Tónia symbolically inflicts the castration that she fears on her colleague, Jenny, a trans woman who has already undergone vaginoplasty. The incident can be read as an assault as the jealous Tónia wounds the body that she desires to have. It can be seen also as the investigation of how one body probes another: the wound is a metaphor for castration, as Tónia embraces Jenny as if to move closer to the physical reality of the operation, and to commune with the open flesh that is the lot of all transgender individuals. The violence of the false connection, the strangeness of the kiss, the solemnity of Tónia's gaze, and the defeat of her bloody face, are combined in this shot to show the irruption of a new visibility that was hitherto hidden, and to carry the shot to a sacred, mystical dimension. To the left of the women we see part of the mirror, on which the poster of a body-builder has been stuck. This juxtaposition creates a sudden clash between two regimes of visibility and corporeality. The kiss on the wound pierces the surface of the exhibited body, drawing out a humor—blood—that is extracted from the depth of the flesh. The gush of bodily fluid refutes the perfect image of smooth skin to reveal the real body of any image as a deep and unformed depth that is concealed by the spectacle.

The film explores Tónia's deepest dilemma: should she continue to imitate, to play, to perform women, in a mimetic manner which posits the Virgin as the inaccessible model (if not in the burlesque mode of caricature, then at least in the performative mode of parody)? Or should she take the step and become a woman embodied in a castrated, open, inverted anatomy? This psychological dilemma is also a problem of theology and figurability, as Georges Didi-Huberman reveals in his reading of Tertullian, and which he summarizes as follows:

> Through the physical struggle of imitation and incarnation, something passes, in Tertullian, that is never theorized, that is never made completely clear; something which would tell us how the visual is torn away from the visible. The visible is the world of idolatry, a world where the image is exhibited, where it becomes representations, despicable performances, satisfied concupiscences. The visual, on the contrary, is what can be seen beyond, in the beyond. The visual characterizes a world where the image is at once present and promised—in short, where it is an aura, the material of the soul.[6]

What Didi-Huberman identifies as the conflict of the visible and the visual intersects with the opposition of the image-body and the body incarnate, the flesh, the phenomenological duality of the lived body, and the object-body. The question of figurability that arises is that of the possibility of embodying an image, or of imaging flesh, as animate, living, spiritual material. However, Didi-Huberman explains that:

the blood that spurts out [. . .] denotes exactly what we could call the incursion of the visual into the visible: that is, here, the irruption from within—the irruption of visceral color, of soul color, in a visible world from which soul and viscera are normally cut off, folded into the depths of the flesh.[7]

The blood that springs from Jenny's wound and contaminates Tónia's mouth is the common matter of their carnal suffering. It is the shared experience of two souls who suffer from their incarnation, and so this kiss is a liturgical ritual that may be understood as the replayed gesture of Catholic Communion. "This is our blood," Tónia says, with her worried gaze turned toward the camera. The imagery is particularly obvious when she kisses Jenny's wound, mixing her lipstick with her friend's blood, and giving to her wound the form of two half-opened lips. Here, the archetypal motif of the representation of the stigmata of Christ also evokes the image of the vulva.

The incident suggested by the visual ellipsis cannot open Jenny's flesh, it only opens a body. Only Tónia's kiss can open her flesh. The kiss is the gesture that transforms the silent body—the big, black back on the screen—into an open wound that is ready to deliver its secret. The kiss is the answer that makes the silent call of the other body heard *a posteriori*. This is the moment when Rodrigues reproduces the figurative obsession of Christian art to make the flesh speak, even though this is one of the great difficulties presented by Christianity, as Jean-Louis Chrétien explains:

> To this thought of a gaze always in ecstasy and a voice always in exodus in its inseparable responses to the call, the very flesh that they raise to their own glory seems, however, to pose a difficulty. Looking and listening put it into play in its integrity; but is it exhausted by them? How would the dark interiority of the flesh be ecstatic, in its suffering or in its joy? How would you offer yourself to a call that would, in advance, exceed it?[8]

The scene confronts precisely this problem of the radical difference between the flesh and the body, and the difficulty of making the flesh talk. Beyond the gaze and listening, beyond the voice and the eyes, the figure makes visible a call and its response, or rather it is the sublime response that makes the inexpressible call be heard.

TO SEE, TO TOUCH, TO EAT

The half-opened lips were the motif around which Caravaggio's painting *The Incredulity of Saint Thomas* was organized. The shot of Rosário's extended body as a dead Christ in the next scene also evokes the style of Caravaggio, and it seems that here the filmmaker takes up Caravaggio's figurative work on the "formula of pathos."[9]

"Unless I see the nail marks in his hands and put my finger where the nails were, and put my hand into his side, I will not believe."[10] To believe the unbelievable, the apostle Thomas asks for proof, which is presented to him in person by Jesus, who offers him the opportunity to see the stigmata of his crucifixion. "Put your finger here; see my hands. Reach out your hand and put it into my side. Stop doubting and believe."[11] Thomas obeys and recognizes his Lord, who then utters his ultimate maxim. "Because you have seen me, you have believed; blessed are those who have not seen and yet have believed."[12] The visible alone does not provide the proof that Thomas requires in order to believe in the resurrection of Christ. Thomas needs the materiality of a touch. Yet Christ's words reduce Thomas's tactile gesture to an act of vision. There is the mark of confusion here, of the recovery of touch through sight in Christian thought: the tangible is not separate from the visible, and, somehow, the visible holds the promise of the tangible. Christian visuality is a "haptology" or "continuism," in the Derridian sense:[13] only vision that leads to contact is full, accomplished, and certain. Vision moves towards touch until the two senses become indistinct: the Christ-like order to "put your finger here; see my hands" seems to be an invitation to look with the hands, to a manual vision. This belief in the tactile nature of the visible is not separable from thoughts of the flesh.

For Thomas, to touch the body of Christ is to confirm the corporeal presence that the vision induces but does not certify: it is to dispel the suspicion of a mirage. It was, moreover, the great theological struggle of one of the first Fathers of the Christian Church, Tertullian. He fought against the Gnostic heresies that considered Jesus to be an ethereal body—a non-body of a spiritual nature or of astral birth—in order to make Christianity the religion of the incarnation as opposed to the perfect images of the Greek gods and the invisible face of Yahweh. Jesus was a God of flesh and blood, born of a woman, and who died by suffering. The flesh is the material and sensitive depth which is the invisible reverse of the body. It is the reality that can be touched, in the double meaning of the word: a physical body on which a hand can be placed, and emotions that can be moved. To touch can be to stroke, to penetrate, or to hurt.

In Caravaggio's *The Incredulity of Saint Thomas*, more than in any other representation of this episode of the Gospel of John (such as Dürer's engraving of 1509), the tactility of Christian visibility is at the very center of the painting. The horizontal framing and the crude frontal light isolate the circle of four bodies against the uniformly obscure background. By narrowing the focus of the scene to only Jesus and three apostles (St. John and St. Peter stand behind St. Thomas to observe his gesture), all of whom are grouped together in a compact whole, the painter concentrates the drama of the picture on the gesture of the penetration of the wound, and he reduces the painting to four bodies that look, touch, and are touched. The entire work of Caravaggio performs a tenebrism that places crudely-lit white flesh against a black background that leaves no room for imagination of the visible extent of the world. The adaptation of the evangelical episode is an opportunity for Caravaggio to represent, almost poetically, the imagination of the visible that produces this new effect of *chiaroscuro*. Looking at the work of Caravaggio as a whole, Louis Marin has noted the radical obscurity in which the figures are immersed:

> The black background is much more than a "background" of the scene. The background is ultimately the surface of the painting itself. Therefore the projection of the light beam on the plane of the painting makes available for the figures only the extreme edge of the surface, the foreground of the picture: the floor of the scene is a foreground and the figures are continuously pushed forward, almost as if we were dealing with figures in relief on a solid wall, the face of the "arcanian" tomb.[14]

This general description of Caravaggio's tenebrism seems to be the key issue of the painting: Thomas seeks to verify that Christ has resurrected and emerged from the tomb, yet Caravaggio situates the scene in a dark non-place that seems to be the very interior of a tomb space. While the painter shows the visible where it should not appear (in the sealed black coffin), Thomas seeks to see formless reality from within the wound and the unrepresentable miracle of the resurrection. The painter therefore organizes the defeat of the eye and consecrates the power of the hand: the hand or manner of the painter who shows the invisible night of the tomb, and the hand of Thomas which takes over from his suspicious eyes.

What the picture shows is the aporia of a view that is always carried towards a greater proximity, towards a truer contact, and towards an endless penetration. Just as the black background which functions as a quasi-surface brings the four figures closer to the spectator, so the four spectators who are represented—including Christ himself, who looks at his own wound—lower their heads to see more closely, as the three apostles have their bodies bent over to bring the eye closer to the rib. Thomas's body is so curved and his head so far forward that his mouth is right in front of the hand that Christ places on his to guide it to the wound. Yet Thomas does not look at the wound, as noted by Giovanni Careri.[15] The figurative problem of the painting can thus be expressed as follows: to what extent are we the witnesses, we who look with and in front of these four actor-spectators?

Thomas touches the wound, but Jesus directs Thomas's right hand with his own left hand. The violent penetration of the wound that resembles two lips is redoubled by the visual impression that Thomas is about to kiss the hand that guides him. The finger seems to dismiss these two lips, but it echoes the virtual kiss, and given the directional gesture of Jesus, it is possible to think that these two lips will swallow the finger. The light amplifies this impression. It comes strangely from the back of Christ, that is to say from the dark place from which it arrives: the tomb of the resurrection. And this marvelous light which comes from the tomb at the left of the painting, behind Christ, illuminates, more than anything else, all of the folds: the white drapes of his coat, which he opens with his right hand to reveal the wound; the wrinkles of the three stupefied foreheads of the apostles; and especially the small tear in the fabric on Thomas's left shoulder, which is the same size as the wound in Jesus's side, a detail which figuratively comes to signify the condensation of the two motifs: the wound and the mouth. Eight eager eyes look at this wound as if it were about to reveal the truth.

There are thus a series of gestures that draw a chain of intensification of vision, and which have as their coordinates the eye, the hand, and the mouth, and as their movements the passage from the eye to the act of touch, and from the touch to eating: to see, to look in order to see better, to move closer in order to see more closely, to touch, to penetrate, to open, to kiss, to swallow, and to incorporate. There are so many gestures that find in the Eucharist the ritualization of this logic which, in Caravaggio, represents violence: to see truly is to be swallowed by the visible. Giovanni Careri connects the Eucharistic logic of the painting to a sermon on the Passion by St. Charles Borromeo, who was famous at the time of Caravaggio. Borromeo was one of the great craftsmen of the Council of Trent who had confirmed the Eucharist in 1563, eight years before the birth of the painter. Speaking in the place of Christ, the Italian cardinal pronounced this exhortation: "Put your hand and also see how deep is the abyss of divine mercies. There you will be allowed to touch and kiss the very entrails of His mercy."[16] The gesture of touching the wound is reflected by Borromeo as a kiss, and the invitation to participate in the pain of Christ is transformed (by the effect of this trope of the kiss that induces reciprocity) into the promise of a gift that is yet to be received: the gift of the infinite compassion of God. The play between the active touch and the shared kiss intertwines the gift and the counter-gift—active participation and the received offering—according to what Agamben called "a use."[17]

The Eucharist is the ritual that suspends activity and passivity in favor of a use thanks to the incorporation of the host by the communicant, an act which is also the incorporation of the communicant into the mystical body of Christ. According to Giovanni Careri, the wound that is touched by Thomas (whose hand is directed by that of Christ) and the amount that is swallowed suggest that this pathetic group prefigures the incorporation of the resurrected body to the Corpus Mysticum until the end of time, according to the Pauline anthropology of the flesh:

> This thought implies an "entry" of each of the chosen ones into the glorious body of the risen one, and if we have to imagine through which opening we will be able to enter the body of Christ, we can only think of the wound.[18]

The curved bodies and wrinkled foreheads of the apostles may be less indicative of the effort to see than they are a resistance to the dazzling truth: in the night of the tomb, the light from the resurrection exposes the flesh and reveals the opaque evidence of the miracle. Truth figures crudely in this space outside the world: in this pre-scene, it is represented by the filthy, obscene gesture of the finger that enters the wound, spreads it, sinks into it, and gets lost in it.

The drama of vision follows from the dogma of the incarnation. To see is always insufficient, suspicious, deceptive, and subject to simulacrum, as long as the vision is not compassion. Since Christ is not an image, but a real and suffering flesh, to see means to believe in what is hidden from all that is visible, that is to say, to believe in the inner reality of his flesh. Vision is always in tension with touch, and, even more, with the act of eating (Didi-Huberman would speak of the "voracious eye").

This ideal of incorporation has a pathetic and obscene side, which is the kiss on the wound. To replay such a scene seems to allow Tónia to go beyond the phantasmal imitation of the Virgin, and to abandon the idolatry that she brings to her cheap icons. She really experiences the carnal suffering that is, in Catholicism, the suffering of all embodied souls, and more particularly the pain of Mary Mother of God and Mary Magdalene when they see the stigmata on the other beloved—the God who became bleeding, open, raw, and dying flesh. From the painting to the film, from the obscure stage of the tomb to the specular backstage of an invisible scene, the wounded flesh is that which escapes the spectacle of the visible world and requires the obscene gesture of a kiss in order to be represented. The only spectacle that flesh can offer is the Communion, understood as the compassionate choreography of the bodies kneeling, gathering together, touching, and kissing one another in celebration of their similar carnal essence.

CONCLUSION

In *To Die Like a Man*, as in Rodrigues's preceding films, the kiss re-enacts the ideal of a sacrilegious communion of damned bodies suffering from the bottomless pit of their desire. The queer utopia of corporal transformations bends, suddenly and ephemerally, in the face of the figurative and blood-stained irruption of the Christian utopia of a single flesh, the great mystical body of Christ, of which each of these bodies would be only a limb. The scene shows a distinct and solitary body that is suddenly made melancholy by this very solitude opening itself to the flesh of a fellow being, and they become absorbed in this common flesh, this universal flesh of those who live, love and suffer. However, this reversal can be read differently, as an act of reappropriation of noble culture by the minor destinies, the *devenir-mineur*, of Christian figures. João Pedro Rodrigues retains only the strangeness of the Christian flesh and iconography: the already-queer monstrosity of a pregnant virgin whose glorious body dies in a spectacular apotheosis like an iconic queen, and the gory, quasi-sadomasochistic martyrdom of the flesh that bleeds, tears, and is kissed.

Love is Stronger than Death: João Pedro Rodrigues's *Two Drifters* and the Ghost(s) of Manoel de Oliveira

José Bértolo

"Yes. I was dead. I've come back from down there."[1]

UNDER THE INFLUENCE OF MANOEL DE OLIVEIRA

The subject of this chapter may be surprising at first glance. When we talk about *Odete* (*Two Drifters*, 2005), João Pedro Rodrigues's melodramatic second feature film, it is unlikely that we think immediately of the work of Manoel de Oliveira. Rather, the affinity to classical cinema in *Two Drifters* is more readily observed, and especially the affinity to classical melodrama, with Douglas Sirk being the first filmmaker to come to mind. Aside from that most obvious reference, Rodrigues's work shows a recognizable debt to other filmmakers, such as Joseph L. Mankiewicz, Rainer Werner Fassbinder, or Pedro Almodóvar.

In this chapter, however, I do not aim to explore the connections between Rodrigues and other melodrama directors, whether classical, as in the case of Sirk and Mankiewicz, or postclassical, such as Fassbinder or Almodóvar. Furthermore, I do not intend to argue that João Pedro Rodrigues is a direct artistic heir of Manoel de Oliveira. I will not even try to prove that Oliveira is a crucial influence in *Two Drifters*, which is a film full of both explicit and veiled cinematographic references to films such as Mankiewicz's *The Ghost and Mrs. Muir* (1947), Blake Edwards's *Switch* (1991), or Jerry Zucker's *Ghost* (1990).

In his published conversation with Antoine Barraud, Rodrigues comments on the work of Manoel de Oliveira. In his discussion of the older filmmaker's influence on his work, Rodrigues highlights the "carnal presence" and the "Buñuel-like perversity" of Oliveira's characters, and the fact that the director seems to believe in "unreality" above all things.[2] According to Rodrigues, the films directed by Oliveira are markedly artificial and "unreal," yet not in a way that stresses that falsity, but rather one that confirms Oliveira's perception of life as artificial and unreal.[3] This relation to a problematic notion of realism is certainly one of the fundamental traits shared by both filmmakers.

In this chapter, I argue that even if the similarities between Rodrigues and Oliveira are not self-evident, there are some crucial echoes of Oliveira's (romantic) ghost stories in the films of Rodrigues, and especially in *Two Drifters*, Rodrigues's queer take on that same genre. My hypothesis is that by studying these two filmmakers simultaneously, who at first seem very different from one another, we may uncover the common ground between them. In this sense, I will consider *Two Drifters* in relation to three films directed by Oliveira: *Benilde ou a Virgem Mãe* (*Benilde or the Virgin Mother*, 1975), *O Passado e o Presente* (*The Past and the Present*, 1972), and *O Estranho Caso de Angélica* (*The Strange Case of Angélica*, 2010). *Two Drifters* occupies the central place in this comparative analysis, which will demonstrate how Rodrigues and Oliveira share a similar preoccupation with crucial questions pertaining to film aesthetics and film theory, and concerning interpretation, figuration, and the nature of cinema as medium and as art.

HYSTERICAL PREGNANCIES (*BENILDE OR THE VIRGIN MOTHER*)

Oliveira's *Benilde or the Virgin Mother* centers on the eponymous Benilde, who is presented paradoxically both as a virgin and as a soon-to-be mother. She seems to believe that she still is a virgin, and that her pregnancy is a mysterious gift from God, which would turn her into a new version of the Virgin Mary. The paradox that lies at the heart of Oliveira's film triggers a meditation on truth, belief, and the limits of knowledge. In terms of plot design, ambiguity is the single most important element of the film, and it is a feature that led the French critic Jean-Louis Schefer to write that Oliveira's film is, ultimately, an "incomprehensible drama."[4]

More skeptical spectators might argue that, as the film progresses, we are led to believe that Benilde was, in fact, raped when she was sleepwalking, possibly by the madman who howls and wanders around the house. However, the film ultimately gives no firm answers, and instead it remains open to an array of disparate interpretations. The film recalls Todorov's definition of the fantastic genre:[5] the script of *Benilde* is written in such a way that it is impossible completely to dismiss multiple readings once we are caught in its interpretive trap. Different, scattered clues may lead us to believe that the pregnancy is indeed a miracle, or that the father of the child is either the madman, Benilde's fiancé, the ever-present priest, or even Benilde's own father. If one of these possibilities of paternity were true, she would presumably know the truth and thus would be lying and saving face by calling upon the grace of God. Nonetheless, since we learn early in the film that Benilde sleepwalks, it is possible that even she may not really know who the father is. Consequently, she may be as much a victim of this interpretive dilemma as the spectators are.

This hermeneutic dilemma is, in fact, staged by the film in narrative terms from a theatrical perspective, since each of the characters believes in a different hypothesis. The doctor thinks that Benilde is clinically insane; being a mundane woman, Benilde's aunt believes that she is lying and had sex with the madman; her father is led to believe that she lost her virginity to her fiancé before marriage; and her ignorant handmaid has no idea what to think about the whole situation.

The most obvious common axis between *Benilde* and *Two Drifters* is the fact that the protagonists of both films have an unusual pregnancy. At the beginning of Rodrigues's film, we see Odete, who works at a supermarket, helping a pregnant woman. She instantly becomes infatuated with the idea of being pregnant, so that she can stop being an "invisible woman" and become the center of attention for those around her. Later, we see her with her boyfriend at home and she asks him to get her pregnant, which he refuses to do since they are not even married. Their relationship quickly comes to an end and she develops an obsession with a neighbor, Pedro, who has just died after being hit by a car, and whom—it seems—she did not even know personally.

In order to understand the importance of the pregnancy in *Two Drifters*, I would like to recall three adjoining scenes: 1) Odete is taking a pregnancy test, which indicates that she is not pregnant; 2) right after the test, she is at the cemetery, prostrated over Pedro's grave and screaming his name, asking him to come—"vem!" [come!], she says—and to have sex with her—"fode-me" [fuck me]; 3) immediately after that scene in the cemetery, Odete is standing by the grave with Pedro's mother, to whom she is now showing her alleged baby bump. At this point we learn that she is pregnant.

In his conversations with Barraud, Rodrigues calls attention to the "old-fashioned" way in which he structures his films: "shot after shot, after shot. Classical. Academic."[6] The filmmaker's observation highlights the fact that most of his films—with the important exception of *O Fantasma* (*Phantom*, 2000)—are made within the codes of classical cinema. That is, as a modern filmmaker he is decisively influenced by "old-fashioned" ways of making movies. This is most evident in the way that he conceives his films within the conventions of certain typical Hollywood genres, such as the melodrama in the case of *Two Drifters* and the musical in the case of *Morrer Como um Homem* (*To Die Like a Man*, 2009). Luc Chessel synthesizes this convergence between classical and modern ways of doing films to argue that, for Rodrigues, "'classical découpage' [. . .] is a sort of model (an organic model) which is impossible to perfectly reproduce."[7] I would like to return to the three consecutive scenes that I described above, now with Rodrigues's classical notion of "shot after shot, after shot" in mind.

On a simple level, the way in which these scenes are edited should not raise any hesitation in the mind of the spectator. First, Odete is not pregnant; then, she asks a dead man to make her pregnant; and finally, she is pregnant. Yet this succession of events is barely believable, since we know that dead men do not father children. In a simple and effective way, the film raises a fundamental problem of interpretation: who is the father of Odete's child? Although in a less emphatic manner than *Benilde*, Rodrigues's film rehearses different views on this pregnancy: Odete seems to believe that Pedro miraculously impregnated her after his death; Pedro's mother believes that Odete will actually give birth to her grandson; and Odete's ex-boyfriend believes that he must be the father of the child. As a result, the spectator is left perplexed and uncertain.

Later on, when Odete's ex-boyfriend takes her to the hospital, he learns—and the spectator learns with him—that, in fact, from the point of view of science, she is not pregnant. The doctor declares that she has been suffering from the rare mental and physical condition called hysterical pregnancy. That is, Odete has all of the symptoms of a pregnancy, but there is no baby inside her.

The interesting point in Rodrigues's film is that the revelation that this was a hysterical pregnancy all along does not entirely solve the riddle at the heart of the film. Just as with *Benilde or the Virgin Mother*, to dismiss Odete as merely a madwoman and a falsely pregnant woman is to overlook the complexity of the film. These characters demand interpretation. The strange opacity of these women requires us to make sense of them and, by extension, to make sense of the films that they inhabit.

Therefore, when we learn that there is no baby, we must return to the three sequences that I mentioned earlier and look at them in a new light. We must remember the second scene, in which Odete is lying on Pedro's grave telling him to "come." If we conceive of *Two Drifters* as a story of the supernatural, when Odete says "come," she is in fact asking the deceased Pedro to come back from the realm of the dead into the world of the living. More specifically, I argue that *Two Drifters* is, in fact, the story of a supernatural possession.

In Portuguese, as in English, the verb "possuir" (to possess) can have a ghostly dimension (to be possessed by a ghost). It also has strong sexual undertones: instead of saying "fode-me" (fuck me), as Odete does over the grave, she could alternatively say "possui-me" (possess me). So when she thinks she is being sexually possessed by this ghost, she is probably, in fact, being supernaturally possessed by him. He enters her, not through sexual intercourse, but by metempsychosis, that is, by the transmigration of his soul to her body. From this moment on, the pregnancy not only indicates "in psychological terms, a classic, Freudian transference of [Odete's] desire, [and] a crazy wish-fulfillment scenario"[8] but also it is the symbol of a supernatural possession.

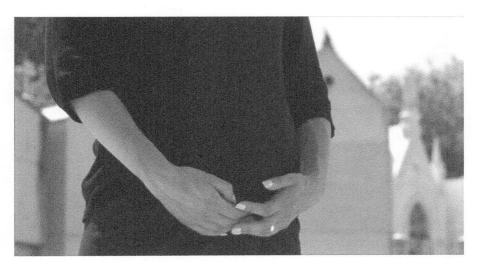

Figure 3.1 Odete's belly

Pregnant women have a new life developing inside them, which is easily visible in the well-known silhouette of the woman with a prominent belly. In Odete's case, this is precisely what happens: she has a new "life" developing inside her. The particular aspect of her case, however, is that inside her belly there is not a material human life form, but another thing, literally a thing from another world. This means that, in Rodrigues's cinematographic universe, the relation between what the spectator sees and the fictional truths of the films is not at all clear-cut. This becomes transparent in *To Die Like a Man*, for instance, where the interplay between essence and appearance is precisely the central point of reflection, in the figure of a human being who clearly has the identity of a woman, but also possesses the sexual organs (and thus, the appearance) of a man. The lesson to be learned is that, in Rodrigues's films, things frequently hold unsuspected meanings. In the specific case of *Two Drifters*, pregnancy becomes the strange index of a possession.

To sum up this first part of the chapter, I conclude that in both *Benilde* and *Two Drifters*, pregnancy works on a symbolic level, which has strong theoretical implications because it reveals that these filmmakers are constantly asking us to interpret characters, situations, and visual signs beyond their literal meanings. Their films are ultimately made within realistic aesthetic models of representation, but they also challenge literalness. This is why the spiritual, the immaterial, and the ambiguous, which are in permanent tension with immanence, materiality, and the physical evidence of the bodies, are so important for Rodrigues and Oliveira. That tension enables the filmmakers to question the unstable nature of reality, and also the uncertainty that characterizes cinema as a medium.

DEAD HUSBANDS (*THE PAST AND THE PRESENT*)

It is interesting to observe that the titles of both of the films discussed so far contain the names of their female protagonists, which inscribes them within a long tradition of works of art titled for their heroines. Among hundreds of other examples are novels and films such as Samuel Richardson's *Clarissa* (1748), Marquis de Sade's *Justine* (1791), Charlotte Brontë's *Jane Eyre* (1847), King Vidor's *Stella Dallas* (1937), Mankiewicz's *The Ghost and Mrs. Muir* (1947), or Fassbinder's *Martha* (1974). This lineage contains diverse artworks and stories, but all of them seem to deal with the tradition of the Romanesque and with the seeming exploitation of the heroine's integrity by placing her in extreme circumstances. With this in mind, it is important to identify one aspect that contributes to the singularity of Rodrigues's film in this respect: namely, that Odete may not be the real protagonist of this story, even if the film's title coincides with her name. The interpretation that I am proposing here is that of the supernatural. This story is mainly a love story between two men—Rui and Pedro—who are separated at the beginning of the film when Pedro dies in an automobile accident. As I suggested earlier, Odete may be a kind of vessel for Pedro, who, by inhabiting her body, is finally able to return from among the dead (to quote the French title of the novel written by Boileau and Narcejac, *D'entre les morts*, that Hitchcock adapts to film in *Vertigo* [1958], and which has some similarities with *Two Drifters*)[9] in order to reunite with his lover in the world of the living. In short, this is a ghostly love story. As such, it is also the story of widowhood, which recalls another film by Oliveira, which in turn can illuminate further aspects of Rodrigues's film.

The Past and the Present begins with Vanda sitting at a writing desk, and holding in her hands the photograph of a man. We quickly learn that the man in the photograph is her ex-husband, who died in an accident. In the present of the film, Vanda is married to another man, whom she despises. She still loves her previous, dead husband instead. Her current husband ends up dying later in the film, and she learns that her ex-husband—the one in the photo, whom she came to love after his death—did not actually die. They reunite and marry again. At the end of the film, she starts to hate her new/first husband and begins to love her previous husband, whom she had hated while he was alive.

This black comedy can be described as follows: Vanda cannot love the man to whom she is married in the present, and she always loves the man to whom she was married in the past, hence the title: *The Past and the Present*. The title also points to the exceptional ontological instability of this character who does not have the ability to live/love in the present, and is thus in a permanent state of non-coincidence with it. In a way, she does not inhabit the reality of daily life, but the realm of the imaginary. She does not take advantage of co-presence, but feeds instead on "figures of absence"—to quote Marc Vernet's celebrated study (1988)[10]—such as portraits. Therefore, she does not love her husbands while they are alive and have physical bodies with real flesh; she only loves them when the only things left behind are the images and memory of them. Consequently, she prefers mediated love to non-mediated love, and she desires intangible objects instead of tangible ones.

The issues that are addressed in *The Past and the Present* have a direct relation with *Two Drifters*, even if such questions are configured differently in Rodrigues's film. First, we must recall that *Two Drifters* is also a film about marriage, widowhood, and remarriage. Oliveira's film opens with Felix Mendelssohn's *Wedding March* in the soundtrack; *Two Drifters* likewise starts with a symbolic marriage. In a remarkable opening sequence, Pedro and Rui exchange rings and vows in the street at night: "In joy and in sadness, in sickness and in health, every day of our lives, until death do us part." It is thus especially tragic, or melodramatic,[11] that Pedro dies in an accident a few minutes later, turning Rui into a widower, if not legally, then certainly at a symbolic level.

However, in Rodrigues's film, just like in Oliveira's *The Past and the Present*, the expression "till death do us part" is not meant to be taken at face value, especially because in the worlds of these filmmakers, death is definitely not the end. Minutes before dying, Pedro tells Rui, "I love you," to which Rui answers, "You will have to prove that to me." The narrative arc that *Two Drifters* builds from this opening sequence until the final moments shows us the proof of this love. Pedro's return from the realm of the dead and his reunion with his lover at the end of the film are precisely the materializations of the proof of his love that Rui requests from him at the beginning. The originality of this film, however, is that instead of showing a common ghost figure—such as Patrick Swayze's figure in Zucker's *Ghost*, for example—Pedro's return is mediated through the body of a woman, Odete. That is, the ghost is embodied within the physical world, which is attuned to the poetics of the flesh that we associate with Rodrigues's work from his first feature film, *Phantom*, in which the body of the actor Ricardo Meneses is on full display for the majority of the film, to the later *To Die Like a Man*, in which the protagonist Tónia cannot decide whether she is willing to complete her sex transition, and indeed, in *O Ornitólogo* (*The Ornithologist*, 2016), where the camera gazes on the naked body of the actor Paul Hamy in an overtly queer reenactment of the martyrdom of St. Sebastian.

In *Two Drifters*, the ghostly possession is gradual. The first important moment is that which I described earlier, when Odete asks Pedro to enter her and then becomes impregnated not by, but with him. The second key moment happens after she finally meets Rui, the widower. Rui tells her how he met Pedro in the club where he still works at night. At the end of that sequence, Odete tells him: "Don't be afraid. Let Pedro return to you." Then, she goes to the cemetery and sleeps on Pedro's tomb, literally taking the place of the dead, and she is awakened there the next day by Pedro's mother, who says, "my daughter."

Figure 3.2 Odete looking through the window

This sequence definitively marks the process of transformation. Instead of "my daughter," the mother could have said "my son."[12] She brings Odete home, and allows her to sleep in Pedro's room. Odete looks out of the window and sees almost the same view that Pedro (if he were alive) would see from the cemetery: the 25th of April Bridge and the Tagus River (Lisbon aptly recalls *Vertigo*'s San Francisco). Showing the same view from the room and from the cemetery suggests an identification of Pedro's room with the cemetery, and, as a consequence, of Odete (in the room) with Pedro (in the cemetery). Over the course of this same sequence, Odete calls Rui from Pedro's phone, which is an uncanny moment for Rui because he sees Pedro's name on his phone screen, as if the ghost of his lover were literally calling him. Then, Odete puts on the dead man's clothes and goes to the hairdresser, where she asks to be styled as Pedro according to a photo that she found in his room.

Odete's metamorphosis recalls myriads of films. Alfred Hitchcock's *Vertigo* is perhaps the most obvious example, but we may also refer to Yevgeni Bauer's *Gryozy* (*Daydreams*, 1915), Kim Ki-duk's *Shi Gan* (*Time*, 2006), Pedro Almodóvar's *La Piel Que Habito* (*The Skin I Live In*, 2011), or Christian Petzold's *Phoenix* (2014), to name just a few. These are all films in which characters suffer physical transformations, which in turn have profound effects on their identities. Yet *Two Drifters* is also very close to Oliveira's *The Past and the Present*, especially in the way that it deals with portraits and images, with the spatial and temporal non-coincidence between lovers, and with the close intertwining of love and death. It is precisely this inextricable association between love and death—of which *Two Drifters* is arguably one of the most striking modern configurations—that brings me to Oliveira's *The Strange Case of Angélica*.

CODA (*THE STRANGE CASE OF ANGÉLICA*)

Like the other films that I discuss in this chapter, *The Strange Case of Angélica* is a story about a haunting. However, in this case, the ghost that haunts is not purely allegorical like in *Benilde or the Virgin Mother*, or in *The Past and the Present*. In *Angélica*, as in *Two Drifters*, the ghosts are real, and they are at the service both of ghostly love stories and the directors' enquiries into cinematographic art.

The Portuguese critic Fernando Guerreiro wrote that even if *Angélica* were not to be the last film that Oliveira directed (he was 102 at the time), it was "his aesthetic confession."[13] For this author, the film can be considered the pinnacle of Oliveira's work, essentially because it expresses the filmmaker's view on the art of cinema. On this same topic, Guillaume Bourgois also argues in his book on the film that *Angélica* underlines several questions that are crucial to Oliveira's film practice.[14] According to these critics, Oliveira's film offers a reflection on cinema as an art form that merges life and death, movement and stillness, the visible and the invisible, matter and antimatter, verisimilitude and the supernatural. For Oliveira, cinema is the result of the confluence between reality and the imaginary, and this makes him a direct heir of Edgar Morin, who discusses cinema in these same terms in *Le Cinéma ou L'Homme Imaginaire* (1956).[15] Such indetermination between the real and the imaginary is at the core of cinema's deeply unstable nature.

This is also one of the aspects that Rodrigues has been exploring since the beginning of his career. His "Asian Trilogy,"[16] for instance, focuses extensively on these matters, exploring the tenuous borders between documentary and fiction. However, we can trace this type of reflection back to his first feature film, *Phantom*, and it persists in his most recent feature film, *The Ornithologist*.

The specificity of *Two Drifters* within this reflection comes from the fact that Rodrigues creates this film within the framework of classical cinema. At first glance, it may look like the story of a hysterical woman; however, if we look at the film closely and try to pursue the interpretive clues that it offers, we discover a complex film that is, ultimately, about the hysterical ontology of film. Like the three films by Oliveira, *Two Drifters* works mainly at a symbolic level. The fact that Odete really transforms into Pedro at the end of the film, while her physical appearance remains structurally unchanged, may be perceived as a sign that cinema (which is a medium that in principle deals solely with the surface of the world) truly possesses the ability to transform reality from the inside. In addition, these films show us that, like cinema, reality is a mutable, porous, and ultimately precarious thing. In an interview, Oliveira observed that "cinema is the phantasm of [. . .] physical reality, but it is [also] more real than reality itself, in the sense that reality is ephemeral, it constantly escapes us, whereas the cinema, although impalpable and immaterial, can capture [reality]."[7]

In *Angélica*, the dead woman is also a symbol for this interplay between cinema and reality. Her ontological instability is represented by the "Mélièsian" technique of superimposition, and it mirrors this conceptualization of film as an unstable medium. In a way, she works as an allegory of cinema, while Isaac, the male protagonist, is just like the spectator, a cinephile. Similar to *Two Drifters*, this is the love story between a living person and a dead person. Also like *Two Drifters*, it enables the couple to be reunited at the end. The difference is that in Oliveira's film, the reunion happens after death and out of this world, while in Rodrigues's the reunion is physical and it happens within this world when, in the final sequence, Pedro and Rui have sex through the body of Odete in an act that further stresses Rodrigues's highly corporeal poetics.

To conclude, I will concentrate on the similarities between the two films. The fact that they both have happy endings is not only striking, but also very relevant, because these endings seem to prove the success of cinema in overcoming the boundaries of reality. In sum, through their highly theoretical plots, both films perform the ultimate miracle of cinema: to reconcile different realms of reality in a single, new, and autonomous reality on the screen, where—as someone mentions in *The Past and the Present*—"impossible things become actually real."

PART 2

Cinematic Landscapes and Territories

Phantoms, Drifters, and Desiring Saints: Landscapes, Soundscapes, and Becoming-queer in the Films of João Pedro Rodrigues and João Rui Guerra da Mata

Andrija Filipović

INTRODUCTION

In *O Fantasma* (*Phantom*, 2000), *Odete* (*Two Drifters*, 2005), *Morrer Como um Homem* (*To Die Like a Man*, 2009) and *O Ornitólogo* (*The Ornithologist*, 2016), João Pedro Rodrigues and João Rui Guerra da Mata create specific relations between landscapes, soundscapes, and what I call becoming-queer. I am using the concept of becoming-queer to describe the ways in which these directors go beyond simple representation of gay or transgender identities to construct milieus that surpass the traditional humanist divisions of human and non-human, or natural and cultural, without naturalizing or denaturalizing queer desire, but constructing a "third way" that goes beyond the linear/non-linear and material/non-material divide. I will argue that Rodrigues and Guerra da Mata create a specific film/world image of becoming-queer. Becoming-queer in this sense is a much broader concept, which surpasses purely LGBTQ+ identity concerns[1] and is much closer to Rachel ten Haaf's concept of "neither,"[2] as developed in her discussion of *A Última Vez Que Vi Macau* (*The Last Time I Saw Macao*, 2012). Moreover, becoming-queer includes the "neitherness" of gender, film style, and locality in these films, while actively creating an ontological openness toward another (filmic) image of the world, which questions any kind of stable boundary.

In the essay "The Age of the World Picture," Heidegger writes that "metaphysics grounds an age, in that through a specific interpretation of what is and through a specific comprehension of truth it gives to that age the basis upon which it is essentially formed."[3] Such metaphysical ground is what Heidegger calls the "world picture." The modern world picture "does not mean a picture of the world but the world conceived and grasped as picture,"[4] which means that it is, first and foremost, "representing man."[5] To represent means "to set out before oneself and to set forth in relation to oneself."[6] For the world to become picture (or image, in the context in which I am using the term) is "one and the same event with the event of man's becoming *subjectum* in the midst of that which is."[7] The modern image of the world, therefore, is essentially the relation between subject and object, where the primary element is man as subject. The becoming-queer of the image (of the film/world), meanwhile, constructs complex milieus with relations that are pluritemporal in their multimaterial differentiation, and that queer any notion of stability. As will be shown, narratives go both forward and backward, and perhaps nowhere at all if we persist with spatial metaphors. In other words, Rodrigues and Guerra da Mata construct an image of materiality that goes beyond the face-landscape assemblage and its organic, all too human, representation of the world.

ON LANDSCAPES, SOUNDSCAPES, AND MILIEUS

As Agamben and Deleuze and Guattari observe in their works, landscape is deeply connected to a certain conceptualization of the human. Agamben argues that landscape is something which is essentially tied to the human being in the sense that landscape offers a feeling of being "at home." Landscape is thus in opposition to the world into which human beings were thrown and where they suffer disorientation. Landscape is a form-of-life. For Agamben, landscape is one of the inappropriables, along with the body and language. He says of landscape that,

> not only is it unclear whether it is a natural reality or a human phenomenon, a geographical place or a place in the soul; but in this second case, neither is it clear whether it should be considered as consubstantial to the human being or is instead a modern invention.[8]

He goes on to describe landscape as "a phenomenon that concerns the human being—and perhaps the living being as such—in an essential way."[9] In order to fully understand Agamben's claim, one has to go back to Heidegger and his existential analytic of *Dasein*. According to Heidegger, animals do not have a world, merely an environment. Animals are just being in the world, while only *Dasein* exists and has or dwells in a world. Due to their immediate relation with other beings-in-the-world, animals are unable to own a world, or to be open to or dwell in the world, but rather they are enclosed in their limited environments or habitats.[10] The essential difference is between the environment and the world. The transition from the environment to the world in the becoming-human of *Dasein* is performed through "a suspension and deactivation of the animal relationship with the disinhibitor."[11] This suspension creates the human, and the opening of the world for the human is "constitutively marked by negativity and disorientation."[12]

The possibility of there being a landscape appears once the environment becomes a world, and when animal becomes human. In that sense, one could write of the coalescence of the terms *human, world, landscape* because they cannot exist without each other. Landscape assumes even greater suspension and deactivation than that required by the concept of the world, to the point that one speaks of inoperability—of the inoperability, that is, the inappropriable. The world itself is suspended in order for the landscape to be produced. For Agamben, landscape is first and foremost an animal environment. It is the "natural world" represented on the landscape, which assumes that animals live in and relate to their environment. Landscape is made inoperable by *Dasein* watching it as her/his own world. World is transformed by becoming a landscape, a world that is *only* watched and contemplated. Negativity that is constitutive of the world, or as a negation of animality in the human and a negation of the animal environment in the world, is dismissed here because "use-of-oneself and use of the world correspond without remainder."[13] Furthermore, landscape "dwell[s] in the inappropriable as form-of-life," and hence "in landscape [the human] is finally at home."[14] Humans are thrown into the world while landscape is home for human beings, it is a refuge from the thrown-ness, given that the human is thrown constitutively into the world and disoriented in her/his constitution as *Dasein*. Landscape, therefore, is essentially connected to the human being; it is what makes us human beings beyond the difference between the environment and the world, although there is no landscape without the environment and the world.

Deleuze and Guattari, on the other hand, argue that landscape and subject are inextricably linked or, to be precise, that what they call the facialization of the body and the landscapification of milieus happen simultaneously so the human is produced as a subject-organism, while milieus become the unified ground for representation in the form of nature-landscape. Since the landscape is produced with the function of subjectification, so too is the soundscape, because sound is produced by the facialized bodies that move through the landscapified milieus. In his analysis of film music, Redner[15] shows the ways in which, when understood from Deleuze and Guattari's point of view, music relates directly to the narrative of a film, thus motivating and supporting the development and structure of the film. While Redner's focus is exclusively on music, I would argue that the same could be said for sound in the film more generally, and especially when considered in relation to the processes of subjectification and landscapification. The sound within the film either produces reterritorializing effects of subjectification/landscapification for both the characters and the viewers of the film, or alternatively, it performs deterritorializations as it opens the lines of flight toward milieus beyond the subject/organism.

Landscapification is inextricably tied to the face and the abstract machine of faciality. As Deleuze and Guattari write, "the face has a correlate of great importance: the landscape, which is not just a milieu but a deterritorialized world."[6] The abstract machine of faciality consists of two axes—an axis of signifiance and an axis of subjectification. These two axes are connected because signifiance "is never without a white wall upon which it inscribes its signs and redundancies," while subjectification "is never without a black hole in which it lodges its consciousness, passion, and redundancies."[7] At the intersection of these two material-semiotic axes, the mechanism of production of faciality appears: the abstract machine of production of the face. In this sense, the face is part and parcel of signifiance and subjectification; that is, it is the product of the relations of power that produce the organism. Production of the face is the result of decoding and overcoding, of the deterritorialization and reterritorialization of material-semiotic flows, which are essentially tied to the social processes that produce an organism from a body. An organism is a functionalized body, the organs of which gain specific functions within the given socius. The head, which Deleuze and Guattari equate with the body, must be facialized:

> if the head and its elements are facialized, the entire body also can be facialized, comes to be facialized as part of inevitable process. When the mouth and nose, but first the eyes, become a holey surface, all the other volumes and cavities of the body follow . . . Hand, breast, stomach, penis and vagina, thigh, leg and foot, all come to be facialized . . . Facialization operates not by resemblance but by an order of reasons. It is a much more unconscious and machinic operation that draws the entire body across the holey surface, and in which the role of the face is not as a model or image, but as an overcoding of all the decoded parts.[8]

The processes of landscapification are almost the same as the processes of facialization, which means that landscape is produced at the same time as the subject-organism. Deleuze and Guattari explain that "Christian education exerts spiritual control over both faciality and landscapity: compose them both, color them in, complete them, arrange them according to a complementarity linking landscapes to faces."[9] Signifiance/subjectification transforms the head into a face, and the organism into a subject, and this transformation runs parallel to the transformation of milieus into a landscape. In these intertwined processes, fluxes of head-body that are common to all beings-in-becoming are deterritorialized into the face, which negates the materiality that is common to both humans and animals, and to living and non-living beings. In the relations between humans and landscape lie the whole ontopolitics not only of what has been overcoded as human, but also of what has been overcoded as animal, plant, and non-organic as well. It is so because, as Deleuze and Guattari write, "the human head implies a deterritorialization in relation to the animal milieu that has itself been deterritorialized (the steppe is the first 'world,' in contrast to the forest milieu)."[20]

However, there are ways of going beyond this state of affairs, and Deleuze and Guattari call these "lines of flight." In the following section, I will analyze the ways in which Rodrigues and Guerra da Mata try to untie the entanglement of milieu-landscape and body-face. I will argue that, in their films, there is a multiplicity of milieus that are connected through co-constitutive multimaterial and pluritemporal relationships rather than a world-landscape that is a single nature in the sense of the One of substantial ontology. This type of filmic image of the world is more aptly described as the becoming-queer of human, nature, film, and so on.

MILIEUS OF BECOMING-QUEER

In *Phantom*, the protagonist, Sérgio goes through a series of transformations, from being a gay man who moves around the city landscape, to embarking on a process of becoming-animal by obsessing about a swimmer, to finally becoming-imperceptible in a machinic-desert milieu. The soundscape changes from the everyday noise of the nocturnal city to the droning of machines and the silence of the desert, and this change signals his passage beyond human representation, at which point the film ends.

Phantom opens with a surprising and confusing scene: a dog barks while its owner is choked to death by a person wearing a black latex gimp suit. It will become apparent that the person in latex is Sérgio, and in terms of a linear narrative, this scene ought to be in the last third of the film. By placing the murder at the beginning of the film, Rodrigues and Guerra da Mata complicate diegetic temporality and simultaneously criticize the linear temporality that lies at the base of the subject-organism.

Sérgio works as a refuse collector. He is taciturn, but demonstrates affection for a dog living at the waste depot. In an interview, Rodrigues explained his interest in exploring the relationship between human and animal "because [Sérgio is] a character that acts a lot by instinct. So, this borderline between humanity and animality, and rationality and irrationality was something I was very interested in exploring."[21] Sérgio's marginalized social position is further underlined when Rodrigues and Guerra da Mata show us Sérgio's Lisbon as a dark and empty space: most of the garbage collection is done at night. Sérgio-as-subject is marginalized by his social class, to the extent that his landscape is made poor: the space that he moves through and lives in is as rich as his class position allows. Like the lifeworld of a tick that Deleuze and Guattari discuss in *What is Philosophy?*,[22] Sérgio's landscape is relationally poor because of his social standing. That, however, starts to change when he lays eyes on a young, middle-class man. He becomes fixated, to the point of following the man to a swimming pool, stealing his swimming trunks and masturbating while auto-asphyxiating under the shower. Social class and sexual obsession intertwine in a scene in which Sérgio breaks into the young man's home and kidnaps him. Sérgio is sexually aroused by the man, and fascinated by his material possessions. He eventually releases the young man, but Sérgio's process of becoming is unstoppable. This is when the scene from the beginning of the film takes place: Sérgio, wearing a black latex catsuit, kills a different man. He then runs through the dark streets of Lisbon to the outskirts of the city outskirts and the desert of the post-industrial milieu.

The term "milieu" is used here to signify the difference of this term from "landscape" and from the processes that are included in the abstract machine of faciality. When Sérgio kills a man, he enters into the process of becoming-animal for the purpose of signifiance and subjectification. He becomes Sérgio-humanoid, and is no longer Sérgio-binman or Sérgio-gay-man. After he runs away to a place that appears to be a quarry, he behaves like someone/something not entirely human, drinking stagnant water from puddles and eating waste. The world ceases to be an urban landscape and instead becomes a wasteland milieu that lies beyond the divide between culture and nature. This outside-ness of the wasteland milieu to the nature/culture binary, created by the work of signifiance and subjectification, is to be found in the way that this milieu was produced by human industrial activity and then abandoned to nature. A post-apocalypse ambience is created: we know that there *were* people there but they are no longer present. Rodrigues says of the location where these scenes were shot:

> This is the north of the city; it's a part of the city that was built in the '50s and the '60s. Before that, there was nothing here. It was just countryside, and there were just like old farms. So there's still a lot of these traces of a past that was not really the past of a city, was more of a past when this was not Lisbon. So I think it's also a borderline. It's a borderline territory, in between urban and more countryside. For me, these places tell stories just by themselves, because they are kind of ruined. You see ruins of old farms. You see ruins of old roads. You see a past that becomes also part of the fiction, in a way.[23]

This is the spatio-cultural-temporal milieu in which Sérgio-humanoid creates his line of flight away from the abstract machine of faciality and its urban landscape. Sérgio enters a factory, where he becomes almost one with its machines. We do not find out what those machines are for or what kind of factory it is, but we hear the (desiring-)machines humming incessantly and we see Sérgio-humanoid almost melting into them. The film is open-ended, as Sérgio-humanoid leaves the factory and its/his machines behind, and disappears into the desert. The camera remains still while, through the open doors of the factory, we watch a black figure running towards the darkness.

It could be said that *Phantom* follows the linear progression of Sérgio's transformation from being gay to becoming-animal to becoming-imperceptible (although the first scene complicates this progression). *To Die Like a Man*, meanwhile, shows a similar process in reverse. Mainstream understanding of transgender discourse is based on the linear narrative of adjusting the body to the desired gender. *To Die Like a Man* takes that mainstream discourse, and twists it and turns it on its head through the story of a trans woman who chooses to die like a man, or perhaps as some other gender, or beyond gender, if such category can be applied in the first place. The central motif of the film may perhaps be found in the line "I want to be plural" that is sung by the main character, Tónia in the graveyard, while António is lying in the coffin next to his/her lover. We first meet Tónia as a trans woman who performs drag shows in a club. Rodrigues explains: "I wanted Tónia to have the aura of the *grande dame* of the drag show. At the same time, in this film I tried to go against the usual films that feature drag queens. I wanted to do something different. I wasn't interested in shooting Tónia's stage performance, at least not until the end of the film when it becomes a special moment; when it becomes something different."[24] Tónia moves between woman and not-completely-woman in her own conceptualization of her body, which the end of the film confirms, by multiplying the body, gender, and ontological statuses between António and Tónia, living and dead, in a single scene in which the camera pans across the graveyard.

The multiplication of milieus is not reserved for gender; it also occurs on the formal level. The film complicates diegetic space and time by twisting its topology through an insistence on the artificialization of landscape. Maria Bakker's house in the woods becomes a milieu around which space and time are organized, but which lies outside both. We meet Maria Bakker within the first ten minutes of the film. Tónia's son, Zé Maria, is on military exercises in the same wood, where he has sex with a fellow soldier; a few minutes later, the two men spy on Bakker and her partner at home, and the comrade asks Zé Maria if his "father" (that is, Tónia) knows these people. Zé Maria then kills him. Bakker does not appear again until the final third of the film. After Tónia and her partner Rosário accidentally stumble upon Bakker in her garden, which contains the grave of the killed soldier, she invites them in for a cup of tea. Maria Bakker is a campy decadent who lives in seclusion from city life with another trans woman,

Paula. Bakker's manner of speaking, her witty jokes at others' expense, and her quotations of German poetry create an air of aloofness and artificiality. In the evening, Tónia, Rosário, Maria Bakker, Paula, and Doctor Felgueiras who came for a visit, go for a walk in the forest looking for snipe, which one of their number has heard are extinct in the area. Suddenly, after the not-so-metaphorical snipe hunt, the whole scene turns red, the characters sit on the ground, and music starts. For the duration of one song, the red remains and the characters sit still. The natural landscape of the forest is made artificial through the theatrical immobility of the characters, the changing color, and the use of music, and this upsets any claim to either natural or artificial, so that the forest becomes a milieu rather than remaining a landscape.

Rodrigues and Guerra da Mata use this scene to underline the artificiality of the whole film assemblage, as well as the artificiality of essentialist ontology with which we approach the world. This scene is key to Tónia's decision to "die like a man," or to "die as a man": after it, she leaves for home, and subsequently for the hospital where she dies. The artificiality of gender categories equals the artificiality of the film's construction, which indicates the artificiality of every construction, including the image of the world. In other words, beyond constructions that aim for unity and wholeness (of body, subject, organism, world), there lies an incessant multiplication of milieus in their becoming. Rodrigues and Guerra da Mata also show the multidirectionality of queer desire because the film does not contain a single straight character. Not only is heterosexuality as such excluded from the narrative, but also non-heterosexual gender and sexual identities are destabilized. Queer desire, then, can never be closed within unified constructions. Or every closing within unified constructions is revealed as artificial in the movement of becoming-queer.

The use of music in *Two Drifters* has the same estranging effect as it does in *To Die Like a Man*. By being ironically too much on point, the music and lyrics appear to underline the mood, together with the special effects of the rain and wind. *Two Drifters* shows how a catalytic event sends Rui and Odete into a centripetal movement of intensive becoming, in which any sense of stable identity is irretrievably ungrounded, including the line between life and death. Rodrigues and Guerra da Mata formally give the film a linear structure (with elements of melodrama, pastiche, and parody), but the content drifts away from the identity categories that ground the production of subjectivity. That is, Rodrigues and Guerra da Mata destabilize the essentialist onto-logics that are produced by the abstract machine of faciality at the level of characters. The film revolves around relations between a woman (Odete), a dead gay man (Pedro), and a living gay man (Rui), although the boundaries between living and non-living, imaginary and real, and heterosexuality and homosexuality become porous, if not altogether redundant, when they are treated ironically in this way through both music and image.

The film opens with a romantic scene in which Pedro and Rui say their goodbyes after exchanging engagement rings, but Pedro dies in a car accident immediately afterwards. The subsequent scenes show his partner Rui suffering, drinking himself into a stupor, engaging in anonymous sexual encounters with other men, and even trying to kill himself. Odete works in a supermarket and lives in the same building where Pedro lived. She accidentally learns about his death and goes to the funeral and the wake. Soon afterwards, she becomes obsessed with the dead man: she starts identifying herself as his girlfriend, visits his grave, sleeps on it, and develops a phantom pregnancy. Odete cuts her hair short and steals Pedro's clothes. She becomes Pedro. The last scene of the film is decisive in destabilizing the essentialist ontology of the abstract machine of faciality. The scene shows a sexual act between Odete-Pedro and Rui, in which Rui is the receptive partner. As the camera slowly moves back, it shows Pedro in a corner, watching the scene calmly and silently.

Rodrigues and Guerra da Mata's multiplication of milieus no longer takes place through locations. This film is shot in apartments, a graveyard, and a supermarket, with a couple of street scenes. Milieus are multiplied at the psychosexual level, that is, at the level of subjectification. Like Sérgio before her, Odete enters into the process of becoming, which leads to further multiplication and moves further and further away from the starting point of socially recognizable subjects. We meet first Odete-the-supermarket-worker, then Odete-the-liar (who introduces herself as Pedro's ex-girlfriend), Odete-the-hysterically-pregnant-woman, and, in the end, Odete-the-man, and a dead man at that, who becomes alive in her body but who is not in her body (Odete-Pedro and Pedro are separate in the last scene). The film could easily be understood as an allegory of the postmodern multipositionality of the subject, especially since it uses the elements of melodrama, pastiche, and parody. However, within the context of this discussion it is understood as the multiplication of milieus to the point of surpassing ontic differences, precisely through the ironic and parodic use of music and other filmic elements and motifs from other films. Odete not only becomes a man, she becomes a dead man. Of key importance here is the surpassing of ontic difference between the living and non-living, which is impossible if the film is read from a postmodern point of view. The becoming-queer of milieus outside the abstract machine of faciality has no regard for the difference between nature and culture, or living and non-living. Everything is open to relationality within the becoming-queer of milieus, no matter the "class" of beings to which a given being purportedly belongs. What is unacceptable and unconceptualizable from the position of subject-organism, such as the ontological non-difference between the living and non-living, is ontological "ground" for becoming-queer. Pluritemporality (the flow of time which is neither linear nor non-linear) and multimateriality (which includes both corporeal and incorporeal and everything in-between) emerge as categories for the description of what is beyond the landscape and of what is constituted by the multiplication of milieus, rather than a postmodern intertextuality that functions simply at the level of signifier and subject.

Alongside *To Die Like a Man*, *The Ornithologist* is perhaps the most complex of the films by Rodrigues and Guerra da Mata that are under discussion here. It is complex because the filmic image of the world is queered through radical multiplication of milieus on every level. The narrative of *The Ornithologist* meanders along with its main character Fernando (and birds and animals) down the river, through the forests, and across the mountains. There is no straightforward resolution of its narrative arc (if indeed there is one), and the film complicates relations between the real, contemporary, historical, mythic, hallucinated, and imagined. The ornithologist travels downriver, and he encounters in turn two Chinese women on a pilgrimage who tie him half-naked to a tree (perhaps in reference to St. Sebastian), costumed revelers performing an archaic folk ritual by firelight, a deaf goatherd named Jesus (with whom he has sex), and a band of Amazons. At the end of the film, a dynamic cut moves Fernando the ornithologist from the forest to the city, where he becomes Rodrigues himself.

The film ties together a multiplicity of milieus, ranging from semi-pagan beliefs in the region where the film was shot, to scientific discourse (an ornithologist watching birds), to mythological and religious discourses (Amazons, and St. Anthony of Padua, whose story Fernando's echoes). By means of these milieus, which appear serially in the film narrative, the focus is placed on the process by which the character of Fernando-Rodrigues becomes a desiring *machinic* saint. I emphasize machinic to point out the relational character of Fernando the ornithologist, who functions as an open desiring-machine in the sense that this concept is described in Deleuze and Guattari's *Anti-Oedipus*: "Producing-machines, desiring-machines everywhere, schizophrenic machines, all of species life: the self and the non-self, outside and inside, no longer have any meaning whatsoever."[25] The binary ontology of subject–object is lost to the disjunctive synthesis of desiring machines. Furthermore, it is Fernando as desiring-machine who connects and multiplies the milieus, since the desiring-machine functions "amid hiatuses and ruptures, breakdowns and failures, stalling and short circuits, distances and fragmentations, within a sum that never succeeds in bringing its various parts together so as to form a whole."[26]

Another element that points to the reversal of subject–object relations and the multiplication of milieus is the birds. The majority of the first third of the film is dedicated to birdwatching, and to birds watching back. Rodrigues and Guerra da Mata set the scene so that the birds watch the ornithologist and, by extension, the viewers of the film. As Rodrigues says in an interview:

When I was looking at birds, I thought "how do birds look at us or look at me back?" The film is also constructed with that, the fact that how do birds look at us? That's why I chose to show the point of view of the birds, as if birds could see different things from other human beings. In a way, they sense this transformation and so I thought it made sense really to . . .[27]

Animals and animal milieus, in other words, possess agency beyond being an object for the human gaze in everyday life or in scientific discourse. That is, by looking back at both Fernando the ornithologist and the viewer, animals are freed from being tied to the objectified environment, while at the same time *Dasein* as human subject possesses the world, and with the world, possesses the animals as beings-in-the-world. The device of showing the animal looking back and reclaiming the agency that is usually reserved for humans unsettles the modern metaphysical framework and points toward a much more complex image of the world.

The final minutes of the film follow a dynamic cut from the forest to a roadside on the outskirts of Padua. The ending brings about the disjunctive synthesis of two thematic series: nature-ornithologist-mythic-religious-animal and director-urban-filmic. Rodrigues and Guerra da Mata create multiple milieus within the first series, since the elements do not necessarily communicate with each other, except in relation to, and through, the focus on Fernando as desiring-machine. However, some of the elements from the first series (if not all of them—after all, what is nature or animal if not convenient construction for a subject/organism?) are fictional because they are mythic or religious, yet they have real material consequences for the character of the ornithologist. Differences between fictional and real, natural and social, human and animal, religious and secular, dead languages and living languages, implode in this pluritemporal and multimaterial becoming-queer of the (filmic) image of the world. As Rodrigues says:

There is this legend that St. Anthony understood every language and when he spoke he was understood by everyone. The idea came from there. Also, I wanted to get inspiration or take elements from different mythologies, so I had this idea that, for instance, this huntress in the end, as they come more or less from Ovid's *Metamorphoses*, they could still speak Latin, as in Ovid's text. The film slowly loses reality and approaches fable. In the end I could permit myself to do things like this: these bare-chested women speaking Latin and him understanding what they say. These animals that are no longer alive, but are the forests' ghosts. It's approaching an unreality that at the same time is real.[28]

The issue of language is further underlined by the use of Mirandese, a regional language that was forbidden by Salazar, yet kept alive by an older, rural population that was out of the reach of the dictatorship. Rodrigues and Guerra da Mata move away from the majoritarian language of Portuguese, and insist on "stuttering" and "stammering" (as Deleuze and Guattari say of minor literatures[29]) within the dominant soundscape/landscape. The soundscape includes the sounds of animals and other natural sounds, together with the music made by a masked troupe of dancers. In other words, there is no non-diegetic music, and the little music that is present is rooted in local tradition, which underlines further the minoritizing processes that are at work in the film. The treatment of St. Anthony, who is associated with marriage and family values, as a body of flesh which "confuses sacred and profane,"[30] and who is at the same time Fernando the ornithologist and Rodrigues the director, also unsettles the majoritarian religious expectations of this sacred figure. The desiring saint's desiring production, then, "is pure multiplicity, that is to say, an affirmation that is irreducible to any sort of unity."[31]

CONCLUSION

Rodrigues and Guerra da Mata create a particular film image that simultaneously functions as an image of the world. I have defined this image as becoming-queer. *Phantom* shows the main character's process of becoming-imperceptible to the abstract machine of faciality. He moves from a marginalized position within the urban landscape/soundscape to milieus that are beyond any kind of social or other form of recognition. *Two Drifters* follows a similar line: it complicates the ontic division between the living and the dead, as well as between genders. With *To Die Like A Man*, the process of becoming-queer intensifies and develops, through both form and content, and explodes the artificiality of entrenched subjectivities and identities, showing the underlying multiplicity of milieus. Finally, *The Ornithologist* forgoes any notion of purpose-driven narrative, and synthesizes disjunctively various milieus and their temporalities and materialities.

What kind of image of the world does becoming-queer offer in Rodrigues and Guerra da Mata's films? Heidegger shows that the modern image of the world is grounded in the relation between subject and object, and that this is a relation which conditions every metaphysics that would offer some kind of understanding of the world. Furthermore, Agamben shows that this type of defining relation to the world conditions the emergence of the human subject who is thrown into the world and shapes it through both negation (as animal environment) and ownership (by transforming it into landscape). Landscape and its soundscape are part and parcel of the becoming-human of the human subject. However, Deleuze and Guattari show that such an assemblage of *world, landscape, human* is nothing but the product of certain relations of power. More precisely, the human subject is an effect of signifiance and subjectification that shape both bodies and milieus. Following Deleuze and Guattari's insights, I have shown that Rodrigues and Guerra da Mata construct an image of becoming-queer by multiplying milieus, instead of by representing unified landscapes and soundscapes. The becoming-queer of milieus points toward multimateriality and pluritemporality that lie beyond the human as subject/organism and its representational image of the world. Instead of a safe humanist subject–object divide, or any kind of simplistic binary opposition, the films of Rodrigues and Guerra da Mata offer an image of the world that is irreducibly multiple, and which challenges viewers to enter into the process of becoming-queer to a world that is made to the measure of the human.

Queer Metamorphoses and Displacements in the Cinema of João Pedro Rodrigues and João Rui Guerra da Mata

António Fernando Cascais

INTRODUCTION

João Pedro Rodrigues and João Rui Guerra da Mata's joint filmography is extremely diverse, but recurring themes do emerge, with the trope of metamorphosis perhaps being the prime example. João Pedro Rodrigues himself has recognized this, as I have explored in a previous study of *O Fantasma* (*Phantom*, 2000).[1] In the present chapter, however, I will demonstrate how, as well as being a recurrent theme in the two filmmakers' oeuvre, metamorphosis is also strongly interwoven with the spatial dimension in their works.

Beginning with their first film, and again in films such as *Morrer Como um Homem* (*To Die Like a Man*, 2009), *Odete* (*Two Drifters*, 2005), and *O Ornitólogo* (*The Ornithologist*, 2016), we witness more or less intense processes of identity transformation, or indeed, actual metamorphoses. The main characters undergo mutations that are sometimes radical, against a backdrop of spatial displacement (places, environments) that is not a mere framework but rather plays an active and instrumental role in these transformations. Changes in space and identity thus become inextricably connected within transformative processes of reciprocal cooperation and improvement. The basic connection between these changes and spaces operates through the characters' actual bodily reality, that is to say, their corporeality. The characters' bodies are the physical loci of their transformations precisely because they function as their point of connection to the spatial environments through which they move and by which they are affected.

The characters are thoroughly engaged in experimental processes of self-fashioning, which ground and revolve around their lived, bodily, sexual, and gender realities, as those realities are experienced in the characters' use of space. Transformations of identity are partially compulsory (they follow external pressure), and partially deliberately sought; but they all affect individuals who are not at ease with their own situation—wherever that may be—and who are also at odds with their own inadequate bodily realities. As subjects, they are the target of some threat to their lives, which confronts them with the imminent collapse of their initial identities, and with the imperative to become-other(s) (*devenir-autre(s)*) and thereby commit to an actual journey, at the end of which they will become different subjects because they can no longer be who they initially were, nor can they stay where they are. We could define this fact of having to change and having to move in a single process as a spatialization of processes of (re)subjectivation in the cinema of João Pedro Rodrigues and João Rui Guerra da Mata. In order to profitably describe such spatialization, this analysis adopts a shift from the more usual perspective that is based on a temporal unfolding, to a perspective that hinges on spatial progression.

BETWEEN THE SELF AND THE OTHER

Deriving from the Greek *meta morphē*, metamorphosis means to go beyond form. It is a change in shape, nature, or structure that is so profound that the being which undergoes it is no longer recognizable: it is altered and becomes *other*. The notion of metamorphosis has always expressed a profound, even radical, transformation: a change on the ontological plane that wholly envelops that which changes, and which transforms its way of being. Metamorphosis turns sameness into alterity, or reveals an internal rupture of the Self, whose duplicity and unraveling into Other was already present, even if it was undetected or unconscious. The themes of metamorphosis and identity are thus indivisible.[2]

A brief overview of the evolution of the theme of metamorphosis in Western culture reveals that in classical antiquity, this gift was reserved for the gods and could be inflicted upon mortals as a punishment. Bruce Clarke has pointed out that metamorphosis is one of the skills attributed to Hermes, who was the emissary and messenger of the gods as well as being the patron of reading and writing, communication, and thievery, and the bearer of a *pharmakon* that could both cure and poison.[3] Hermes is constantly in transit, and is therefore *enodios* (of the road) and *hodios* (of the journey). This characteristic establishes a connection between metamorphosis and journey. He is also frequently associated with Aphrodite, and their connection is given form in their son Hermaphroditus.[4] These stories predate the medieval Christian demonization of metamorphosis as one of the evil powers of Satan, the great trickster and master of appearances who could take on the form of an irresistibly handsome young man in order to lead sinners into temptation. The Renaissance reclaimed classical mythology, especially in its creation of the human beast—the werewolf—which later came to be appropriated in literature and film that deals with the theme of the *Doppelgänger*, and even more recently in science fiction, where technically-mediated shapeshifting is both celebrated and feared.

Science fiction plays with several modes of "fiction of terminal identity."[5] Such fiction is a genre within science fiction that deals with the end of the metaphysical, substantial, and unitary subject, and the emergence in its place of new hybrid subjectivities or "hybrid entities" that are at the interface of the biotechnoscientific manipulation of the body. Hybrid entities are currently particularly apparent in the prevailing domains of info-biological research, the flux of postcolonial subjects, the emergence of digital mediascapes and e-spaces, and an erotic attitude (or "erotitude") in relation to the post-human *mindful-body* and non-procreative behaviors. In these domains, hybrid is a synonym of fluid identity, diasporic subjects, cultural syncretism, and a plurilogical perspective, as noted by Massimo Canevacci:

> *Info-biology, postcolonialism, technoscape, e-spaces, erotitude* are converging toward a visionary, constructivist, de-centered meaning of hybrid, no more condemned to regressive imaginations. Hybrid cultures favor liberational bodyscape, spreading syncretic cultures, diasporic subjectivities and hybrid identities.[6]

Fiction of the terminal subject is actually firmly embedded in the spaces of the post- and trans-human that are so relevant to postmodern thought. It provides the postmodern apology of post-humanism with fictional content that is teeming with cyborgs, androids, and interspecies man-animal or man-machine hybrids, and at times is transgendered and transsexualized, and at times has markedly queer tones. Hybridity implies that the Self and the Other are interdependent and belong to each other. Henceforth, identity and alterity come to be explicitly constitutive not of the individual, but of a construct which has been labeled "dividual" by some commentators, and "multi-vidual" by others.[7] This concept clearly abandons the typical binarism of the dualistic logic of fixed and immovable identities that is frequently based upon biological or social determinisms:

> *Self-representation is hetero-representation: it is a production of a visionary hetero-logic, an altered logic, a strange dislocating cluster of logics. I would*

like to stress the shift from autonomy to *heteronomy*: it makes explicit the idea that *nomos* (law) has an authority based on the static logic of mono-identity. That's why nomos should be moving toward the fluid brightness of the anomic "otherness": *heteronomy a desiring crossing toward the otherness*.[8]

Canevacci also notes that within the Western tradition, the concept of hybrid has both a mythological and a genetic cultural matrix. He states that "[e]very universal is partial—every singular is plural—every purity is hybrid—every history is polyphonic—every taxonomy is anomic."[9] In other words, according to a hybrid logic, rather than being in opposition to the Other, the Self is the Other.[10] This concept has a cultural lineage that owes much to Rimbaud's "Je est un autre" ("I is another.").[11] Much like the atom, which was believed in the past to be physically indivisible, in contemporary times the individual is no longer held to be the indivisible minimum unit in social and psychic terms:

hybrid culture shifts the concept of the border from an either/or situation to a not-only/but-also one. This means the end of the dichotomies that have substantially determined modernity and its concept of identity, physicality, time and space.[12]

Melanie Puff adds:

Hybridity means an amalgamation of heterogeneous elements in a single organism, whereby the resulting condition retains the separation of the individual components. This implies that the Self is continually dependent upon the Other due to cognizance of the fact that the Other is part of itself.[13]

IDENTITY METAMORPHOSIS

Rodrigues's cinema is not (techno)science fiction, but it does reflect various ways of disassembling and fragmenting the Self. It endeavors to do so, however, through mythical-cultural allegories—first and foremost, metamorphosis—rather than resorting to the program of queer performativity, which he does not embrace. The methodologies of queer theory apply only marginally to his cinematographic framework. In this respect, Bruce Clarke reminds us that metamorphosis is a metamorphic allegory, that the metamorphic body is an allegory of the allegorical, and that the classical tradition (from which modern narrative and consequently film narrative descend) featured significant formal and thematic relations between allegory and the trope of metamorphosis.[14] These thematic relations can therefore stand for burning human issues, such as the construction of gender and sexual conflict, family and class identities, cosmological, economic and social structures, moral affects, and intellectual ideals:

> In the development of modern science and technology, the scene and control of physical transformations gradually shift from a hermetic occult and an anthropomorphic *Natura* to a capable and culpable humanity. By the same token, agents wielding metamorphic powers shift from supernatural to human. Through science, human agents acquire literal technologies for the range of super-natural functions: for meta-morphosis, modes of material transformation; for uncanny productivity, automation; for prophecy, electronic communication; and for daemonic flight, aeronautics and space travel. That is, through science, humanity confirms its daemonic status.[15]

Rodrigues has revealed in several interviews that he is not comfortable with his cinema being labeled as "gay." Nonetheless, the film critic Vincenzo Patanè insightfully notes how much Rodrigues is indebted to a gay imaginary, and all the more so in *Phantom*:

> Insightfully playing with the imaginary that is most valued by gay cin-ematography—from *Pink Narcissus* to Genet, and from *The Blood of a Poet*, by Cocteau, to Kenneth Anger's *Scorpio Rising*—the film force-fully revisits the subject of the double, one of the paramount subjects of twentieth-century culture.[16]

In the same line of thought, João Ferreira states that:

> Considering the various expressions of gay cinema, sexual affirmation, and the validation of sexuality [. . .], his films are not born of the canon, but the canon appropriated itself of them [. . .]. It certainly is not the politics of identity but rather exclusively the politics of desire. Homo-sexual desire, without a doubt [. . .] but it does not stop there. From this perspective, Rodrigues' films are more directly the offspring, at least conceptually, of the N[ew] Q[ueer] C[inema] foundations laid by the first works of Gus van Sant and Todd Haynes.[17]

SÉRGIO

In *Phantom*, Sérgio is a Lisbon refuse collector who is introduced in the opening scene of the film as an insatiable sexual predator. Dressed in a skin-tight, full-body, black latex suit, he rapes another man who is naked and handcuffed, behind a closed door. On the other side of the door, a Doberman barks and scratches. The scene portrays the end point in Sérgio's metamorphic process, which is then explored by the narrative in flashback. Sérgio works the night shift on a refuse collection truck. He moves through the streets of a crepuscular, labyrinthine, and claustrophobic Lisbon: "an almost imaginary place, shadowy and lugubrious, the natural habitat for the film's main character Sérgio"[18]—an environment that clearly alludes to the dungeons of leather and S&M bars.

In the many night scenes, the aural background features perpetually barking dogs, which enhances the pervading atmosphere of violent animality and unbridled sexual desire. Gary Kramer remarks that, "while there is plenty of hard-edged realism in the film [. . .] Rodrigues includes elements of magical realism in the drama."[19] Sérgio's animality surfaces immediately in his humane and tender relationship with his dog Lorde, with whom he shares a bowl. This provides a shocking contrast with his behavior towards his girlfriend Fátima, whom he answers by growling when she annoys him, and when she attacks him, Sérgio reacts by whining. Their only sexual relation is a violent simulation of penetration by a bell weight. *Phantom* is not a silent film, but it is certainly a film of few words, while its proxemics are very eloquent: the film is set against the background of the nocturnal urbanscape, "representing the impossibility of communication between human beings, except through pure physicality."[20]

Sérgio is an awesome mastiff who moves from being prey (when he submits to consensual rape by his supervisor) to becoming a predator, when he sexually molests the uniformed policeman upon whom he stumbles, handcuffed and gagged, in a patrol car. When the two meet again, their roles are reversed. While he awaits the shift distribution, Sérgio smells his hand and licks traces of semen from it. The ever-growing abjection of his becoming-animal throughout the film can be read as a metaphor of the all-encompassing abjection that was historically imposed upon the figure of the homosexual, who was gradually removed from social interaction by stigma, and marked by a taint that envelops all of the space and time of his being within heteronormative society. In parallel to these scripted and consensual sex games, which are clearly indebted to S&M imagery, Sérgio also goes cottaging in an increasingly aggressive posture that leads him to harass his colleagues explicitly in the changing rooms. In the only, undeniably pornographic (or perhaps, we might concede, post-pornographic?) close-up of the film, which is unprecedented in modern Portuguese cinema, Sérgio forces his occasional partner to suck his erect penis in the public restroom. While he is working, he spies on the people who inhabit the houses from which he collects garbage, in an act that strongly recalls Gide, whose exclamation fits Sérgio's apparent perception like a glove: "Familles, je vous hais!" ("Families, I hate you!").[21]

Sérgio meets João, a young man who becomes the target of his obsessive desire and the driving force behind his becoming-animal, and whom he
stealthily shadows. When Sérgio approaches João and reveals himself to the
young man, the latter clearly becomes annoyed. Sérgio follows him everywhere
by day, and prowls around his house at night. He rips open João's garbage bags
with his teeth, and retrieves a pair of used motorcycle gloves, which he uses
to masturbate, and a pair of ripped underpants, which he smells. Despite his
obsession with João, Sérgio also continues to have casual sex with other men.

After leaving one of his occasional partners, who is seen taking a shower still
with an erection, Sérgio's naked body is seen against the background of a clear
blue sky while he sits at the window of his attic apartment. This is probably one of
the most symbolic scenes of the film, and it is certainly unique in its full daylight
setting. Sérgio climbs onto the roof, in an excursion from the almost fully crepuscular world of the film. Before doing so, however, he slips into João's underwear
and, thus clothed, climbs above his room and out of the darkness as though he
were a crawling animal. He moves around the roof on all fours, and is filmed
from behind and in close-up with the bulk of his scrotum hanging between his
legs as it would on a dog. However, in a signal of his inability to endure his ascen-
sion into the light on the edge of a social and human world to which he no longer
belongs, Sérgio quickly returns to his cave-like sanctuary, and to his obsessions
which abhor daylight, in a clear allusion to the night-time metamorphosis of the
werewolf. This return explains the notion of the "clothed body" (*corpo rivestito*)
which is presented in the form of the latex body suit as a symbol of the shedding
of skin,[22] which in turn denotes the change in his ontological status.

We meet Sérgio again in the shower room of his workplace. He is wearing
João's underwear and, with his hand inside it, he is masturbating frantically
while choking himself with the shower pipe. The act is not shown crudely, but
rather suggested; however, its spasmodic intensity puts it on the same level
as the earlier scenes of rape and violent sex. Sérgio begins his pursuit once
more, but he is caught by a policeman (presumably the same man whom he had
encountered previously) who scares him away.

Sérgio then follows João to the pool at his gym, where Sérgio swims after
everyone else has left. Once more, his nudity is examined thoroughly by the
director, who films his testicles and anus in close-up when he turns to dive.
Sérgio finally dares to break into João's home, and he sprinkles his urine on the
young man's bed to mark his territory or perhaps to signal his desire to mate. He
jumps out through a window when he hears João approaching, but he is caught
by the policeman, who cuffs and subdues him. Sérgio bites the policeman's trun-
cheon, licks the protuberance between his thighs, and pulls his underwear out
from the undone zipper on his trousers with his teeth, but the policeman leaves
Sérgio when he senses that João is approaching. Sérgio appears handcuffed in
front of João and asks for help, but the latter questions him about his pursuit.

When Sérgio tells João not to fear him, João is furious and pushes him away. We are not shown how Sérgio breaks free of his handcuffs; we merely see him roaming among garbage trucks that have been set alight, perhaps as revenge against him, possibly by João, whose refusal to surrender "not only symbolize[s] João's rejection, but also a more global rejection by society as a whole."[23]

The final sequences hark back to the beginning of the film: João is handcuffed and gagged with duct tape and, in his own room, he is raped by Sérgio. The film ends with Sérgio, dressed in a full-body latex suit and with his transformation into "phantom" complete: he roams an enormous landfill on the outskirts of Lisbon. He arrives there at night, having jumped onto one of the garbage trucks on which he used to work. This final journey takes place after he has drunk from the pool in a garden in the deserted city: "the landfill is his last haven, a space outside the world to which he retires when the mask comes to be all that he really is. The phantom becomes real."[24]

The landfill is a repugnant depository of the waste removed from human bodies. It becomes the social reprobate's permanent habitat, which he enters through a hole dug under the barbed wire surrounding it. He crawls around the site, warms himself at the fire that is burning in a metal drum, and rolls on the floor next to it. He feeds on leftovers from garbage bags and captures a live rabbit, which the film suggests that he kills and eats. He drinks water from a puddle, then vomits it up. He takes shelter in the landfill premises at night to sleep, and this is the only time when he removes his latex mask. He unzips the suit to relieve himself, once again exposing his genitals. Fearing exposure, he furtively roams the deserted landfill and hides when he hears the trucks approaching. His metamorphosis into a non–human is fully accomplished.

ODETE

In *Two Drifters*, as in *Phantom*, Lisbon has an active role in the plot of the film. On the night of their first anniversary, Rui and Pedro say their goodbyes. The latter heads for home, while the former goes to his night job in the gay bar area of Príncipe Real. Soon after, however, Pedro dies in Rui's arms following a car accident:

> By focusing on this moment as the pivotal point in the metamorphosis that Pedro undergoes over the course of the film, we are able to see the greater complexity of his ritualized passage from life to death (he dies in this sequence).[25]

Johnny Mercer's lyrics for "Moon River" "add two important ingredients to JPR's recipe [. . .]: the idea of a crossing ('moon river, I'm crossing you') and that of the two lost souls ('two drifters, off to see the world').”[26] We will learn later that Pedro's ring featured the engraving "2 drifters," and of course the expression also became the international title of the film. Finally, the inclusion of Joni Mitchell's "Both Sides Now" in the score reveals, according to Bértolo, a program that is developed by the film on several different fronts: "The *two sides* simultaneously explored by the film are multiple: life and death; body and soul; sanity and madness; the realization and impossibility of love; male and female; truth and lie."[27]

The cemetery is a non-profane space, which serves as the ritual point of access between the worlds of life and death. Near Pedro's grave, Rui meets the extravagantly grieving Odete, a young woman who is obsessed with the idea of having a child, and whose boyfriend refuses to help her conceive. She rolls around frantically on Pedro's grave, howling his name, in an apparent attempt to impregnate herself with a presence that no longer is: with a life that no longer lives. She then declares herself to be pregnant by Pedro, both to her boyfriend and to Rui. The locus of mutation in *Two Drifters* is Odete's body: as her pregnancy progresses, she becomes increasingly masculine in her attire, her short haircut, and her lack of make-up. Odete goes as far as to meet Rui in the gay bar where he works, and she simulates anal intercourse with him while instructing him to call her Pedro. All of this takes place in front of Pedro, whose back we see as he witnesses the scene. The film "is also part of a philosophical and ethical approach, one that accounts for the experience of the minority at the same time as it questions the issue of gender and sexual norms,"[28] and this "radically inscribes it in the queer ethics that refuses to frame the body within normative categories of identity."[29] The penetration scene is essentially a simulation; in keeping with Beatriz/Paul Preciado's true counter-sexual utopia, it does not reach the literality of a radical rupture with Odete's biologically female body.

TÓNIA

By contrast with these earlier films, the case of Tónia in *To Die Like a Man* is quite different. She is frozen midway through her process of change as if both she as a character, and Rodrigues as director, had halted in the face of radical, irreversible change because they are somehow unable to deal with the hardships and challenges that such change brings. The metamorphic process in Rodrigues's cinematography seems to become ever more circumscribed and tentative as it evolves from Sérgio's extreme identity change, through Odete's limited gender change, all the way to Tónia's toying with gender characteristics. At each metamorphosis, the changes are less and less profound and extensive, and ever more limited, superficial, and reversible instead, and the characters that undergo these changes seem to become ever more insecure about them and unsure of themselves.

There is a murder in the opening sequence of *To Die Like a Man*. During night-time military exercises, the young soldier, Zé Maria, who is the son of the seasoned transvestite Tónia, shoots a comrade with whom he has had sexual intercourse. They are close to the country house of the sophisticated and mysterious Maria Bakker, who finds the dead soldier and buries him in her garden with the help of her foolish but devoted partner, Paula. Tónia's life revolves around the queer nightlife in Lisbon. She has tempestuous relationships with her transvestite colleagues Irene and Jenny, her agent Teixeira, Zé Maria, and her partner Rosário, who is the same age as her son. Rosário is a hopeless addict, while Tónia's health is compromised by HIV and by a noticeably suppurating, infected breast implant. Fernando Curopos is right to observe that:

> [h]er physical metamorphosis is carried out by means of a self-"glamorization," a fitting into the idealized image of her innermost gender that directs her towards a hyperbolic femininity, all the while dressing as a "woman in good order" (she's getting closer to her fifties), through a mimetic desire to fit socially, to become a "regular" woman.[30]

We cannot but agree with Curopos when he notes Tónia's aspiration to normalcy, which leads her to mimic a strongly binarized, heteronormative, heterosexual relationship with Rosário in which she performs the role of the mother–lover; yet Rosário insults her by telling her that she is neither man nor woman. Divided between her faith—which holds her back from undergoing gender reassignment surgery—and her desire to please Rosário, Tónia is caught in the trap of compulsory heterosexuality, yet she is unable to employ true queer performativity to overcome it and the constitutive shame that it entails. Tónia's experience thus corresponds closely to what Eve Kosofsky Sedgwick identifies in her critical discourse.[31]

In one scene, which foreshadows their common fate, Tónia and Rosário are seen at night against the background of the monumental Prazeres Cemetery in Lisbon. These characters are adrift and in permanent conflict with themselves and those around them. They exude a *difficulty of being* which reappears as a surface effect: they cling to one another by any means, but they find both themselves and others abhorrent. This difficulty of being is almost constant in Rodrigues and da Mata's characters. In the attempt to escape their stifling environment, Tónia and Rosário go on a road trip during which they get lost in the woods around Maria Bakker's house, and are taken in by her.

The forest space is marked as labyrinthine: it leads all of the characters, involuntarily and unconsciously, to the same spot; they become lost and completely unable to find their way back to where they belong, and they find themselves trapped in the forest that did not looked threatening before. Bakker claims that she only contacts the world of the living through the mysterious Doctor Felgueiras, who recites Paul Célan with her in the original German. Bakker, whose cosmopolitan cultural references provide a strong contrast with Tónia's folk-religious devotion, suggests a surreal evening of snipe hunting. The full moon then reddens, and floods the scene with scarlet: all of the characters are seated. They are transfixed: caught by the camera in a still pose as though they were in a rural portrait while the sound of Baby Dee's "Calvary" is heard in the background. The time and place suggest a transfiguration that transports us to another possible world. This is a world that we perceive as pacified and redeemed—possibly heterotopic, as defined by Michel Foucault.[32] At this moment, Tónia flees. Her sudden departure raises suspicion both on the part of the other characters in the movie, and for the audience of the film. Later in the movie, it becomes obvious that she feared the forest because she was unable to adapt to it, much as she fears a complete gender reassignment, which she confides in an exchange with Jenny Larrue, who, unlike Tónia, has actually gone all the way in her sex change. The forest gives her the chills: "There is something wrong here," she comments. We may be assured that it is not merely the presence of the body of her son's victim, of which she is unaware. She simply does not belong in this world. Fernando Curopos answers this question definitively when he states that:

> Tónia unconsciously dreams of herself as being "plural" but never manages to free herself from the many chains that restrain her. Although she enters a 'heterotopic' world where neither the law of gender nor the pre-established identity categories prevail as they do in the other spaces that she is used to, nonetheless she ends up leaving it, acknowledging that "there is something wrong here."[33]

We could also note that Tónia senses the black wings of death hovering over Bakker's residence (something similar occurs in multiple other locations in the cinema of João Pedro Rodrigues). She attempts to dispel the threat by resorting to her religious beliefs (according to which the sexes were designed by God in the strictest of binary systems), which are very much in conflict with her life as a transvestite. Bakker employs erudite culture to the same end. The movie is based on the true story of the famous Portuguese transvestite, Ruth Bryden, who was known to suffer from a deep conflict within herself, and who ultimately demanded to be buried in men's clothes so that s/he would present himself before God in total compliance with His divine design of two different sexes, in contradiction with the lifestyle that Bryden had pursued during all of his/her life.

After Tónia has been hospitalized, Jenny Larrue comments: "We are all just passing through. None of this is the end." When Teixeira attempts to soothe Tónia, he implicitly alludes to AIDS: "No one ever dies of the illness anymore." To this, she replies, "I'm no longer in charge. I lived like a woman, now I want to die like a man." Tónia's wish to be buried like a man is fulfilled, and she is laid to rest next to Rosário, who is found dead from a drug overdose on the beach. In the final scene, Tónia's ghost hovers over the burial plots during their joint funeral, singing "Oh, how I wish to live in the plural."

FERNANDO, JOÃO PEDRO, AND ANTÓNIO

In *The Ornithologist*, Fernando's change represents yet another turn in the metamorphic process in Rodrigues's cinema. This is a turn that reasserts its evolution towards the loss of ontological depth, as it points—in the case of this particular movie—to the religious supernatural.

In fact, *The Ornithologist* revisits the symbolic spaces that were once inhabited by religion: the relationship between man and nature, and the relationship with oneself, that is, the connection between the individual and his very own Self. En route to the habitats of the birds that he intends to observe, Fernando is unaware that he is stepping over a threshold as ancient as Western mythologies. In such mythologies, the forest is the seat of the supernatural, where all wonders are possible, and especially metamorphosis. However, the crossing of the border between the human world and the woods is signaled by two events of crucial symbolic value. First, it is foreshadowed by the loss of his cell phone signal, which keeps Fernando from communicating with the person who regularly reminds him to take his medication (these reminders, according to Roth-Bettoni, implicitly downplay AIDS, making it seem simply a chronic, non-fatal disease).[34] This event once again introduces the notion of incommunicability between humans and, more widely, between worlds. Then, he falls into the rapids, which drag him to the *other side* and leave him at the mercy of super-human forces. All of this points to the fact that re-establishing contact with the human world is a question of ritual observance rather than one of technical proficiency, meaning that the borders in question, while they are not insurmountable, always require an ontological transition from one state of being to another. The impossibility of being untouched and unscathed at the end is typical of the journey narrative—whether it is the passage through initiation, the expiatory peregrination, the philosophical quest, or even the seafaring exploration. This impossibility is clear from the initial, adventurous rescue of Fernando by the two mysterious and treacherous Chinese women, who are lost on their way to Santiago de Compostela. They drag him out of the water, only to tie him to a tree (using knots that are reminiscent of the ancient Eastern technique of *shibari*). Later, they rob him before they vanish, fearful of the prodigious space of the woods that echo with the maleficent sounds of haunting.

After this first episode of transition, a second episode is introduced during the night in which Fernando in his flimsy tent is surrounded by threatening, dancing *caretos* who wear the allegorical masks typical of Portuguese and Galician popular culture (but which are also present in other regions of Europe), and which evoke the fauns of mythology. The camera lingers on the ithyphallic shape of one of the *caretos*' masks. In a sequence which moves towards an oneiric dimension, Fernando is woken from his dream by a young, deaf and mute shepherd with whom he interacts in gestures—and again, the theme of incommunicability is present here. The young man is irresistible and explicit in his nakedness. He invites Fernando to bathe in the same river into which Fernando had previously fallen. Fernando surrenders to a kiss with this pagan shepherd-faun, who nonetheless bears the very Christian name of Jesus. Later on, Fernando will unintentionally murder Jesus in an argument over an unfounded suspicion (Fernando does not even allow Jesus to try and explain why Fernando's stolen property is in his possession). Fernando will then wander to what looks like an ancient, abandoned hermitage. This is an especially symbolic place that is associated with purifying contemplation, material deprivation, and the absence of human contact. He sees a white dove, which is a symbol of purity and divine grace, and he adopts the behavior of a hermit: presumably, the same hermit whose skull he is holding in a scene that is evocative of the Christian *memento mori*.

Fernando thus finds the path to redemption from the guilt that we are led to believe haunts him. He mortifies himself by cauterizing the tips of his murderous fingers with a hot iron, and thus seems to attain appeasement, which he makes explicit by disposing of two highly symbolic objects: his ID and medications. From a biopolitical point of view, the ID formally confirms his belonging to the socio-political community (the *bios*), while the second keeps him connected to biological life (*zoe*). The *pharmakon* that he seeks is actually quite different, as we perceive in the parody of the Sermon of St. Anthony to the Fish, which is directed at a water tank. Fernando goes deeper into the woods, and meets a group of androgynous Amazons who have come from a different place and time—somewhere in pagan antiquity—to hunt boar, which is a symbol of triumphant virility in pre-Christian myth. They communicate in Latin with Fernando, who appears to be touched by the Holy Spirit, once again in markedly Christian fashion.

Fernando is longing for Jesus's forgiveness (for having killed him) when he stumbles upon Jesus's dead body. He touches the fatal wound in the same manner as Christ instructed the apostle Thomas to touch the wound that had been caused in his side by the Roman's spear. However, Fernando is surprised by the young man, who resurrects before his eyes and—now clearly speaking

Galician—reveals that he was the *careto* with the ithyphallic nose, that he is actually called Tomé (Thomas), and that he lost his life in a careless knife game with his mates. Tomé receives an answer that comes not from Fernando the ornithologist, but rather from the director João Pedro Rodrigues himself, who suddenly replaces Fernando and who, furthermore, has become a transmuted being who claims to be called António, like the Portuguese-Italian saint who preached in medieval Padua. Fernando/António/João Pedro Rodrigues thus appears to pay the blood price for his crime. He says, "Look at my fingers: I no longer am that man. And I know I am here to right that wrong." In a reversal of their mythical-religious positions, he urges Tomé to believe him, just as Christ did with the apostle of the same name: "It's no use trying to understand certain things. They happen, one believes." These final sequences leave one wondering quite uncomfortably whether Rodrigues the filmmaker is dealing, in a meandering and morose manner, with some kind of self-consciousness, if not even personal guilt (but for what, exactly?). Redeemed and reconciliated, and with their fingers lovingly intertwined, João Pedro Rodrigues and Tomé make their way to Padua to the soundtrack of António Variações's "Canção do Engate" ("The hookup song"), where these two characters meet the two Chinese women from earlier in the film, who are returning from the city that they decided to visit instead of Compostela, for they no longer believe in Santiago.

CONCLUSION

A plausible hypothesis about the cinema of João Pedro Rodrigues and João Rui Guerra da Mata is that they employ the trope of metamorphosis as an allegory of the homosexual (and, by extension, the transsexual and transgender) who deserts the social world. Metamorphosis represents the transformation from one state or mode of being to another. This transformation also unfolds across space, and in the journey between one space and another, since the difficulty of being what one truly is also envelops the difficulty of being in any place where one might happen to be. In Rodrigues and da Mata's cinema, the identity changes that are undergone by each of the characters (Sérgio, Odete, Tónia, and Fernando) represent many different thematizations of otherness as an evolving metamorphic process.

In this sense, Sérgio's metamorphosis is archetypal for its depth and radicalness, which lead him beyond the borders of the human. This is not so with the rest of the characters, who cannot help but convey an ever-growing feeling of tentativeness and lack of daring or assertiveness in their metamorphoses. At each change, each character appears to take a step back and refrain from being as daring or going as far as the last. The changes become ever more limited and superficial, as well as reversible. The case of Tónia is illustrative in this respect, because she finally wishes to die like the (oh-so-binary) man that she has never really ceased to be. Furthermore, the metamorphic process in these movies always entails, and is tightly intertwined with death (whether it is the principal character's or someone else's), if not even murder, suggesting that metamorphosis implies that someone has to pay the ultimate price for the change that is at stake. The plot of the film leaves one wondering whether Fernando is not, deep down, overwhelmed by guilt. Metamorphosis therefore has a murderous tone: it comes ever more suggestively to call for some kind of supernatural or spiritual redemption. This becomes all too obvious in the latest movie, which deploys João Pedro Rodrigues himself, positioning him as a filmmaker who is on a personal journey towards appeasement and closure.

Neo-Baroque Landscapes: João Pedro Rodrigues's Docu-fiction and Ecosophical Kinships in *The Ornithologist*

Hyemin Kim

> No matter how small, each body contains a world pierced with irregular passages, surrounded and penetrated by an increasingly vaporous fluid, the totality of the universe resembling a pond of matter in which there exist different flows and waves.
>
> Gilles Deleuze, *The Fold: Leibniz and the Baroque*[1]

INTRODUCTION

Even while internationally there have been sporadic curations and discussions of Portuguese "landscape" films (centering around works by Manoel de Oliveira, Paulo Rocha, António Reis and Margarida Cordeiro, Pedro Costa, and Miguel Gomes, among others), the meaning of "landscape" in the geographic, historical, and cultural surroundings of Portuguese cinema remains largely obscure to the Anglophone film milieu. The idea of Portuguese landscape, as philosopher Adriana Veríssimo Serrão elucidates, carries a spiritual lyricism of "yearning" that "oscillates between finitude (limited) and infinity (unlimited)" of land as it evolved in the development of Portuguese modernity, owing in large part to its physical location on the fringe of the European continent.[2]

Bearing in mind the country's geographical status as the Western frontier of Europe, the Portuguese aspired to both preserve and expand their territory for the development of Portuguese national (and transnational) identities. This desire animated the practice of complex symbiosis between nature and culture and came to embody a singular sanctuary in the conceptualization and visualization of the Portuguese landscape. As opposed to the idea of uncultivated nature, the landscape in the Portuguese context illustrates a mixture of the contemporary with the mythological (the supernatural or poetic elevation), as has been shown distinctively in the Portuguese tendency towards "docu-fiction" in landscape films. This view is supported by scholars and critics who have attempted to introduce a group of Portuguese films to American and other international audiences (well beyond the Iberian Peninsula) in the past decade. For instance, the film critic and programmer Dennis Lim, in his spring 2012 essay for *Artforum*,[3] addressed a legacy of "docu-fiction" in Portuguese cinema by emphasizing the evocative combinations of documentary and fictional or poetic narratives in the films of António Reis and Margarida Cordeiro. A similar critical direction has been taken by the scholar Patrícia Vieira, who has also looked at landscape-driven Portuguese films to address how the "environment" is embedded dramatically in the genealogy of Portuguese cinema, and how this corresponds in turn to the socio-economic and political transformations of modern Portugal.[4]

This chapter continues the endeavor of recognizing the legacy and traits of Portuguese docu-fiction (or ethno-fiction) in contemporary film studies and modes of filmmaking. It explores filmmaker João Pedro Rodrigues's *O Ornitólogo* (*The Ornithologist*, 2016) and the mythopoetic aspects of the film through the lens of Deleuze's conception of "the Baroque," which he illustrated in *The Fold: Leibniz and the Baroque* (1993). Drawing on Deleuze's thoughts on "the Baroque," in which space and time are rendered in Borgesian cryptographic and curvilinear folds, the myriad paths of landscape and memory in *The Ornithologist* can be also interpreted as a continuation of (Neo-) Baroque[5] cosmology and historiography, concepts which are often vernacularized as "magical realism" in a broad sense. Even while the definition and application of "magical realism" as a term has been vague in literary and film criticism to date, it can be framed in relation to the four required elements of fantastic literature in Borges: "the work within the work, the contamination of reality by dream, the voyage in time, and the double."[6] This parallels the way that Deleuze, in *The Fold*, conceptualizes the Baroque as the expressive enfolding or spiraling of a world from *within*, which would figuratively resemble Japanese origami or the tornado vortex. This concept of the world and time is meant to bend the actual topography and linearity that are often conceived within the more realist conventions of geohistorical studies.

In order to configure "the Baroque" in *The Fold*, Deleuze takes Borges's short story "The Garden of Forking Paths"[7] as a pivotal example. He draws attention to this story in which Borges revisits the labyrinthine book of the Chinese philosopher-architect named Ts'ui Pên in the Leibnizian cosmology of "pleats" (Le Pli), which contains and affirms all inflections, bifurcations, and curvatures of incompatible paths and their confluxes. In Deleuze's philosophical rhetoric, this cryptographic space (which also leaps through time) is a distinctively Baroque apparatus. In his reading of Borges's story, the labyrinth is also concretely illustrated as the encounter with monstrous and uncanny figures at each transitory moment between different spatio-temporal coordinates. Such encounters involve horror, disaster, and death, as is illustrated in the works of these three figures—Borges, Deleuze, and Rodrigues. The presence of monsters (supernatural animals, the dead, ghosts, and otherwise non-human powers), as well as the anamorphic figurations of encounters with them, play prominent roles both in Borges's and Deleuze's work, and they can serve as prototypes for the interspecies relationships with birds and forests that are central to the storytelling (both verbal and figural) in *The Ornithologist*.

Underlying its apparent story, the supernatural force of the elements identified above is presented captivatingly through the camerawork and cinematography, and attracts viewers with the eerie and intimate gaze of the unknown. This gaze is interspersed with the voyage of the avian archivist Fernando in the *Parque Natural do Douro Internacional* (Douro International Natural Park). Further, within that ornithologic survey, the film's protagonist, Fernando, who transforms himself into a queer avatar of St. Anthony of Lisbon, manifests his own animality and the mythological contours of "the Baroque" by revealing his enigmatic stories of incarnadine humiliation. The metamorphosis of Fernando into St. Anthony is vividly exhibited in his erotic encounters with some Mirandese men, who are abiding mysteriously in their indigenous land, the *Terra da Miranda*, in Trás-os-Montes in the northeast of Portugal.

However, seeing these figurations of the Baroque raises a particular question: who would be the subject—or dreamer—in this picturesque experience of curvilinear time travel that is presented in *The Ornithologist?* In other words, what kind of subjectivity or intersubjectivity would be alluded to if one were to reflect on the Baroque images of *The Ornithologist* using the framework of Deleuze's ontological notion of "assemblage" of the subjects? In the film, which is reminiscent of Deleuze's exposition of Leibniz's monads, various extraordinary vignettes, which involve multiple subjects (a pilgrimage story of Chinese girls; a tale of shepherd twins; Jesus and Thomas; a mystery of an injured bird; a displaced presence of koi fishes and a skull; and, most evidently, a doubling of Fernando and St. Anthony), bifurcate, mobilize, and envelop the mode of infinite inflections within the Möbius strip of the miniaturized, haunted forest.

The camera and its perspective, both horizontally and vertically, shift between the positions of the ornithologist (and his binocular camera), the birds, and other elliptical characters, eschewing the voyeuristic, focused gazes of spectators. It is difficult to pin down the central subject (as well as the observer) of this filmed landscape and the events that occur therein. Although it derives seemingly from the documentary or ethnographic tradition of fully capturing indigenous people and their preserved habitats, the film does not simply anchor itself in the factual relationship between reality and record, nor does it construct itself completely as a fictional work in which a reliable narrator sutures the storyline and transfers what is to be seen and construed to the audience.

However, the complexity of the film is not merely a postmodern narrative contrivance. The hybridization of fiction with documentary embraces the proximity to reality (similar to the experiential observations in films by the Harvard Sensory Ethnography Lab), and complicates and attenuates the determinative operation of the film's narrative (and cognitive production) and affect. The fusion of fiction and reality in *The Ornithologist* opens up the film itself to a whirlpool of unexpected and dense imaginations of the truth, of dreaming, and of relationality (which extends to the relation between humans and non-human inhabitants) in the landscape that the film portrays. As in the Borgesian enigma of topology and memory of the Adelph, the central force of this vortex of journeys and relationships is hidden even while it offers erotic suspense and exuberant puzzles to the audience.

THE ORNITHOLOGIST, BORGES, AND DELEUZE

João Pedro Rodrigues's *The Ornithologist* is the director's fifth feature film. It explores a river valley area (the Douro International Natural Park), which is adjacent to leafy forests in the northern, medieval region of Trás-os-Montes, Portugal.[8] The film follows Fernando, the ornithologist of the title, who becomes distracted, loses his kayak (in a shipwreck), and goes astray during the course of his journey to observe birds in the preserved wilderness. After the brief intertitle giving the mythopoetic, prophetic story of St. Anthony of Lisbon in the thirteenth century, the film commences with imagery that is reminiscent of National Geographic Channel documentaries: the camera observes birds in their nesting areas, with minimalist frames and *mise en scène*. Even as the film relies on the documentary footage of the habitat, the minimal camera movements and tones (in colors and sounds) enable the sequence to achieve a singularly illusive quality that immerses its spectators in the dream state of "nature" and of birds residing fictively in the thirteenth century.[9]

Later in the film, when Fernando has digressed from the marked birdwatching route, he is more susceptible to his surroundings than he was to the habitat of the birds that he initially intended to observe. In an inversion of encyclopedic desire, the dense "fabric" of the torrential auditory and visual features of the landscape and weather defines the ornithologist's figure and his consciousness. Furthermore, the man finds himself out of his depth in the winding rapids, and the Baroque journey deviates to the ritualized forest, which in turn renders the ultimate transformation of the ornithologist into the mystic St. Anthony of Lisbon, under the elliptical gaze of the birds in their habitat.

Figure 6.1 *The Ornithologist* (2016)

After the kayak accident, Fernando, who is possibly dead, encounters a Chinese-Christian lesbian couple who are on a pilgrimage to Santiago de Compostela. After rescuing Fernando, the sapphic pair intoxicate him and tie him to a tree in a BDSM image that also carries the threat of castration. Fortunately, Fernando escapes from them and goes on to meet a young, deaf shepherd named Jesus whom he befriends and kills. The truth (the fact of murder or not) is obfuscated later in the film when Fernando meets Jesus's twin brother, Thomas. While Thomas also appears to be killed in a regional ritual of sacrifice at full moon, Fernando convinces him that he (Thomas) is still alive and allows Thomas to murder him (Fernando), thus contrasting with the murder that he might have committed in contact with Thomas's twin, Jesus. The cut (the slit in Fernando's throat that is inflicted by Thomas) results in Fernando (with the alternating faces of the actor Paul Hamy and director Rodrigues) undergoing a bloody transformation into St. Anthony, and the story shifts to St. Anthony and Thomas's amorous co-drifting on the idyllic, mundane streets of Portugal at the end of the film.

In terms of the narrative, above all, the film complies with Borges's four elements of fantastic literature that were mentioned above: "the work within the work, the contamination of reality by dream, the voyage in time, and the double." In *The Ornithologist*, there are multiple stories overlaid within the broader story, and these establish an opaque maze of interzones where discordant stories converge without any single resolution emerging over several other alternatives. There is a contamination of reality by the dream, which in turn is infused with the peril of calamitous and colorful eroticism (the wreckage of the kayak, castration, a stab in the chest, the finger in the wound, the slit in the throat, and blood). This danger is repeated in the encounter with "the double," which evokes an intensity that is characteristic of Caravaggio's Baroque paintings, which vivify seductive crime scenes and in which ominous colors protrude from within.[10] Overall, *The Ornithologist* is not about the voyage of the ornithologist: the film itself is an incarnated and textured voyage that envelops and traces the world and which is interlaced with multiple different paths of crimes and concomitant ritualistic eroticism.

Turning to the topological interiority of *The Ornithologist*, the film gives a remarkable presentation of landscape images of Trás-os-Montes that traverse the past, the present, and the future in the style of Baroque collagists. These images phantasmagorize the realistic images (which resemble images from Google Maps) as though in a panorama. Even while there is an observational and at times rough realism that relies on the surviving "untouched" landscape of Trás-os-Montes, the cinematic juxtaposition and the rhythm of the images twist the illusion of hard realism and its representation into a subconscious coil of dreaming and awakening, beneath the chronological passage of time. For instance, the palimpsestic sequence of arraying multiple slides of Trás-os-Montes across time, with the Chinese girls confronting the landscape after wandering around in the forest, stands out for its vivid suggestion of the "dysnarrative" docu-fiction of Trás-os-Montes. This sequence presents Trás-os-Montes in audiovisual terms as somewhere that is located virtually in the pleats of memory, among the layers of cryptographic images of landscapes: the iconographies of medieval Christianity, the dead and their graves, the nature that is preserved as though in a terrarium or in hyperreal taxidermies, traffic signposts, contemporary Chinese travelers, and so forth. Through these cerebral (and sensory) pleats of cinematic memory that combine photographic observations, dreamlike collage, and pacing, the film's spectators may navigate the multilayered immanence of the landscape across time.

ANTÓNIO REIS AND MARGARIDA CORDEIRO— LANDSCAPE AND LANGUAGE

Trás-os-Montes (1976) (the first feature film directed by Rodrigues's mentors António Reis and Margarida Cordeiro) engaged with similar ethnographic concerns to Rodrigues's and also merged those concerns with a time-traveling poetic drama. In addition to the shared location of Trás-os-Montes, Reis and Cordeiro, and later Rodrigues, followed in similar fashion the styles of ethno-fiction that diagrammatically blend observed reality with the "persistent murmuring of the myth" which appears as episodes of poetic fragments.[11] At the beginning of *Trás-os-Montes*, a cheery little shepherd boy appears. He prefigures the deaf-mute shepherd Jesus in *The Ornithologist*. The boy of *Trás-os-Montes* is calling his sheep using a subdialect that seems to hide the ancient or primitive language of his tribe, and which the sheep appear to understand thanks to the directors' poetic invention of mythological relationality. Interlaced with background views of the mountain ridge that seem to echo the past, the film is infused from the very start with the desire (both mythological and poetic) to search for the autochthonous language that survives the passage of time. Indeed, the boy also sees an inscription on a rock, which seems to refer to a language from the Neolithic. In his 1977 interview on *Trás-os-Montes* with *Cahiers du Cinéma*, Reis recalls this shepherd in particular:

> The first (shepherd), the one you're talking about, is a force of nature. He is like a Fulani in Africa and a shepherd in the Middle East, a shepherd who had a profession, a code with his sheep, who walks in the night, who still belongs a bit to the Neolithic age. What he says to his sheep is a code where it is difficult to separate the music, the phonetic and lexical aspects: you feel a shock between these elements. And he speaks a subdialect older than Portuguese.[12]

In fact, in order to film *Trás-os-Montes*, these independent filmmakers deliberately befriended this non-professional actor (as they usually did with other non-actors) to the extent that the camera became like an everyday tool of which he would not feel afraid. This practice of getting close to untrained actors (which extends to the intimacy with non-human actors such as birds, sheep, and dogs in *The Ornithologist* that I discuss in the next section) continues in the collaborations with non-professional actors throughout Rodrigues and João Rui Guerra Mata's docu-poetic works.[13] The tender and "natural" smile of the shepherd that the camera captures in *Trás-os-Montes* comes from the fact that the filmmakers were living in the field of their subjects. Such cohabitation in the actual landscape is the condition that enables the weaving of an undulating intersubjectivity across the filmmaker, the subject, and the audience. The audience can also *witness* a similarly shimmering, mythopoetic relationality in the bucolic presentations of images of a town where little boys are breaking icicles near the frozen creek. In that scene, one of boys finds "lighting stones" which, as he explains in inexplicable and serious enchantment, "came out from the dark by drilling through the earth." The other boys look back at him in a mix of awe and surprise. This unique combination of experiential fieldwork and mythopoetic enunciation is also manifested in the same filmmakers' 1982 film, *Ana*, which explores the abandonment of a small village at the edge of Portuguese modernization. The late French critic Serge Daney commented on one pivotal moment of that film:

> There's a wonderful moment when, wearing a cloak trimmed with ermine, she passes through the countryside with the muffled elegance of a Murnau character. The version of Bach's *Magnificat* we're hearing

is at the right height of the beauty of this advent. The old lady, from the back, cries out a name: Miranda! Blood then comes to her mouth, she looks at her reddened hands, she knows she will die. Miranda is the name of a small village nearby and it is the name of a cow that has strayed and that we find again in the next shot. There are always many things to respond to a word. There is a risk of dying, crying out alone in the countryside. Always poetry.[14]

Although the films *Trás-os-Montes* and *Ana* display a much less surreal texture and a more natural tone in comparison with *The Ornithologist*, the landscape portrayed in those films nonetheless stands somewhere between concrete material from an observed reality (as in the photographs and documentary) and a poetic vortex of time and memory. The temporal coils in these films correspond to the phantasmatic in the Borgesian-Deleuzean dream-machine that enunciates nearly obliterated poetic signs and names for the virtual remembering of the other. It is relevant to note that, in the story of "The Other,"[15] Borges inserts a story of a dream-encounter within a rather realistic frame of history. In this work, Borges emphasizes that he is awake in the concrete present of Argentina, and he simultaneously divagates into a dream-dialogue with the younger Borges from the past, who is living in Geneva. The dreamed loop of the story thereby opens a question about Argentina, and it can be dismantled only by the impossible number of the year 1964 on the bill. The evidence provided by the number "1964," however, does not imply the victory of linear hard realism. Even while the number of 1964 destabilizes the dreamed story, by way of its narrative-penetration it also takes the readers to the cryptographical realm of the enfolded present, which is already contaminated by the layers of unfolded dialogues between the "two Borges."

In a similar move, the eponymous location of Trás-os-Montes is already infiltrated and narrativized by both séance-like (in other words, invoking the past and the dead) and prophesizing accounts of stories and encounters, which continue in the Trás-os-Montes of *The Ornithologist*. Similarly, under the influence of Reis and Cordeiro's hybrid ethnographic filmmaking of quotidian life and poetic narratives, Rodrigues's previous films have also dealt with Portuguese mythopoetic figures such as the shepherd in *O Pastor* (*The Shepherd*, 1988), and Portugal's first king (Afonso I), gay men, and birds in *O Corpo de Afonso* (*The King's Body*, 2012).

Well before he directed *The Ornithologist*, and in what can be seen as an homage to Reis and Cordeiro, Rodrigues directed a short film entitled *The Shepherd*, which is filled with the reverberating sounds of old sheep-bells and long takes that portray the daily life of a shepherd who is forced to retire. This film allegorizes the act of remembering the ecology of human (shepherd) and non-human (sheep) co-dwelling in the old, rural landscape of Portugal. That remembering also connects to the act of memorializing the forgotten or victimized *other* in the modernizing world that is present in Reis and Cordeiro's films. While the political intention of the ornithologist Fernando's encounter with the shepherd Jesus in a utopically preserved realm is merely insinuated, it also serves as a cinematic séance for the dead shepherds and their companions (sheep, goats, and dogs) as well as portraying the serenely rural surroundings of the present. The film thus enfolds and transports these rhetorical intentions into the time of eon with its heavenly forms, styles, and tones of images and sounds.

In his later experimental short film, *The King's Body*, Rodrigues juxtaposes the story of Afonso I, which is read by undressed, mundane (low-income or unemployed), gay men, with background images of both an antiquated and modernized Portuguese-scape. The background images then shift to a flock of birds flying, which evokes the atmosphere and drama of Borges's essay, "The Simurgh and the Eagle"[16] (borrowed from Attar of Nishapur's *The Conference of Birds*). This chapter describes birds that go on a voyage to search for the king named Simurgh in order to overcome his anarchy; at the circular end of the story, they realize that they themselves are Simurgh (which means "thirty birds" and "the bird"). In the mythologized and simultaneously prophesized plane of eon that is *The Ornithologist*'s Trás-os-Montes, the enigmatic "togetherness" of a shepherd, a king, and the birds in premodern Portugal is revived in the images of the present. This *enfoldment* renders visible the imaginary book or archive of transcultural signs (which includes the imagery of Fernando's cellphone and of contemporary Chinese travelers), which also suggests (both enchantingly and critically) the deterritorialized dream of unknown survivors in the future.

GOPRO, THE BIRDS' GAZE, AND NON-HUMAN EMBODIMENT

In *The Ornithologist*, the illumination of intimacy (which is expressed both mythologically and technologically) with non-human actors, the effect of the unreal, and the unknowability of that intimate dream are amplified when Fernando (alternately with Rodrigues) encounters birds. While the story of meeting with avian creatures might already suggest something inordinate and divergent, it is also important to note that the anamorphic cinematic images—most evident in the scene of an owl's static gaze at Rodrigues from a high angle at one point—of those special encounters are created by a different lens, a GoPro. Rodrigues chose to use a GoPro for filming the birds in order to try to present a bird's-eye perspective. In an interview about the film, Rodrigues recounts:

> it's shot in a different camera—a GoPro. It has these stupid lenses that are round and they deform the space. [. . .] they [birds] do see a bit larger

than us. In a way, physically, [the lens] would be something that would be similar or closer to how they see. I also wanted to create this different texture in what they see—to concentrate—because they focus more in a way, even if they see larger, they focus more on a point. That was done in the colour correction stage of the film.[17]

Indeed, the anamorphosis of the birds' gaze or point of view that recurs in *The Ornithologist* takes place inside the eye of a different camera. This in turn corresponds to Deleuze's thoughts on Baroque visibility through the consideration of what is inflected in the monad.[18] In the case of filming *The Ornithologist*, Baroque or Neo-Baroque visibility is expressed through the non-human monad of a GoPro which metaphorically and mechanically connects the birds' gaze to a cinematic point of view. Alanna Thain in her essay "A Bird's-Eye View of Leviathan," recognizes the benefits of using GoPros in order to perceive experientially animals' sense of vision. She points out that there are even experiments that attach "this lightweight and body-mountable equipment" to animals, "in an attempt to establish empathy with or get an embodied sense of the animal perspective."[19] Even though Rodrigues did not literally attach the GoPro to the bodies of birds, he used it in every moment of encounter with birds to give to the audience the materiality and sensation of the birds' gaze. Rather than relying on naturalist ideas and strategies of filming the non-humans in their actual environment, the use of a lens with a specific, optical structure implies that *The Ornithologist* consciously embedded the camera as a rhetorical tool of Baroque storytelling that traverses non-humans and humans in search of their shared desire and dream.

To return to the question posed in the earlier part of this chapter, one can ask, who is the subject or dreamer of this anamorphic view? Of course, one

Figure 6.2 *The Ornithologist* (2016)

cannot identify the subject through the framework of Borgesian-Deleuzean thoughts on Baroque images because the subject is variable and inflects from within. However, an experiential intersubjectivity that is imagined as being positioned in the camera obscura for the presentation of cinematic time-images can provide a conceptual answer to that question. As Damian Sutton states in *Photography, Cinema, Memory: the Crystal Image of Time* (2009), the Deleuzean "subject" (or precisely, "superject"[20]), as opposed to Cartesian solipsistic subject that relies on the given object,

> finds its instruments in the Baroque camera obscura in which the viewer is placed inside the cell of the camera. The viewer inhabits a variable perception within the camera obscura and watches the image that is a reflection of the variable outer world on its walls.[21]

More precisely, this reflection of the variable external world on the interior walls of the camera can be construed as a Deleuzean inflection: following the argument outlined in *The Fold*, the outside is wrapped and multiplied within the monad in the Baroque worlds.

While the superior or godlike mind is symbolized as the souls of birds in *The Ornithologist*, its unconsciousness and intersubjectivity of dreaming are rendered visible in the immanent plane of the camera obscura. This optical dark room in turn makes virtual the assemblage of time-image that is on the screen and which envelops the world, as well as the mode of being in the world. Although the representational functions of filming the pro-filmic world are not rejected here, it is evident that the screen also transports through this mechanism the historical and cultural representation of worlds to the fabric of the moving image. Within itself, this matter of the cinematic images layers the palimpsestic bifurcations of symbols, fiction, and desire that exist at the borderline of reality and illusion. In this sense, *The Ornithologist* is a work of Baroque cinema that deploys a symbolic technology (the GoPro camera) of non-human vision as a means of materializing the (virtual) fold of multiple archival signs and systems that make up the concrete yet mythological landscape of Trás-os-Montes and its inhabitants.

SENSORY ETHNOGRAPHY AND ECOSOPHICAL RELATIONALITY

Returning to "A Bird's-Eye View of *Leviathan*,"[22] Thain's work offers an insight into the plethora of ethical and cognitive relationality that observational (and co-habitational) aims and methods have brought to practices of sensory ethnography and, by extension, to *The Ornithologist* through the use of a GoPro camera. In my conversation with Rodrigues,[23] the director explained that he did not specifically work with the Harvard Sensory Ethnography Lab for the development of *The Ornithologist* during his fellowship (2014–15) at the Radcliffe-Harvard Film Study Center. However, the film's emphasis on an affinity with the birds' gaze through observation and its transformative effect on the audience's perceptual capacity resonates with the SEL's projects which prioritize visuality and embodied experience over didactic anthropological knowledge in ethnographic filmmaking practices.

Borrowing from Raymond Ruyer's conception of *vague,* as well as from Félix Guattari's ecosophical practice as addressed in *The Three Ecologies,* Thain argues for the immersive effect of observational, close-up methods in research on sensory ethnography. She also emphasizes that these methods embrace the observer's own sensory and perceptive engagement with the subject, and as such that they differ from the predetermined operation of observation for authorial or objective knowledge production. The gist of ecosophical cognition is in its observational agency of generating the film as an action that encompasses the subject and the observer together, instead of representing the world that is intended or regulated by the observer. Indeed, Ruyer's notion of "action," which coincides with "being," serves as a conceptual framework for Thain's assessment of the film *Leviathan* (Lucien Castaing-Taylor and Véréna Paravel, 2012) in the sense that it forcefully blurs the distinction between the subject (birds) and the film's cognitive reception (on the side of audience) through the amplification of the sensory (both sonic and visual) output.

Similar to the way in which Rodrigues uses a GoPro camera in *The Ornithologist,* *Leviathan* also uses this "small, cheap, rugged, and waterproof device with fixed focus and no viewfinder"[24] to enact intersubjective and circumstantial (which is often torrential and chaotic) embodiment. In this experiment of embodiment, there is no object to be extracted as the background for anthropological knowledge. Moreover, through the specific medium of the GoPro, *Leviathan* addresses the proximity and vitality of observation in a static moment that is separate from the frenetic voyaging and fishing scene on the surface of the sea with its seething waves. Regarding the long-take scene of a wounded bird in *Leviathan,* Thain writes:

> We cannot look away from the bird and what it is doing: it actively and repeatedly fails as a symbolic stand-in or preformed political subject in this scene because we return again and again to the urgency and persistence of its embodied situation. The length of the scene, and the suspension of intervention except by looking, the way that the camera searches the featured folds of the bird's body from a dispassionate proximity afforded by the GoPro's tiny size: this too-long and too-closeness

also keeps us from simply reading the bird as an isolated subject whose lifeworld is backgrounded.[25]

Drawing from this, one can recalibrate the notion of the unknowability that was proposed earlier in order to read *The Ornithologist* in a more actively relational sense as a film that accompanies the ethical implications of co-actions and co-world-building between the cinematic subject (birds) and the audience. The unknowability that the viewer can experience and speculate on—even participate in—in the films (both *Leviathan* and *The Ornithologist*) is not a passive resignation of knowledge of the other, but an engaged failure in possessing an authorial position over the subject that is on view for an emphatic crease (*pleat*) of sensorial understanding.

Even before the use of the GoPro camera, Castaing-Taylor directed *Sweetgrass* (2011) in collaboration with his spouse Ilisa Barbash. The film is in alignment with his advocacy of non-linguistic or non-textual depictions of ethnographic reality in his 1996 essay "Iconophobia."[26] Castaing-Taylor's "Iconophobia" boldly contrasts film with prose and written anthropology in particular, even while it admits the paralinguistic qualities of film that come from its narrative and syntagmatic features and other textual compositions. The director contends that "if the rules of the film resist formulation, [. . .] it may be that the relative syntactic poverty of the medium is precisely its semantic strength, that which allows it to respond to the diversity and density human experiences as flexibly as it does."[27] Indeed, the durational presentations of corporeal indices in *Sweetgrass* resemble the genre and subjects of *The Ornithologist* (as well as *Trás-os-Montes* and *The Shepherd*), and they undermine the authorial interpretation of anthropomorphic symbolism as the film reproduces audaciously the interspecific hardship of sheep ranching in Montana's Absaroka-Beartooth mountains for the eyes and ears of the viewer. Beyond the ocular navigation, the sound designs of *Sweetgrass* contribute to the voluptuousness of ecosophical cognition.

Rather than seeing the illustrative qualities of film as the medium's weakness in its capacity to describe for the production and operation of knowledge, Castaing-Taylor argues for the expansion and plenitude of lived experience and sense through "thick depictions"[28] (as opposed to "thick descriptions") in film. He connects the perceptual virtue of dense depictions with the possibility of "local knowledge," since to depict or to show in film is to compose "a series of *indices*"[29] of life and the flesh of the world. As opposed to the dominant ways of reading, the abundance of indexicality in sensory ethnographic practice (of using an observational optic of the camera) permits "an ambiguity of meaning"[30] that the interdependent positionality of the subjects and the spectators of the film co-generate as they submit themselves to the excessively sensorial field of the local (yet deterritorialized) environs and their ecosophy.

Of course, the ethno-fictional legacy of Portuguese "landscape" films that was addressed earlier is characterized by its poetic cryptography of using both text and image, as well as by its Borgesian-Deleuzean Baroque cosmology and historiography of folds. That literary and philosophical puzzle and palimpsest serve as a phantasmatic lens by which it is possible to approach the questions of interspecific memory and relationality in *The Ornithologist*. However, the Baroque exuberance of the SEL's sensorial methods (which are also used in *The Ornithologist*), along with Guattari's and Thain's ecosophical modes of being "together" with non-humans in rhizomatic habitats, complicates in cognitive terms the mythopoetic dimensions of the films that have been discussed in this chapter alongside *The Ornithologist*. The intimate and hazy methods of cognition that arise from the use of the GoPro and other audiovisual apparatuses in *The Ornithologist* add interspecifically desiring textures of attentive knowledge to the ethno-fictionality of Portuguese landscape films. In *The Ornithologist*, this *thick* fusion (which is a Baroque mode) of bifurcating mythopoetics of time, supernatural non-humanness of topology, and anamorphic optics of the GoPro takes place in ways that advocate and render the Trás-os-Montes that survives in cinema with a "magical realism" of ecosophical cohabitations and kinships.

Failure, Erasure, and Oblivion in João Pedro Rodrigues and João Rui Guerra da Mata's Asian Trilogy: *Red Dawn, The Last Time I Saw Macao,* and *Iec Long*

Juan Antonio Suárez

INTRODUCTION

João Pedro Rodrigues and João Rui Guerra da Mata's "Asian Trilogy" comprises the films they co-directed in and about Macao, the former Portuguese enclave in southeast China. The films are relative oddities in the directors' filmography, especially when contrasted with the flamboyant melodramas that preceded them (*Odete* [*Two Drifters*, 2005] and *Morrer Como um Homem* [*To Die Like a Man*, 2009]) and the oneiric, spiritual odyssey that followed them (*O Ornitólogo* [*The Ornithologist*, 2016]). While Rodrigues is the exclusive director of these better-known feature films, the "Asian films" are joint directorial efforts with Guerra da Mata, Rodrigues's art designer and occasional co-writer. The collaboration is based in part on Guerra da Mata's biographical connection to Macao, where he spent his childhood.[1] The "Asian films" are the first ones that Rodrigues produced on digital video rather than in his preferred format of celluloid, and he made them with a small crew, rather than with the larger ensembles that he used in the narrative features.[2] Beyond such particularities of production, other traits differentiate the Asian Trilogy from the rest of his films. While Rodrigues's single-author titles emphasize the protagonists' corporeality, the jointly-made "Asian films" tend to elide it. The characters in *A Última Vez Que Vi Macau* (*The Last Time I Saw Macao*, 2012) remain off-screen, or are replaced with animals. The individual protagonists of the feature films are replaced in the Macao films by unseen or vague collective subjects, such as the market vendors and customers of *Alvorada Vermelha* (*Red Dawn*, 2011), or the factory workers and anonymous Macanese crowds of *Iec Long* (2015). The fictional orientation of earlier and subsequent features is abandoned in the Asian titles in favor of documentary (in *Red Dawn*) or of a combination of essay film, fiction, and actuality (in *Iec Long* and *The Last Time I Saw Macao*). The documentary gestures hark back to Rodrigues's early career, and in particular to his diptych *Esta É a Minha Casa* (*This Is My Home*, 1997) and *Viagem à Expo* (*Journey to Expo*, 1998), about a migrant Portuguese family living in Paris and their holiday trips to their country of origin. At the same time, the nocturnal ambience of the "Asian films", their focus on marginal characters or little-noticed corners of social life, and their cinephiliac allusiveness—especially prominent in *The Last Time I Saw Macao*—align them with the rest of the directors' titles.

Of the Asian titles, only *The Last Time I Saw Macao* has been discussed at length, while *Red Dawn* and *Iec Long* have received little scholarly attention. Criticism of *The Last Time I Saw Macao* has explored the transnational character of the film, its generic mixture, its formal and thematic ambiguity, and its constant filmic references. *Variety* called it "a Chris Marker-esque essay film disguised as a deconstructivist noir," while James Quandt detailed its cinematic debts and intricate generic filiation: "conspiracy thriller, neo-noir, city symphony, travelogue, apocalyptic sci-fi, autobiography, essay film, experimental home movie, meta-memorial, and cultural critique."[3] In a lengthier discussion, Jimmy Weaver has treated *The Last Time I Saw Macao* as an example of contemporary transnational film, using as a blueprint Thomas Elsaesser's definition of the genre.[4] Rachel ten Haaf has explored the film through Samuel Beckett's trope of "the neither," as a fusion of opposites that results in a hybrid compound. Beckettian "neithers" are evident in the genre of *The Last Time I Saw Macao* (film noir plus documentary), the gender of its protagonist—the trans performer, Candy—and the postcolonial space of the city, with its combination of colonial Portuguese architecture, futuristic casinos, and corporate towers.[5]

However insightful they are, these critiques nonetheless leave significant elements in *The Last Time I Saw Macao* untouched. They have surprisingly little to say about the film's queer affect, which radiates well beyond Candy's identity; they do not explore the peculiar reading of contemporary Macao in the film; and they pass over its cataclysmic temporality and apocalyptic ending and its related animal subplot. Moreover, existing critiques fail to connect *The Last Time I Saw Macao* to the other films in the trilogy, despite the group identity that is conferred on them by the repetition of visual motifs, settings, and shots. These disparate thematic strands of queer affect, Macanese urban space, and cataclysmic temporality have in common a concern with breakdown, erasure, and oblivion that makes the trilogy an example of what Judith Halberstam has identified as "the queer art of failure." Failure in the film—or in Halberstam's work—is not a trait to be decried. The obstructionist, disintegrating pull of failure towards blockage, negativity, and confusion is also enabling and generative. As it blocks the habitual avenues of identification and intelligibility, failure promotes alternative paths of desire and cognition.[6] Failure in these films is personal as much as it is social and historical. It affects the bungled search for the abducted trans performer, Candy in *The Last Time I Saw Macao*, and it also defines Macao as a living space that is oppressively fixated on novelty and as the endgame of decolonization and of former emancipatory projects. The Macao of the film is caught in the cyclical temporality of underworld ritual murder, mindless renewal, neocapitalist spectacle, and gambling, which is the island's main source of revenue. Like its protagonists, Macao has nowhere to go but into the evocation of a past that can only be recreated as a bygone utopia or as a tourist attraction, or into a post-human future where people have vanished and only animals remain. *The Last Time I Saw Macao* is the central, lengthiest, and most complex piece in the trilogy and its concerns radiate to the other two Asian titles. For this reason, it will be the point of entry for my analysis of the three films.

NOIR FAILURE, QUEER FAILURE

The Last Time is an example of the contemporary validity of what Paula Rabinowitz calls the noir "template" to express the dislocations and disquiet of modernity and its aftermaths. Rather than a film style or a cycle, as it had long been characterized, noir was, for Rabinowitz, "a political theory of America's problematic democracy disguised as cheap melodrama."[7] Its scenarios translate

Figure 7.1 *The Last Time I Saw Macao* (2012)

into privatized plots certain forms of aggression that were endemic to American political life, particularly racial violence and "the suppression of working class organizing."[8] In Rabinowitz's wake, Justus Nieland and Jennifer Fay have applied this view of noir beyond American borders and have shown the global validity of this template as a means to encode different kinds of social and political trauma. Prominent in global postclassical noir are the tensions arising between receding traditions and forms of community and universalizing modernity, as well as the clash between the different temporalities and developmental rhythms associated with each of these.[9] Part of the ideological work of noir resides in the way in which it raises and resolves—or not—these tensions in a manner that combines sexual and epistemic closure. The conflicts raised in classic noir are ultimately appeased through the heterosexual couple, which is often affirmed by the end of the film, and through the resolution of the enigmas.[10] Neo-noir, by contrast, belongs to an era of increased complexity and fewer moral and epistemological guarantees. It often keeps tensions unresolved: couples are not necessarily con-solidated and mysteries are not always entirely clarified by the end of the film.

As a characteristic neo-noir artifact, Rodrigues and Guerra da Mata's film moves toward crisis, mystery, and failure, rather than toward appeasement and transparency. The protagonist of the story is also called Guerra da Mata. He is a current resident of Lisbon who lived in Macao as a child and returns after a thirty-year absence in response to a cry for help from his friend Candy (Cindy Scrash, who has a secondary role in *To Die Like a Man*). Candy is a trans night-club performer who had moved to Macao years earlier; she had been drawn to the island "by exoticism or by the promise of an easier life," as the narrator-protagonist muses. However, "once again" she has become involved with "the wrong men" and after the recent death of a friend, which was disguised as an accident that took place during some "innocent 'war games'," she feels that she may be the next target of a criminal gang led by Madame Lobo. Candy has dis-covered that the members of the gang have been transforming themselves into animals with the purpose of assuring their survival after the New Year when, according to a Buddhist tradition, humans will disappear from the face of the Earth and only animals will remain. Once he is in Macao, Guerra da Mata is unable to reach Candy by telephone, misses appointments with her and her friend Mr. A-kan, and fails to prevent her murder. A letter from Candy reaches Guerra da Mata after her death, asking him to go to "the pirates' cave" in a remote part of the island to find the book of the apocalypse and the "sacred bird cage." Guerra da Mata does as Candy has requested and, once in the cave, he witnesses how a man turns himself into a dog by lifting the cover of the cage and exposing himself to the light that emanates from its interior. Guerra da Mata panics and flees, forgetting the purpose of his expedition. After hours spent wandering through rural Macao and a night immersed in the New Year celebrations, he decides to play the gang at its own game. He buys a gun and kills one of the minions who guards the cage, which he takes to his hotel room and uses to transform himself into a kitten. At the close of day, as the sun goes down, a white glare floods the sky, signaling the end of the human species and the dawn of animal domination. The final sequence of the film shows birds, cats, and dogs as the only dwellers of spaces that are devoid of human presence.

The story abounds in dead ends and unsolved mysteries. The "book of the apocalypse" that Guerra da Mata is encouraged to retrieve from the pirates' cave is never found and its contents or purpose remain undisclosed. After Candy's death and Guerra da Mata's incursion into the cave, two more murders take place. A couple, whose relation to the rest of the plot is completely obscure, are gunned down as they hastily close their fish shop and try to escape. Shortly afterwards, the agonizing screams of a woman are matched to takes of a building that is partly covered in billowing plastics; her body and circumstances, however, remain off-screen and unexplained. It is also unclear whether these casualties belong to Madame Lobo's gang or to a rival mob. When da Mata purchases the gun, kills the gang member, and takes possession of the cage, he suddenly realizes the deeper reason for his return to Macao after such a long time: the search for "happiness." Yet he does not explain what he means by happiness: perhaps it is his way of referring to his new state as an animal in the imminent feral regime.

Not all of the enigmas are related to the central storyline. The main narrative is punctuated by unmotivated sequences that thicken its cryptic density. Guerra da Mata's search for witnesses as to Candy's whereabouts is capped by the image of a siren that touches a scorpion fish and dissolves in the water. This is perhaps an allegory for Candy's flirtation with an enticing but dangerous crowd. (Similar sirens appear in the fish tanks at the marketplace of *Red Dawn*, imbuing the routines of the market with a touch of the fantastic). During the New Year's celebrations, an adolescent couple take selfies in front of an historic building while, concurrently, two young men in black training gear sprint down the same solitary street. These unrelated images confer on the film a degree of absurdity and looseness and evoke the life unfolding beyond the claustrophobic murder-cum-apocalypse plot in which da Mata and Candy are entangled, but because the images are unexplained, they contribute to the mysteriousness of the film. Not only do the centrifugal details enhance the mystery; so does the oneiric cohesiveness of the film. Motifs are repeated in a way that portends, without clarifying, their significance. Most prominent among such motifs is the "sacred" bird cage, which gang members pass back and forth among themselves in a baffling choreography that takes place all over the city and the surrounding countryside. The cage motivates several conversations, much plotting, and some killing, but its contents remain secret. Its function is revealed only belatedly when Guerra da Mata witnesses its use in "the great ritual of the chosen ones." The sacred cage is also replicated in the many other cages that the inhabitants of Macao carry around, hang from trees, or set on the grass in parks and gardens in an ancient Chinese custom that seeks to keep caged birds happy and healthy through their exposure to the open air. Madame Lobo plays with wooden animal figurines that represent some of the characters: her gofers describe her as a dragon and "the Portuguese man" as "a lamb among wolves," and likenesses of these animals are seen on her table. However, her manipulations are charmingly opaque. Painted dragons recur at various points in the story although their meaning is uncertain: their images are matched to off-screen voices that describe Madame Lobo as a dragon— perhaps alluding to her power—and they are glimpsed inside the pirates' cave and in the montage showing the countdown that ushers in the animal era.

The mystery of the film is heightened above all by its most salient formal feature: the decision to leave the faces and bodies of the characters off-screen and to narrate the story through da Mata's first-person testimony and incidental ambient sound. Da Mata's voice is the guiding thread throughout the film, but his face is never actually shown. Only his hands and feet are glimpsed when he picks up glasses, telephones, the evidence of Candy's murder, or the mystifying bird cage. Candy is only viewed at the beginning of the film, when she lip-syncs to "You Kill Me" (which was one of Jane Russell's song numbers in Josef von Sternberg's *Macao*, 1952) in front of several caged tigers. Afterwards, she is only heard: when she phones da Mata and when she reads her goodbye letter in voice-over. Her murder is staged off-frame and conveyed only through sound: the victim's cries, reports from a gun with a silencer, a splash, and screeching car tires. Candy's enemies are similarly invisible: we glimpse the front of Madame Lobo's embroidered tunic and her manicured, bejeweled hands as they shift the animal figurines, and of her minions we see only hands, feet, midriffs, and backs.

The relegation of characters to invisibility connects *The Last Time I Saw Macao* with the aesthetics of film noir and with some examples of experimental cinema. The consistent concealment of characters in Rodrigues and Guerra da Mata's film brings to mind Robert Montgomery's classic noir *Lady in the Lake* (1947), which was filmed partly from a subjective, first-person perspective that allows us to see the protagonist only when he approaches a mirror, while the rest of the characters are only visualized when they enter his field of vision. While Montgomery's film hides the detective throughout the film, most other examples of film noir keep the criminals or decisive evidence out of sight, only to reveal them at the end. Two canonical instances in this respect are the identities of Miles Archer's murderer in *The Maltese Falcon* (John Huston, 1941) and of the person who plants a bomb in a car at the beginning of *Touch of Evil* (Orson Welles, 1958). The mystery in both of these films revolves around the discovery of the perpetrators, and the plot moves towards rendering visible what had remained hidden.

In modernist cinema, off-screen space was also one of the trademarks of French filmmaker Robert Bresson, one of Rodrigues's influences. However, it was Masao Adachi and Chantal Akerman who used it in a manner that is closest to that of Rodrigues and Guerra da Mata in films that narrate through disembodied voices the circumstances of unseen individuals. Adachi's *Ryakushô: Renzoku Shasatsuma* (*A.K.A. Serial Killer*, 1969) relates in a detached, monotonous voice-over the life of serial murderer Norio Nagayama. The narration is heard over neutral shots of the locations where he lived and committed his crimes, and it contrasts Nagayama's chilling insanity with the ordinariness of his environs while hinting at the connection between his actions and the muted violence of everyday life in contemporary Japan. Mixing the documentary and the autobiographical, Akerman's *News from Home* (1977) combines street views of New York with her own mother's voice reading fragments of the letters that she sent to her daughter during her time in the city. Akerman's later video *Là-bas* (*Down There*, 2006) juxtaposes the filmmaker's disembodied reflections on family history, the holocaust, the state of Israel, and the circumstances of her sojourn in Tel Aviv with views from her windows and occasional glimpses of the city. In all of these examples from both film noir and experimental cinema, the withdrawal of the protagonists' bodies is tied to scenarios of rupture and loss. Yet while classic film noir ends up supplying the missing elements and completing the cognitive puzzle, experimental film tends to insist on the irreparability of loss and the inevitability of partial knowledge, incomplete stories, and failure.

Failure is, in the end, the final word in *The Last Time I Saw Macao*. Guerra da Mata may succeed in finding happiness through his cross-species metamorphosis but he fails at everything else. He bungles Candy's rescue. He is late for a meeting with Candy's friend A-kan (who is supposed to take Guerra da Mata to Candy) but he cannot warn her because he forgets his cellphone at the hotel. His inquiries constantly lead him to dead ends. At the casino where Candy sings, no one wants to talk to him. She has not been seen for days at the Military Club where she often dines, a rundown place where he only finds shadows from the past. Candy finally calls da Mata while he is having dinner at the inner port and urges him to come to her apartment, but once again, he is too late. The lights are on but no one answers the door. A call from A-kan directs him to the port— "Save Candy!"—but by the time he gets there she has already been killed.

In the end, then, the film is a parable of loss: of Candy, of the solution to assorted mysteries, of satisfactory closure, of the faces and bodies of the characters, and even of the human species altogether. Lost, too, is the heterosexual couple that is concomitant with, and symbolic of, ideological, epistemic, and narrative closure in classical film noir. Yet even if Candy had found her way to da Mata's arms and all mysteries had been solved in the end, theirs would not have been a conventional union by the standards of classical cinema, and not only because of her trans identity. What binds them together seems to be friendship: a more indefinite, less goal-oriented affection than love or sex. Friendship is less an object to be attained than an atmosphere in which to bask, and, precisely for that reason, it is less amenable than love or sex to conventional plotting. Candy remembers in her final letter "the crazy years" that they shared in Lisbon, and Guerra da Mata's voice distills warmth and concern for her. At the same time, Candy's disappearance, which is due to da Mata's failure, does not end their relationship, but detours it through scattered objects and memories, and through the mission with which she entrusts him: to find the book and the cage and "save himself," and thus to accede to a different form of existence. Loss and failure, then, are not entirely subtractive, but also additive, for they open alternate avenues of relationality and affect.

Affect radiates beyond Guerra da Mata's relationship with Candy to a renewed rapport with his past and to a dialogic connection with his interlocutor (played by João Pedro Rodrigues), whose voice enters the acoustic space of the film during Da Mata's childhood reminiscences. Guerra da Mata's trip to Macao is a return to the world of his childhood. His affection for Candy, then, triggers a horizontal search in the present and what might be called a vertical exploration of his past. Architectural traces of those years are still standing, if drastically transformed. His former school (Santa Rosa de Lima) is now a girls' school, his classroom has been turned into a storage space, and the building where he lived, the Moors' Barracks, is now a government building and heritage site. Contemporary views of these locations are combined with faded photographs of da Mata and his family in the early 1970s. During this sequence, Rodrigues's disembodied voice asks Guerra da Mata about the games he used to play, the hiding places for his toys, and the secret band that he formed with his friends ("The Fire Dragon"). As the camera shows the spaces that are mentioned in their conversation, it replicates the movements that Guerra da Mata reminisces about, skirting along a wall, jumping into a courtyard, going around a corner to hide the toys. Memory becomes dialogic, and the radius of friendship and intimacy expands to this unseen interlocutor, who enquires about memories with which he appears to be familiar. The effect of the dialogue rests in part on extra-filmic knowledge about Rodrigues and Guerra da Mata's longstanding relationship, but even without such knowledge, the exchange exudes closeness. In this respect, the affective currents in the film surpass heterosexual coupling to include a queer profusion of non-exclusive forms of relation.

READABLE, UNREADABLE MACAO

The backdrop of Guerra da Mata's repeated failures in *The Last Time I Saw Macao* is a city that presents a problem of legibility. It is a vague place where "nothing is what it seems" and guesses often go awry. An off-screen comment (in Rodrigues's voice) describes Macao as "an architectural jungle with two sides, like the coins that the slot machines swallow at a hallucinating pace: one calm and smiling, the other secret and veiled." It is "the kindest" and "the cruelest" of cities. Candy moved there looking for exoticism and "easy" living, but found herself in the midst of "strange and frightening" developments. Macao is both Chinese and Portuguese, and duplicity is part of its legacy, even though the traces of Portugal are faint at this point ("Four hundred years of Portuguese presence in Macao and no one speaks Portuguese," complains Guerra da Mata).[11] In synchronicity with these assertions of heterogeneity and fracture, Guerra da Mata arrives in Macao during the Eleventh National People's Congress, when official pronouncements ceased to refer to China as a "harmonious society."[12]

The narrative bears out such disharmony. The criminal plot plays out against a peaceful landscape of crowds of tourists milling around the historic center and anonymous locals exercising in parks, shopping, working, walking, or eating. Alongside people, the film also captures the material particulars of everyday life: fish drying in the sun, traffic, temples, small altars on street corners, churches and cemeteries, and the New Year decorations of smiling, cartoonish tigers that are present all over the city.[13] In addition to communicating the misleadingly calm surface of Macao, these snapshots reveal the documentary origins of the project, which, as the filmmakers have pointed out, quickly veered into crime fiction.[14]

Macao has long been connected in the popular imagination with gambling, prostitution, corruption, and crime. Josef von Sternberg's *Macao* exploited this imaginary, as did later British productions such as Lewis Gilbert's *Ferry to Hong Kong* (1959) and Guy Hamilton's *The Man With the Golden Gun* (1974), which is part of the James Bond saga. (Guerra da Mata recalls the shooting of the Bond film in the streets of Macao when he was a child).[15] Macao sometimes lived up to its legend. The city did become crime-ridden and triad-dominated in the years prior to the Portuguese handover of the territory to China. This was mainly due to gang disputes over the exploitation of gambling concessions. Order was eventually restored by the Macanese authorities after the transfer to China in 1999, when Macao, like Hong Kong, became a Special Administrative Region (SAR) under the close supervision of the Chinese government.[16] Since the late 1990s, the Macanese authorities have sought to attract film production to the area as a means of generating good publicity and promoting a pleasant image of the island, but most of the films set there have been financed by Hong Kong studios and have remained focused on Macao's shady side.[17] Some examples are Johnnie To's crime thrillers *Joi Gin a Long* (*Where a Good Man Goes*, 1999), *Fong Juk* (*Exiled*, 2006) and *Fuk Sau* (*Vengeance*, 2009); Tat-Chi Yao's *Aam Fa* (*The Longest Nite*, 1998); and Billy Tang's peculiar *Ho Kong Fung Wan* (*Casino*, 1998). This latter is a thinly fictionalized biopic of the real-life triad boss Broken Tooth Kai, who financed the film: it was intended to glorify his trajectory but ended up being used in court as evidence for his eventual indictment on various criminal charges.[18] Given this cinematic legacy, it is perhaps not surprising that the urban landscape of Macao suggested predominantly noir plots to Rodrigues and Guerra da Mata.

The fascination with crime and with the threateningly enigmatic nature of the city is also a way to puncture the contemporary façade of Macao. Macao is now the Las Vegas of the East and a UNESCO "World Heritage City" (a status granted in 2005). It is a city of pleasant surfaces and easy consumption, and a major tourist destination, and it now sells—very profitably—the excitement of gambling and the image of its past.[19] As a "culture city," it markets itself as a melting pot of East and West, and a place where, in the words of a 2002 text by the Macao Secretariat for Social and Cultural Affairs, "Chinese culture and other cultures are mutually accommodating and the ethics of tolerance, openness and diligence flourish."[20] This identity had been already promoted by the Portuguese government since the time of the Sino–Portuguese agreement of 1987, which stipulated that Macao would return to China under the same conditions as neighboring Hong Kong. In the last decades of its existence, the Portuguese administration engaged in heritage recovery projects and utilized the old city as a way of fostering a positive legacy. These projects have been continued by SAR authorities as a form of city branding that seeks to attract tourism and investments. The image of Macao as a city with a distinctive culture of fusion and tolerance has also helped to erase the memory of the recent violence of the triads. The paradox is that violence was also used to produce the city of culture: older neighborhoods were drastically modified and gentrified; they were transformed from complex, hybrid living spaces into postcard-like settings devoted to tourist-related services.[21]

Macao also has a long history as a gambling haven, which, in some cases, it may have wanted to dissimulate rather than foreground. The Portuguese authorities in Macao granted the earliest gambling concessions in the 1850s to offset the migration of commerce to Hong Kong after the first Opium War. However, the main boost to the gambling industry started in the early 1960s, when the *Sociedade de Turismo e Diversões de Macau* (STDM/Tourism and Entertainment Company of Macau Limited), controlled by Hong Kong entrepreneur Stanley Ho, won the monopoly on gambling on the island. The STDM modernized gambling and increased its scale and appeal. It replaced small-scale dens with large casinos (like the Casino Lisboa) and introduced greyhound, horse, and car races; it used hydrofoils and speedboats to bring clients from Hong Kong; and it offered strip shows and gambling tables already on the ferries.[22] STDM's monopoly ended in 2002 when its concession was not renewed and local authorities allowed the entrance into the island of other investors, particularly from Las Vegas. The Las Vegas investors introduced "gaming" as a more wholesome, family-oriented concept of gambling and delivered new concepts in casino design.[23] Tim Simpson maintains that in contrast to the partitioned, darkened, sequestered rooms of earlier casinos, the new Las Vegas-inspired themed establishments were designed to convey a sense of openness, "transparency," and "panopticism."[24] Both the new casinos and the beautified, historic core of the city reshaped Macao. The ambiguous, lived-in city of old became streamlined, readable, and easily consumable. Only the areas that were untouched by gentrification, such as the unkempt streets surrounding the historic core and the inner port, retained their former intricacy and flavor.

Against the backdrop of these changes, crime is a fictional conceit that the film employs to evoke the porous, enigmatic city that has been largely erased by the new Macao of chromium and glass, architectural simulacra, and franchises. In fact, the setting of the criminal activity in *The Last Time I Saw Macao* is not the beautified old city nor the fisherman's wharf in the exterior port with its potpourri of Western architectural styles; nor is it the fantasy land of the new casinos and malls in Cotai and Coloane, the southern districts of the island. The action unfolds instead in abandoned industrial sites, rundown alleys, modest restaurants and shops, humble hotels like the one where Guerra da Mata stays, and, during a brief interval after the escape from the pirates' cave, in country areas dotted with rusty workshops and dilapidated buildings. The historic center and the new landmarks are glimpsed in passing. After the first failed appointment, there is a disconcerting shot of the Venice casino complex, which contains a replica of a Venetian canal where a Chinese gondolier lip-syncs to Sinatra's "Smile" in a sardonic comment on Guerra da Mata's fiasco. Macao Tower rises above the land "stolen from the sea," and is filmed from one of the old social hubs of the city: the tree-lined promenade of Praia Grande, which is now empty, much of its former surface covered by a highway. The lotus-shaped hotel and casino Grand Lisboa, which looms above the city center, returns as a visual refrain, but it is always viewed partially and indirectly, reflected on the water or glimpsed through the bathroom window at Guerra da Mata's hotel. The action, however, and the focal points of the film, remain distant from these markers of the new Macao.

Red Dawn and *Iec Long* prolong this interest in an unspectacular Macao, although not through crime but through the celebration of local environments and habits and through the recovery of a non-monumental past. Nonetheless, this is once again a past of failure and decline that, like a noir plot, also involves violence. *Red Dawn* portrays the activity in Macao's Red Market—located near the inner port—from the early hours before the market opens to the public until the late afternoon, when it is hosed down and closed until the following day. The film portrays spontaneous activity that rises from below rather than being administered from above. This activity is both mundane and extraordinary. Shopping for food is shown as a prosaic, cyclical need that is easily satisfied, but the film also shows in lush detail the animal holocaust that such satisfaction entails. From early in the morning, sides of pork are brought up to the butchers' stalls to be cut up and displayed; chickens are bled to death, plucked, boiled, and gutted with mechanical indifference; and fish are slit open, halved, and filleted while they are still thrashing and gasping. The "Red" of the title refers as much to the blood that trickles abundantly as a matter of routine as it does to the color of the market's exterior. Much like Georges Franju's *Le Sang des Bêtes* (*Blood of the Beasts*, 1949) about a Parisian slaughterhouse, this film reveals the concealed, unexamined violence that underlies mere eating.[25] Yet while Franju's film is both symbolic of the bloodshed in the recent World Wars and surreal for its odd configurations of lined-up carcasses and body parts, *Red Dawn* is literal, hyperreal, and detached.

The film links the brutality of the market place to that of *The Last Time I Saw Macao* through an enigmatic opening shot: a close-up of a black pump that looks like the ones worn by Candy. The pump is abandoned in the middle of the road near the market and eventually run over by a car—as also happens to one of Candy's pumps on the dock where she is murdered. This visual rhyme is stretched across two films that were produced some time apart. It may have been vexingly obscure to spectators of *Red Dawn* until they saw—if indeed they did—*The Last Time I Saw Macao*, which premiered a year later. The shiny artificiality of the shoe contrasts sharply with the exhibits of bleeding, mauled nature that are for sale on the stalls, yet it is equally subject to violent assault. At the end of *Red Dawn* the pump is recuperated as an homage to Jane Russell, the star of von Sternberg's *Macao* whose death is announced by a fleetingly seen newspaper headline. In the opening sequence of *Macao*, Russell throws one of her black, high-heeled shoes (which is almost identical to the ones in *Red Dawn* and *The Last Time I Saw Macao*) at a drunk harasser. The shoe misses him but ends up hitting the character played by Robert Mitchum, prompting their meeting and triggering the ensuing story in which he becomes her love interest.

Iec Long is less about quotidian, unquestioned violence than it is about memory, but retrospection brings with it different forms of aggression, such as exploitation, death, conflagration, and loss. Like many of the plot elements in *The Last Time I Saw Macao*, or like the black pump that opens *Red Dawn*, *Iec Long* is in part a puzzle with a long-delayed solution. The meaning of the title and the topic of the film are only gradually unveiled and the implications of many of its motifs are not fully revealed until the closing titles. The film starts with the bland musical number of a chorus line of five young women who boogie lackadaisically to a screechy band in what might be a street celebration or a modest casino show. The next scene shows exploding fireworks and crowds of people lighting crackers and sparklers. Later scenes alternate between ruined factory buildings, quotations of classical Chinese poetry, and shots of a model of the factory compound, all of which are accompanied by the intermittent spoken testimony of a former worker whom we seldom see. The contemporary views are interspersed with grainy black and white shots of children standing in the ruins, who are ghostly counterparts of the worker whom we hear speaking and of other child workers who still haunt the site. Posters, labels, and calendars advertising the factory's products indicate that the ruined buildings housed a cracker and firework factory. A title at the end of the film imparts the information that fireworks were among Macao's main exports until the 1970s, when their manufacture began to be phased out in favor of textiles. Black and white photographs provide the testimony of the difficult, dangerous nature of the work and of child labor, for children's small fingers were especially adept at sticking wicks in the crackers. The worker reports that he started working at the factory when he was only six years old and that he stayed for decades, earning low wages and without health insurance or the right to compensation in the case of an accident. Fatal explosions punctuated the history of the company. In the end, the danger of manufacturing these products was the reason for the closure of the factory.

The disused factory, the worker's testimony, the abandoned workshops and tools, and the colorful advertisements for *Iec Long* crackers are remnants of the past that lack the monumentality of old colonial buildings and are easily covered up by Macao's glossy façade. They are emblems of passing and impermanence, like the dust of history; the debris that time leaves in its wake. They are plural and swarming, like the trifling, multifarious activity of the marketplace in *Red Dawn*. They are contradictory, too: on the one hand, they are mementos of a simpler time that is evoked in the naïve designs of the labels and advertisements, and of the magic of the fireworks as markers of celebrations and festivities, but they also embody a memory of pain, of dangerous, uncomfortable work, and of labor abuse. These minor memories are all plowed under to build the geometric masses of glass and steel that rise in their place. Several shots at the end of the film frame the ruined compound against new high-rises under construction. These images corroborate the passing of the old Macao at the same time as they hint at the continuity between old and new. The business of the island remains ephemeral enjoyment and illusion: once it was fireworks, now it is tourism and games. The production of these passing delights is always achieved at a cost. Not the least of these is the erasure of complex, embodied memories and the selective recalling of what can be capitalized on as spectacle. To recreate history as spectacle means to erase its asymmetrical, uncomfortable remains—its pastness—and to acknowledge only what is already known. However, a history that only repeats what is known abjures its temporal dimension and its responsibility to the past and the future with the result that it perpetuates the present and remains locked in a loop.

THE ANIMAL END OF HISTORY

Walter Benjamin connected gambling to oblivion. In the popularity of games of chance in mid-nineteenth-century Paris, he saw one of the traits of the local bourgeoisie: the fascination with always starting again, free of the weight of tradition and accumulated knowledge: "On the boulevards it was customary to attribute everything to chance." Chance, like betting, has for Benjamin the shock-like, adventitious character of the events that are detached from what he called the "context of experience."[26] By contrast with the short temporal cycles of gambling, experience (which in Benjamin means embodied, integrated experience, or *Erfahrung*) involves longer narrative arcs of recollection and futurity. Experience entails "the wish": a projection into the future that rests on memories of place, of the body, and of feelings, and contains a utopian desire to amend the faulty past.[27]

Rodrigues and Guerra da Mata depict Macao as a monument to forgetting, where memory is replaced by euphoric gambling and the chance of starting from zero with every bid. Chinese tourists flock to Macao to forget the past and to catch a glimpse of the future, which is represented by the West and its consumerist wonders. In the Largo do Senado, the old Portuguese civic center that is filled with brand-name stores and is decorated for Christmas, they have their picture taken against a cardboard cut-out image representing Mao Zedong surrounded by revolutionary soldiers and leaders. Guerra de Mata ponders the incongruity: the tourists from the mainland act "as if history could be erased

Figure 7.2 *The Last Time I Saw Macao* (2012)

with the click of the cameras that obsessively freeze history and fantasize about happiness." However, the fact of the matter is that history *is* erased by the click of the cameras that fantasize about happiness in individualistic and presentist terms: a happiness that comes from travel, consumption, and prosperity, and is divorced from the past and the future, and from the kind of collective emancipatory project that gave rise to the People's Republic of China. The dream of the Chinese revolution washes up on the shores of Macao, where the vision of a collective future has dissolved into a present without memory and without an ulterior motive. In parallel, one of the photographs of Guerra da Mata's childhood included in the film was taken at a rally of the *Centro Democrático de Macau* (CDM/Democratic Center of Macao), a center-left organization that was founded only days after the April 1974 revolution in Portugal. The present of the film (the years 2011 and 2012) is marked by jadedness and attrition and by severe economic crisis and the intervention in the economy of Portugal by the infamous Troika (the European Commission, the European Central Bank, and the International Monetary Fund). From this vantage point, the photograph of the CDM rally is a memo from a time of hope, for it recalls a national project that foundered momentarily in the murky waters of bankruptcy. Like China, Portugal also suffered the erosion of utopian politics in an era of out-of-control neoliberal capitalism. The sequence in which the CDM photograph appears is followed by images of official buildings that prominently—ironically?—feature the motto of the Portuguese navy, "Honor your country because your country watches you." Immediately afterwards, Guerra da Mata's attention turns to the ubiquitous dogs: "It seemed that all the dogs in Macao were chasing me." The animals, which become more prominent as the film advances, point towards its conclusion: the end of history as the coming of animal time. This may be the happiness that Guerra da Mata pursues through his transformation into a kitten: a timeless time that is freed from the failures of recent history and self-enclosed in immediate sensations and needs.

For its reflection on a time of diminished expectations and retreat, and for its attention to animals, *The Last Time I Saw Macao* bears some relation to Chris Marker's *Sans Soleil* (*Sunless*, 1983). This parallel has been mentioned in passing by some critics but has not been substantially developed.[28] *Sans Soleil* compares the East (Japan), the West (France, Iceland), and Africa (the Portuguese colonies of Angola and Cape Verde) as three locations from which to reflect on the waning of the grand emancipatory projects that guided leftist politics in the previous decades. Marker's earlier *Le Fond de l'Air Est Rouge* (*A Grin Without a Cat*, 1977) chronicles the rise and fall of unofficial leftism—that is, leftism exempt from Soviet guidance—in the late 1960s and 1970s. As a sort of follow-up project, *Sunless* is a melancholy meditation on how to live, and what to live for, in a time of failed utopias and narrow horizons. The Pac-Man videogames that the protagonist of the

Figure 7.3 *The Last Time I Saw Macao* (2012)

film—who is also represented as a disembodied voice—first encounters in Japan contain the "impassable philosophy of our time": "even though it is quite an honor to win many rounds, eventually, things always end up badly." The youth who congregate in the Shinjuku neighborhood in Tokyo and the teenagers in futuristic gear who perform their robotic dances in unison in Yoyogi Park "know that they are not on the launching pad to the true life; [they know] that this is a life to be consumed quickly, like raspberries." They inhabit "a parallel time" that is not too different from the time bubbles which the protagonist of the film tries to rescue from the ruins of the past in a manner that recalls T. S. Eliot's *The Waste Land* (1922): moments of illumination and images of happiness found in minute occurrences and small folds of history. One source of comfort is animals. They are emblems of the unexpected ("Did you know that there are emus in L'Île de France?") and of affection and care—a Japanese couple make an offering to the gods so that the soul of their lost cat may find peace. Animals are also images of utopia. Cruelty to animals signals catastrophe: a giraffe bleeding to death ushers in a reflection on the dissolution of anti-colonial resistance into fierce internecine struggles. At the end of *Sunless*, the black cat "with the white socks" that crosses the road in an Icelandic village supplements the image of happiness that was shown at the start of the film: three children from the same village walking together in the sun and smiling at the camera. When it is revisited years later, the village has been partly buried by ashes from a nearby volcano, and it serves as a reminder that happiness is always partial and that nature occasionally lights sacrificial pyres. Yet even in the midst of the disaster, one can still catch a glimpse of utopia in the form of a cat settling comfortably among the imperiled buildings.

Sunless ends in suspense, with fragmentary images of happiness shored against the ruins of recent times. By contrast, *The Last Time I Saw Macao* presents a more drastic vision: the total eclipse of humanity. Guerra da Mata becomes a kitten shortly before the entire island—the entire world?—becomes devoid of humans and is turned over to animals. The animal end of history is also an elegant, if radical way out of the present impasse. When there is no future to look forward to, the past is streamlined into spectacle, and history goes into a loop, the world as we know it might as well end, ushering in a new order of being. Rodrigues and Guerra da Mata's films often end in radical transformations. When conflicts become unlivable and characters can no longer cope, they morph. The protagonist of *O Fantasma* (*Phantom*, 2000) ends up living in the garbage dump outside Lisbon dressed in a rubber body suit that makes him look like a humanoid; Odete, in *Two Drifters*, transforms herself into Pedro, the dead gay man with whom she has been obsessed throughout the film; the transvestite Tónia reverts to António, her masculine self, at the end of her life in *To Die Like a Man*; and in *The Ornithologist*, Fernando's ordeals are a pathway—or ascesis—towards sainthood.

Unlike these films, *The Last Time I Saw Macao* depicts both an individual and a collective transformation. It is a transformation triggered by an overlapping series of failures: by Guerra da Mata's bungled mission and by the societal inability to create a livable present, respect the past, and imagine a different future. However, failure in this case is not necessarily tragic. In Macao, if we remember Candy's words, myths are not simply stories, legend becomes reality, and failure is not the end but a chance to start all over again from entirely different premises.

CHAPTER 8

Space and Memory: The Window as Freeze-frame

Carlos Alberto Carrilho and Rita Gomes Ferrão

This is freeze-act, as elsewhere one finds the freeze-phrase (the fragment which fixes the writing) or the freeze-frame in cinema, which fixes the entire movement of the city. This immobility is not an inertia, but a paroxysm which boils movement down into its opposite. The same dialectic was already present in Chinese opera or in animal dances—an art of stupor, slowness, bewitchment.[1]

From the beginning of João Pedro Rodrigues and João Rui Guerra da Mata's collaboration, the city of Lisbon has been at the core of both Portuguese filmmakers' work, while Macao has also been a focus in some of their more recent projects. Their intriguing characters are lonely city dwellers whose stories are projected onto the urban space, even when they move beyond it. Working within the heritage of a postmodern local community that developed in the aftermath of the Portuguese *Estado Novo* (New State) dictatorship (1933–74), Rodrigues and Guerra da Mata align their private memories and domestic space with the social and historical urban space. In doing so, they emphasize a connection with the past as a means to evoke previous practices that allow for a better understanding of the present. Taking this into account, this chapter seeks to decipher the domestic and urban territories that exist off-screen in Rodrigues and Guerra da Mata's works[2] and to read the multiple ways in which their experiences[3] relate to encounters or ruptures with the urban space.

The processes of filming, staging, scoring, and editing a film always result in the act of revealing, cutting, organizing, and modeling a space.[4] As such, from its inception as a form of art and mass entertainment, cinema has been a privileged medium through which to problematize the mechanisms of spatial perception and to form new geographies in the interstices of reality and imagination. This is also what Stephen Barber argues when he associates the birth of cinema with the movement of ghostly human bodies in urban space, and the cinematic city with an entanglement of image and language, and of life and death:

> Film began with a scattering of gesturing ghosts, of human bodies walking city streets, within the encompassing outlines of bridges, hotels and warehouses, under polluted industrial skies. The first incendiary spark of the film image—extending across almost every country in the world, around the end of the nineteenth century—propelled forward a history of the body that remains inescapably locked into the history of the city.[5]

Barber also points out that, during the late 1920s and before the development of sound synchronization, the city had taken over cinema, fixing the hallucinatory quality of the image in the eyes of the spectators and displaying the urban bustle and motion of silent figures through ghostly apparitions and fabulous mirages.[6] The street film was developed in the Weimar Republic as a subgenre of the city film that offered melodramatic narratives based on the street "as a space of random encounters, violent crime, urban surveillance, and ambiguous morality and sexuality, the emerging social space and public sphere in modern urbanism."[7] Technological developments such as street lighting enabled radical transformations in the urban space by making visible the streets at night, thus designing a new dimension for the interaction between characters.[8] On the other hand, urban symphonies that were produced during the silent era, such as Walter Ruttmann's *Berlin—Die Sinfonie der Großstadt* (*Berlin: Symphony of a Great City*, 1927), portrayed modernity as a psychic and visual experience without relying on a conventional narrative.[9]

In urban symphony films, the city is not presented as a random setting for a given action. Rather, it is suggested as a collective entity that does not focus on an individual, a city square, or a sequence of facts or actions. Its inhabitants do not participate in vital insurgencies and convulsions, for these are only generated within the visual matter of space. The cinematic images alternate between examinations of the surfaces of buildings and of the nature of perception in the city, with the ephemerality of day and night represented in its road networks. The images thus follow the gaze of the city's inhabitants over its endless spectacular display.[10] With the end of World War II, new images of destroyed European cities came to be imposed as previous urban cinematic representations were replaced by scenes of eviscerated courtyards or destroyed palaces, as well as by human and architectural debris.[11]

Portugal was not an exception to this shift in perspective, and we find urban symphonies in Portuguese cinema as well. José Leitão de Barros's *Lisboa, Crónica Anedótica* (*Lisbon, Anecdotal Chronicle*, 1930) and Manoel de Oliveira's

Douro, Faina Fluvial (*Labor on the Douro River*, 1931) are good examples of this genre. The latter film was shot in Oporto and is a poetic portrait of the vitality of the Douro River banks. It was "inspired by Ruttmann and by the montage theories," in an "improbable modernity of processes that set the (then) spluttering Portuguese cinema at the level of a yet unknown contemporaneity."[12] In the former film, Lisbon is the main character. Indeed, and as the opening intertitle explains, *Lisbon, Anecdotal Chronicle* "is not a documentary but rather an anecdotal tale of some aspects of ordinary people's lives in Lisbon." *Lisbon, Anecdotal Chronicle* is divided into episodes that depict urban daily life. The film uses renowned Portuguese theater actors to recreate fictional scenes in which documentary images of city life intersect with images of the most emblematic public spaces of the city. Lisbon is shown to lack the remarkable features of new metropolises, such as those documented in other examples of urban symphonies from foreign cinema. The film stages the city as a point of arrival from the rural world, and it establishes "the tendency to convert Lisbon into a privileged source of inspiration for Portuguese cinema, where it appears as unique and traditional."[13] In the words of João Bénard da Costa:

> Leitão de Barros created again, better than anybody else, what he later called the "poor but happy side of the fatalism without rebellion of the riverside people of old Lisbon." With a brisk appearance (the "live scenery"), what appear in this "chronicle" are the closed horizons of a city with a dead end, slave of its own tricks and traps that would forever insinuate itself, in filigree or as a predominant note, in almost all the films (comedies or drama) that had Lisbon as the main scenery. [. . .] it should be looked for in all those Portuguese films, in which Lisbon is painted as a "dark" city, starting with the Barros production, certainly one of the most ruthless views of ourselves, made by ourselves.[14]

Leitão de Barros was a key figure in the construction of the image of Portugal during the authoritarian New State regime led by António de Oliveira Salazar. During World War II, Portugal declared its neutrality and Lisbon was not affected by the bombings that were inflicted on other European cities. António Ferro, the head of the Secretariado de Propaganda Nacional (National Propaganda Bureau), created the so-called "política do espírito" (politics of the spirit) in an attempt to articulate popular and modernist ideas. In this sense, culture was seen as a form of propaganda for the ideology of the regime as it aimed to construct a national, folk culture. Although Ferro advocated the production of historical and educational films for the purposes of nationalist propaganda, the city of Lisbon was the stage for a set of popular comedies in the first decades of the New State, in the era of sound cinema.[15] These comedies were tolerated but never endorsed by António Ferro, and they would become the canon for a particular under-standing of Portuguese popular cinema. The films depicted picturesque urban spaces that evoked the simplicity and solidarity of rural life (values that were cherished by the regime) under the watchful eye of the censors. On the other hand, the modernizing impetus of the New State was brought to light in projects that linked engineering with architecture, such as the Instituto Superior Técnico building, which was presented as an example of the modernist city in newsreels and fiction films including José Leitão de Barros's *Maria Papoila* (1937) and António Lopes Ribeiro's *A Revolução de Maio* (*The May Revolution*, 1937).

In the early period of the New State, housing needs increased in large part due to a higher level of rural–urban migration and changes in the coexistence of different social classes. The city limits were considerably widened from the tra-ditional neighborhoods. Urbanization projects such as the "Plano das Avenidas Novas" (Avenidas Novas Plan) and the "Bairro de Alvalade" (Alvalade Neigh-borhood) were put underway in an effort toward the modernist reconstruction of Lisbon. The parish of Alvalade in the northeast of Lisbon, for example, was transformed from what had been until then a mainly agricultural area. From the 1930s onward, major architectural projects, such as those carried out in the Avenida de Roma and the tower blocks of the Avenida dos Estados Unidos da América and the Estacas neighborhood, have completely reshaped the urban design of the area.

In 1958, the Café Vává opened at the intersection of the Avenida de Roma and the Avenida dos Estados Unidos da América. It was named after a famous Brazilian soccer player of the time. For more than a decade it served as a meet-ing place for university students and for many of the filmmakers who formed the Portuguese *Novo Cinema* (New Cinema) generation. The café brought together those individuals in legendary cultural and political gatherings dur-ing which the foundations of the dictatorial regime were subtly questioned. It is said that the director Fernando Lopes signed the contract commissioning *Belarmino* (1964) in this café, and that it was written on a napkin by António da Cunha Telles, "the extraordinary producer of quite a number of works in this new wave."[16] The gatherings were attended by critics and filmmakers such as António-Pedro Vasconcelos, João César Monteiro, and Paulo Rocha. Paulo Rocha lived in the same building in which the Vává was located. He recalls:

I had arrived from Oporto, and my parents had bought a flat on the eighth floor of the Vává building. It was the era of intense focus on cinema. I was looking for a script to make my first film, and read the news of a crime of passion. The incident had happened next door, which affected me greatly. I walked around the neighborhood and discovered a cobbler's workshop that had a beautiful cinemascope window overlooking the street. I ended up filming on that stretch of road between the Avenida dos Estados Unidos da América, where I lived, and the Vává café.[17]

Thus Paulo Rocha's film *Os Verdes Anos* (*The Green Years*, 1963) was born "at the intersection of the Avenida dos Estados Unidos da América and the Avenida de Roma, which in the 1960s was the symbol of modernity, of international life."[18] The film is celebrated as the inaugural moment of the Portuguese New Cinema.[19] Shot in black and white, *The Green Years* reflects on the concept of social and economic dualism that is characteristic of developing countries,[20] where distinct, traditional, economic and social ways of life persisted in the small, modernized centers. According to the researcher Adérito Sedas Nunes,

> to understand such dualism, in terms of both its structure and the dynamics of its development, is to establish one of the basic frames of reference of the national problem. Rural exodus and emigration, which take on proportions of "social hemorrhage," can only be conveniently located within such a system.[21]

The first shots of *The Green Years* capture the environment in and around the newly developed Alvalade neighborhood. Indeed, those shots portray Lisbon undergoing a process of transformation, caught halfway between the rural and the urban with agricultural fields and vegetable gardens, with a population dedicated to the small agricultural economy in the foreground, and new, tall buildings in the background. The narrator begins by pointing out that:

> The first time I saw the city of Lisbon, I thought to myself: this city is like a broad that has to be handled with great care. Don't hurry it, don't fondle her too soon [. . .] Better take it slowly, eyes wide open and without smelly feet. Better remember, above all, that you were born in a backward village, and you need to learn to hang on.[22]

Rocha's prosopopoeial approach eroticizes the city and synthesizes the challenges faced by those who come from rural areas. The cobbler's assistant Júlio (Rui Gomes) is new to the city, having been warned about its pleasures but also about its dangers. His romance with the housemaid Ilda (Isabel Ruth) is the premise for countless journeys through a new, developing city. In this film, Lisbon encompasses agricultural fields with elegantly shaped olive trees, which would soon give way to new constructions that put an end to any sign of a rural economy. The new city comprises modern buildings, sidewalks that cross over landscaped spaces, modern clothing shops, and sports cars. A sought-after city life is formed in a Lisbon where "inhabitants pay more for a place to sleep in than they do to eat,"[23] although such a lifestyle is inaccessible to the lovers Ilda and Júlio. The urgency with which they seek to change their life evokes the title of Paulo Rocha's subsequent film *Mudar de Vida* (*Change of Life*, 1966). Yet their attempt to break free from the ties that hinder social mobility and which prevent them from enjoying the idealized modern way of life ends in an unavoidable tragedy, about which the viewer is repeatedly warned earlier in the film.

In this sense, the most disconcerting aspect of the film is the window of the cobbler's workshop, which corresponds to the cinemascope view of the street. As suggested by Paulo Rocha, the workshop represents an island at the center of the new urban development, and it has a magnificent view over the inaccessible modernity of the street. A similarly shaped window is found later in Odete's (Ana Cristina de Oliveira) room in *Odete* (*Two Drifters*, 2005). This is João Pedro Rodrigues's second fiction feature film, and it was shot in the basement of the building where the filmmaker lives. The room was designed by the art director Guerra da Mata. At first sight, the window of the room seems to have a conventional shape; however, when the character draws the curtains, we see a walled surface with a wide, horizontal opening that provides a street-level view. The basement windows in both films allow us to glimpse the feet and shoes of passers-by: for Júlio, the utilitarian quality of the window seems convenient; however, to Odete, it serves almost as the window of a den, behind which she lurks and hides at night. In reality, these two windows are located only a few blocks away from one another. Although he filmed it differently, Rodrigues inherited Paulo Rocha's city.

In *The Green Years*, images of the modern city also focus on the artworks that are integrated in the surrounding architecture. Paulo Rocha films Almada Negreiros's[24] engravings at the Cidade Universitária (Lisbon University Campus), the tile panels by Menez[25] at the Vává, and the ceramic-tiled portico of the Rampa store, which was designed by Querubim Lapa.[26] In contrast to the modesty of the cobbler's workshop, the protagonists of the film are shown visiting these artistic interventions as they stroll about the city and cross the Tagus River, with the camera presenting a panoramic view of the city and the river.

The relationship between Rodrigues's work and the Alvalade neighborhood that is portrayed in Rocha's *The Green Years* began in 1997. At that time, Alvalade was inhabited mainly by liberal professionals and middle- and upper-class families. It is also the location of the apartment in which Rodrigues shot *Parabéns* (*Happy Birthday!*, 1997), his first short film after leaving cinema school. Francisco, the protagonist, is an architect played by Guerra da Mata, Rodrigues's life and work partner.[27] In the first scene, we see the bottom of a window and the top of a bed in which Francisco is sleeping. Before that, in black screen, we hear Francisco's girlfriend singing *Happy Birthday* on an answering machine that is also playing a piece of music by Iánnis Xenákis.[28] The previous night, Francisco had been sexually involved with a young man, João (Eduardo Sobral) who shares his first name with both Rodrigues and Guerra da Mata. In the film, the two characters lie next to one another. They had met at the Alcântara-Mar nightclub, which was one of the most famous late-night haunts in the city in the 1990s. The club is representative of an eclectic, cosmopolitan Lisbon where the customers of the exclusive club Frágil coexist harmoniously with the transvestite clubs in the Príncipe Real neighborhood[29] or the prostitutes in the Rua Conde de Redondo.

Francisco utters apologies to his girlfriend on the phone, but leaves out the fact that he is not alone. Meanwhile, João fools around with him. We watch Francisco's body in the shower through the transparent filter of the curtain with a world map printed on it. Meanwhile, João guides the viewer on a journey through the architect's flat. He picks at whatever food he finds, listens to music, dances, watches the Japanese animé series *Dragon Ball Z* that is playing on the television and mimics the robotic gestures of the characters, oscillating between a cartoon character and an untamed animal. João's inexhaustible energy contrasts with Francisco's hangover, as the latter seeks relief in an invigorating shower.

The coded territory of the architect's flat is reinvented by the young man from Almada, a peripheral city in Greater Lisbon that is located on the south bank of the Tagus River. Guerra da Mata lived in Almada when he was younger, and he used to cross the Tagus to work as a bartender in the Bairro Alto, the neighborhood that was at the core of cosmopolitan Lisbon nightlife. João's character might therefore be perceived as a representation of Guerra da Mata in the recent past. When João opens the window, domestic intimacy is invaded by the impersonal marks of the city. Signs of the urban public space enter the flat through the light, the traffic noise, and the buzz of the city, as well as through the animal sounds that João tries to mimic. Sonic, the director's cat, walks on the windowsill and is startled by João's feline posture.[30] When the window is opened, the outside world that is printed on the shower curtain is projected violently into the flat. The window thus establishes a boundary between private and public spaces, with the latter being the off-screen space to which we are not given access. *Happy Birthday!* was filmed in the flat where Rodrigues and Guerra da Mata still live together. The setting resulted from the redesign of their domestic space in the building that was constructed by Rodrigues's grandfather, and where both of his grandparents had lived since the 1960s.

The strong references to the Lisbon of the 1980s and early-1990s in the work of Rodrigues and Guerra da Mata is an appropriate testimony to the legacy of the postmodern Lisbon generation that emerged after the fall of the New State dictatorship in 1974. This community stemmed from the flourishing underground culture that developed between the neighborhoods of Campo de Ourique and Alvalade (the birthplace of the Lisbon punk movement) and, at night, in the Bairro Alto, where new dance clubs and design and fashion shops were located next to the old brothels. The area is also close to the gay bars and clubs of Príncipe Real. The proliferation of exhibitions and contemporary art galleries, experimental and pop-rock concerts, and fashion shows coincided with the birth of a new generation of filmmakers, which included Pedro Costa, Edgar Pêra, João Canijo, Manuel Mozos, Joaquim Sapinho, Teresa Villaverde, Ana Luísa Guimarães, Joaquim Leitão, Vítor Gonçalves, and Joaquim Pinto.

The Bairro Alto was constructed from the fifteenth to seventeenth centuries as a set of urban agglomerations, and as such it constitutes "the first modern neighborhood of Lisbon."[31] The mansions and palaces of the neighborhood were built according to "erudite architectural standards [that] have adapted to both the physiognomy of the streets and the traditional design of existing dwellings, giving rise to a harmonious architectural ensemble."[32] Even though the 1755 earthquake did not destroy the Bairro Alto, the neighborhood did nonetheless lose some of its aristocratic features after it came to be occupied by lower-class groups. In the 1830s, it was one of the areas in Lisbon where prostitution was permitted, both on the street and in specialized establishments. Around the same time, the Conservatório Nacional (National Conservatoire) was founded in the Convento dos Caetanos (Theatine Convent). This institution was dedicated to the teaching of the arts. The separation and autonomy of the Conservatório's different schools and artistic disciplines was decreed only in 1983, and this followed by the establishment of the Escola Superior de Teatro e Cinema (Lisbon Theater and Film School). From the late eighteenth century, the press came to occupy many of the empty palaces, which further contributed towards the development of a bohemian atmosphere that brought together thugs, journalists, politicians, and later, filmmakers, artists, and intellectuals, who wandered around the Bairro Alto and patronized its brothels, restaurants, and taverns.

The descendants of the middle and upper classes that, in the 1950s and 1960s, had settled in the modern buildings around the Avenida da Roma also came to frequent the streets and recreational spaces of the Bairro Alto. The neighborhood fostered an unusual freedom of expression that could not be found in other areas of the city. In the late 1970s, several visionary entrepreneurs invested in nightclubs in the neighborhood, where food, music, and fashion were in line with the cosmopolitanism of other European capitals. In 1982, the nightclub Frágil opened and it would become one of the most legendary night spots in Lisbon. It featured a dance floor and a bar where people could drink and socialize. The decoration of the club was "equally inspired by the industrial and the baroque"[33] and its design underwent several artistic interventions by visual artists, designers, and architects. The venue was further boosted by small-scale, yet irreverent and bold cultural events, including fashion shows, theater plays, and concerts. For instance, the musician and hairdresser António Variações (whose songs feature in Rodrigues's films *Morrer Como um Homem* [*To Die Like a Man*, 2009] and *O Ornitólogo* [*The Ornithologist*, 2016]) was invited to Frágil as a resident hairdresser for a week. According to the founder of the club, Manuel Reis, at Frágil one could live and think freely, without constraints. The visual artist Pedro Cabrita Reis was a famous regular customer and one of the originators of the artistic interventions at the club. He remembers it as a "place of amusement, [where] amidst the drinks, tobacco smoke, and dancing, new ideas arose that would spread out to the whole city."[34]

In an emotional newspaper column that was published at the time of Manuel Reis's death, the Portuguese film and music critic Augusto M. Seabra highlighted the cosmopolitanism of Reis's vision when he chose the infamous Bairro Alto for the establishment of his businesses. The location allowed Seabra not only to bond with architects and visual artists, but also to meet future filmmakers and to mingle with other relevant cultural personalities. Seabra concluded that, although various mayors, architects, cultural institutions, and creators contributed to the consolidation of the new Lisbon cosmopolitanism, Manuel Reis, together with his mindset and the spaces that he created, is of particular importance to the city.[35] Over the following two decades, modernity would coalesce with the traditions of the popular neighborhood as other nightspots, fashion shows, designer and music shops, independent music labels, and art galleries were opened throughout the Bairro Alto.

Other areas of the city would echo and nourish such developments. In the mid-1980s, João Peste, the founder of the Pop Dell'Arte band, brought together a group of musicians and bands on the compilation album *Divergências* (1986), which was the first release by the groundbreaking Ama Romanta label. This double album featured an interview with the sociologist José Paquete de Oliveira as the opening track of the B-side of the first record. In it, Paquete de Oliveira quotes Pier Paolo Pasolini in a reflection on the threat of the new cultural dictatorships: "The fascism of cultural dictatorships will be that which is imposed through the oppression of the people, who will be kept in a state of ignorance or away from new knowledge, lacking a critical consciousness." These words would turn into a kind of manifesto for the influential record label, which focused on marginal projects and Portuguese independent music. Ama Romanta was also well connected to other areas of artistic creation, including to the film directors Manuel Mozos and Joaquim Pinto, as well as to the graphic designer and filmmaker Nuno Leonel. In cinema, some major events included the opening of the Fórum Picoas and King film theaters,[36] the birth of the Lisbon Gay & Lesbian Film Festival (1997) [now Queer Lisboa, the International Queer Film Festival], and the organization of transnational events such as Europália 91, Lisbon: European Capital of Culture 94, and Expo 98. All of these events were showcases for the production of knowledge about Portuguese contemporary culture and for the development of fertile contact zones between Portuguese and international art productions and audiences.

In this context, Rodrigues gained his earliest professional experience in cinema. He collaborated with other filmmakers and directed his first short films, *O Pastor* (*The Shepherd*, 1988) and *Happy Birthday!*. Like other film-makers from the same generation, he was taught by some of the major fig-ures of Portuguese cinema at the Lisbon Theater and Film School, such as Paulo Rocha and António Reis. As such, he "received technical and aesthetic training that reflects many of the values of Portuguese 'new cinema,' and in particular aesthetic intransigence, a markedly authorial character, and an affiliation with the principles of modern art-house cinema."[37]

The Shepherd is a college project that claimed the heritage of António Reis and Margarida Cordeiro, whose work "although aesthetically and ethically homogeneous, presents a conscious evolution: the progressive eschewal of the documentary genre and all its conceptual boundaries, and the tendency towards a poetic, dreamlike approach."[38] In a reflection on her work with Reis, Cordeiro states that:

> The great mistake of cinema is to simplify reality. There is a clearing in the visual field that has to be resolved. A rigorous reorganization of the real, a rigorous one. Reality, as we film it, is not simplified; it is com-plexified—so much so that the film has no reality: indeed, it has many realities. [. . .] Therefore, we try to take on reality and create another one, a complex one. We need to grasp the real and add what we feel, which has nothing to do with neorealism. And cinema is this "giving something else." Giving anything that makes us live.[39]

Two documentaries mediate João Pedro Rodrigues's change of focus from the short form to the long-running fiction format. Both of them have Guerra da Mata as assistant director: *Esta É a Minha Casa* (*This Is My Home*, 1997) and *Viagem à Expo* (*Journey to Expo*, 1998). In these films, Rodrigues explores a labo-ratorial methodology. He observes the visit of a Portuguese emigrant family in Paris to its place of origin in rural Trás-os-Montes, which is one of the most remote and poorest areas of Portugal. Indeed, it was in that northern Portuguese region that Cordeiro and Reis filmed their most famous work, *Trás-os-Montes* (1976): "a pantheist and telluric film, where the scenery and ancestral culture are religiously contemplated, in a pilgrimage of the imagination that recovers the dimension of the myth in each gesture, each ritual or each saga."[40]

In Rodrigues's documentaries, the family's relationship with Portugal is materialized into a "romantic nationalism" that Paulo Filipe Monteiro identified as a part of a Portuguese national identity, and which is "frozen in the *Estado Novo* [New State], and then reactivated in the face of emigration, exile, European integration, or economic and political interests that mobilize it around major cultural festivals."[41] The return to Portugal involves a trip from the countryside to the city of Lisbon along the highways that were developed after the accession of Portugal to the European Economic Community (which became the European Union) using European funds aimed at reducing regional asymmetries. Furthermore, the film portrays a visit to the Expo 98, which was an event that enabled the redevelopment of eastern Lisbon and aimed to revamp its international image as an entrepreneurial and innovative country at the same time as it celebrated Portugal's historic relationship with the ocean.

In 2000, Rodrigues directed *O Fantasma* (*Phantom*) with Guerra da Mata as art director and costume designer. This was his first feature film, and it was also filmed in the vicinity of the flat that he shared with his partner, near the cinemascope window of *The Green Years* and which, as noted above, is also part of the off-screen space in *Happy Birthday!*. The film title of *Phantom* appears over a night shot of a garbage truck around the Alvalade neighborhood. The young Sérgio (Ricardo Meneses) works the night shift in the Lisbon waste disposal service. He develops an erotic obsession with João (André Barbosa), who despises him. Sérgio indulges in several anonymous, random sexual encounters. Four decades after *The Green Years*, Lisbon is shown to have undergone profound changes. In his working time, Sérgio collects household objects that have been left on the sidewalks. These are not only fragments of the modern city that have been rendered obsolete, but also represent consumerist excesses in late capitalist society.

The movie is filmed in color and set in a mostly nocturnal environment that coincides with Sérgio's work schedule. The banality of the unsheltered canebrakes, with their precarious constructions in wood and cement, replace the elegance of the 1960s olive trees that used to be found in the hills surrounding Alvalade. Within this kingdom of shadows, a huge ghostly patch of darkness seems to emerge from the skyline of tall, somewhat degraded modern buildings. This darkness haunts the urban fabric of the other side of Alvalade, which consists mainly of small buildings and houses. Like many of the characters in Rodrigues's filmography, Sérgio has no history. We do not know where he comes from or where he is going, nor whether he is hostage to his own mysterious past, which is hinted at, but never made explicit. Likewise, we have little notion of his future. He lives in a guesthouse that is named after another European city, Sevilha (Seville), and which is located in the historic center of Lisbon, near Príncipe Real and the Bairro Alto.

The only steady, affective relationship that Sérgio has is with Lorde, the dog from the municipal sanitation services whose gestures he mimics when he barks, growls, licks, walks on all fours, uses his sense of smell as a primary sense, and marks territory with his own urine. The film employs an almost documentary approach: it provides a new mapping of the old neighborhoods that were built during the New State, which is outlined by the modern circuits of waste management. Among urban waste, danger, and pleasure, Sérgio seems to live in a post-apocalyptic city as a collector of personal objects, food, and erotic fantasies. He customarily seeks other men, with whom he performs sexual activities in both private and public spaces, and the city is displayed as a sexual playground in a series of tableaux onto which Sérgio's fantasies are projected. Sérgio's existence is like that of a phantom. He is a disposable object who becomes visible only when he is integrated into the social structure as a sexual commodity. His immateriality emerges when he is seen through glass, when water dilutes his features, or when his body swiftly and gracefully climbs hedges or walls.

Finally, the night takes him, handcuffed and imprisoned in the latex suit that outlines the curves of his body yet nullifies his facial identity. The garbage truck transports him to the waste management center. Like a dying animal, he warms himself beside burning containers, hunts small mammals, and feeds on recyclable materials. Once the cycle of recycling is over, instead of being reintegrated into the socio-economic space of the city, Sérgio enters through a door into a disturbing scenario in which all of the characters have disappeared: a black hole that seems to have consumed all signs of life. Devoid of romantic diversions, *Phantom* reinterprets an urban space that is traditionally known for its modernity, and portrays it as seemingly anachronistic and sexualized by the projection of multiple desires, but also as violent and ghostly, following a postmodern approach.

A decade later, Alvalade is shown again in *Manhã de Santo António* (*Morning of Saint Anthony's Day*, 2012). Rodrigues is the director of this film, with Guerra da Mata once again as art director. Alvalade is shown in a different light in this film, which was made during daytime and employs mostly high-angle shots that do not disassemble the geography of the space. Under the watchful eye of the statue of St. Anthony in the main square of Alvalade, an initial shot shows the enormous shadow that is cast by the statue, at sunrise, over one of the buildings. The timeline of the film coincides with the feast of St. Anthony, which is celebrated annually on the night of 12 June. In this festival, crowds of people from in and around Lisbon file into the streets of the city's traditional neighborhoods. The city is adorned with garlands, balloons, and bush basil, and the revelers dance and eat traditional Portuguese soup ("caldo verde") and grilled sardines. The starting point of the film is the tradition of lovers exchanging small pots of bush basil, which are adorned with carnations made out of colored paper and little paper flags that carry love poems. Although these are traditionally folk verses, in *Morning of Saint Anthony's Day* the camera focuses on a basil pot in which the viewer can read a poem by Fernando Pessoa, one of the main figures of Portuguese Modernism. The poem thus creates a symbolic territory that lies somewhere between tradition and modernism.

A group of young people emerges from an underground station into an almost empty neighborhood. They represent a disenchanted image of youth. They walk slowly and in uncoordinated fashion, and these images recall the figure of the undead or the zombie, as well as of the political allegories from George A. Romero's "Trilogy of the Dead." On the one hand, the small paper flag carrying Pessoa's poem may point to the US flag that is seen waving in the cemetery of *Night of the Living Dead* (1968). On the other hand, the group of youngsters brings to mind the scene from *Dawn of the Dead* (1978), in which zombies take refuge in a shopping center where they wander through the corridors among the passive mannequins and water fountains. As in Romero's film, and despite their zombie-like movement, these young people undergo a sort of choreography in which they search for familiar places and objects that might hold significant memories. This search is most apparent in the skateboarding activities and the obsession with mobile phones that are portrayed in Rodrigues's film.

In the second feature film directed by João Pedro Rodrigues, *Two Drifters*, there is a change of focus as this film does not give preference to the historic center of Lisbon, nor to the modern urbanized neighborhoods. In fact, and similarly to other Portuguese films from that period, *Two Drifters* sometimes moves towards the city limits, as if it were following an urge to escape Lisbon, as pointed out by João Rosmaninho:

> With narratives distributed around both central and peripheral areas of the city, Lisbon now seems to be exerting pressure to escape the historical center. It is as though the center, which is usually represented as clean, monumental, and bourgeois, is no longer of relevance for the development of new narratives. [. . .] Lisbon remains outside the frame, but it is imperceptible to us. Yet, the journey appears to be always from the center of the city to its outskirts, or vice versa. [. . .] In spite of everything, what is visible in these shots is not the movement but rather the closed (albeit glass) interior. In *Two Drifters*, the protagonist Odete is always alone as she moves between Ajuda/Restelo and the hypermarket where she works. She sits at the back of the bus and leans against the window as an alternative to running away. [42]

This convergence towards the outskirts of the city was also outlined by the filmmaker Alberto Seixas Santos, one of the thinkers of the Escola Portuguesa

(Portuguese School),[43] for whom Rodrigues had worked as assistant director on the film, *Mal* (*Mercy*) in 1999:

> The city of today is dead, somehow. What remains is a series of adjacent towns, new and increasingly large commuter towns, and the only possible cinema for this new city is a cinema of transit, a cinema of movement, between peripheral dormitory towns and the places where people work.[44]

However, instead of fixing themselves in what is "the urban territory of the contemporary world par excellence, the suburbs,"[45] Rodrigues and Guerra da Mata turned once more to private memories, mainly those of da Mata. Born in Lourenço Marques (present-day Maputo, the capital city of the former Portuguese colony of Mozambique), Guerra da Mata spent part of his childhood and adolescence in Macao, before moving to Lisbon. Guerra da Mata and Rodrigues's *A Última Vez Que Vi Macau* (*The Last Time I Saw Macao*, 2012) represents the return to Macao of the homonymous character played by Guerra da Mata, for the first time since his childhood. The action takes place thirty years after his departure from the autonomous region on the south coast of China.

Macao has been a Special Administrative Region of the People's Republic of China—as is Hong Kong—since 20 December 1999. A powerful trading post for Europe and Asia, it had been administered by Portugal prior to this date, in accordance with the interests and will of the Chinese authorities. The legalization in 1847 of the previously clandestine gambling business contributed to the development of the territory, which was transformed into a leisure center for wealthy merchants, and halted the economic decline imposed by the growth of the British colony of Hong Kong. Astonishingly, in 2006 Macao surpassed Las Vegas in gambling revenue: the city of Macao may be regarded as the "Monte Carlo of the East," as portrayed in Josef von Sternberg and Nicholas Ray's film *Macao* (1952), or as the "fascinating Las Vegas of the East," such as in *The Last Time I Saw Macao*.

During the shooting of *The Last Time I Saw Macao*, the directors searched for the places of Guerra da Mata's memories, as Rodrigues observes:

> I always start by going to places that are related to my life. I need this intimate connection. Even Macao—I did not know the place at all—was all about João Rui's childhood, all those memories that he had told me. [. . .] The paths leading to the places of his childhood were completely different; we constantly had to detour around town, as we would discover other places. The film was constructed around these detours, this labyrinth, this density.[46]

The return of Guerra da Mata's character to Macao is instigated by an email from Candy (Cindy Scrash), a friend of his who had come to the city for unknown reasons; perhaps she was drawn to the idea of exoticism and ease of living. In the email, Candy writes that a friend of hers has been killed in a game simulating a military operation, and that she could be the next victim. It becomes apparent that, once again, Candy got involved with the wrong men, and this trope is common to the genre of the film noir. *The Last Time I Saw Macao* expands on an experiment between sound and image, and between diegetic and extra-diegetic sound. It summons private memories and historical facts and mingles them with the fictional intrigue of a noir-like criminal organization.

Guerra da Mata acts as a faceless detective, like Phillip Marlowe (Robert Montgomery) who is hidden by the subjective camera in Robert Montgomery's *Lady in the Lake* (1947).[47] Prior to the evocative scene of her friend's death, Candy lip-syncs "You Kill Me," which is also sung by Jane Russell in *Macao*. Candy is cast as the inevitable *femme fatale*, in a dress with a provocative neckline and standing in front of a tiger cage. Yet, the music seems to come from an old record player that is located at the back of the room. This scene was not shot in Macao but rather in Almada in the winter, inside a circus tent where only a hanging net separated Cindy Scrash from the roaring tigers. Scrash also evokes another Hollywood sex goddess: Ava Gardner in John Ford's *Mogambo* (1953), who is shown walking by a group of caged felines that are excited by her presence. The dividing net in *The Last Time I Saw Macao* is highlighted by a small spotlight, which also evokes one of the best scenes in *Macao*, in which Robert Mitchum is chased by the local mafia, and steps onto small floating boats in a maze of hanging nets.

The film not only explores the boundaries between film genres and between reality and fiction; it also problematizes sexual identity and the place of women in film noir by inviting a transsexual performer, as an evocation of Andy Warhol's Superstar Candy Darling, and who worked in Príncipe Real clubs, to reinterpret the Jane Russell song. Candy's scene in *The Last Time I Saw Macao* was the only one to be staged in a somewhat controlled environment, unlike *Macao*, which was filmed mostly in American studios, except for the documentary shots of the city that were aimed at creating the location of the plot. Nevertheless, *Macao* is not one of Rodrigues and Guerra da Mata's favorite von Sternberg films. In a major survey of von Sternberg's film oeuvre at MoMA (New York), Andrew Sarris stated that he, too, was not particularly enthused by *Macao* (which was directed by Nicholas Ray in the later stages of production):

Even with a mechanically meaningless assignment like *Macao* his [Josef von Sternberg's] visual signature smiles through the veils and nets like the Cheshire Cat *à la* Chautard. [. . .] Sternberg's contribution to *Macao* is exclusively stylistic, and there is no evidence, internal or external, of any deeper involvement than that. The objective core of the plot is moldy even by the sordid standards of the genre and it would be difficult to argue that Sternberg's few visual coups constitute a triumph of form over content.[48]

The way in which Rodrigues's memories of *Macao*[49] represent how the Orient is entangled with Guerra da Mata's childhood memories established the directors' leitmotif for making *The Last Time I Saw Macao*. In line with the tradition of stereotyping that is exploited by the film industry,[50] the Portuguese community of *Macao* looks strangely Hispanic, and Sarris considers the only interesting characterization to be that of the descendant of Spanish emigrants, Thomas Gomez, a corrupt police officer.[51] Rodrigues and Guerra da Mata note with regard to the fascination with the East as a source of inspiration in Western cinema, that "the representation of the Orient undergoes a more or less exotic revision of the real, now adapted to the imaginary, to iconography, and to the codes of the different cinematographic genres."[52]

Rodrigues and Guerra da Mata's wish to visit Macao at the time of the transfer of sovereignty from Portugal to China was only fulfilled much later, after the making of *China, China* (2007), in which speech is mainly in Mandarin. *China, China* is their first co-directed film, and it is also their first work in which Oriental references are presented through the reconstruction of a universe that has Chinese influences and is located in the vicinity of the Martim Moniz square. Martim Moniz is a multicultural area in the historical center of Lisbon, which has a considerable population of Asian descent. China is the name of a young, dreamy woman of Chinese origin who meets a tragic end in Lisbon amid the stylized violence of John Woo's Hong Kong-based film productions that are depicted on a television.

The film tackles, in a particularly puzzling way, the issue of cultural miscegenation in the city, and the crystallization of the concept of cultural identity. In one shot, the camera travels very slowly over a night view of an illuminated metropolis (New York City), which we suddenly realize is a poster hanging on a bedroom wall. In another shot, the young woman hedonistically dances on top of the bed to "Sonhos Pop" ("Pop Dreams") by Pop Dell'Arte. This song was released in 1988 by the music label Ama Romanta. It forms an unrecognizable musical reference for most of the Portuguese population at the time the film was released, despite being part of the cultural background of the filmmakers. However, upon clicking her gilded shoes, the Martim Moniz square materializes on screen. This is an act reminiscent of Dorothy's ruby slippers in Victor Fleming's *The Wizard of Oz* (1939), but which does not cast the "there's no place like home" spell by means of which Dorothy returns to Kansas. Ultimately, and as suggested by a previous panning shot that stops at the foundations of a construction site, the film reconstructs the city as a dynamic structure in which globalization posits cultural identity as a changeable concept that defines the individual and the community to which s/he belongs.

Guerra da Mata directed his debut work in 2012: the short film, *O Que Arde Cura* (*As the Flames Rose*). The film brings into play the experience of the filmmaker as a graphic designer. It presents a challenging graphic display that encompasses a complex assemblage of projections, TV monitor images, and overlapping images. The play between the real and the virtual is accompanied by a significant set of references, as well as by images and graphics, such as posters or album covers. *As the Flames Rose* comprises a monologue disguised as a dialogue, in a cinematic transposition of the device used by Jean Cocteau in *La Voix Humaine* (*The Human Voice*, first performed in 1930), the text of which served as inspiration for the script of *As the Flames Rose*. Yet, the film also recalls the confined location and camerawork of Rainer Werner Fassbinder's *Die Bitteren Tränen der Petra von Kant* (*The Bitter Tears of Petra von Kant*, 1972).

Instead of a female protagonist who speaks on the phone with her lost lover, as in *The Human Voice*, the film features Rodrigues's first role as the protagonist, talking with his ex-partner, with whom he has ended a three-year-long relationship. The narrative takes place on 25 August 1988, when a powerful fire broke out in the Chiado area of Lisbon, a part of the old historical center and a privileged entrance route to the Bairro Alto. As the heart of Lisbon burns, the remnants are the image of a broken relationship. The city that will be reborn mirrors the hypothetical reconstruction of a relationship based on common memories. These are also the memories of a particular social and historical space: the experiences of two young people in the nightlife of post-revolutionary[53] Lisbon.

Written by Guerra da Mata and Rodrigues, the film refers to a set of events and evokes situations that were experienced by both directors, although it does not claim to be autobiographical. Contrary to the usual construction of characters in the films that are directed solely by Rodrigues, and in which the characters seem to have neither a past nor a future because the only authentic time is the present, the common past and the hypothetical future play a fundamental role in *As the Flames Rose*. The evocative tone of the dialogue refers to a form of melancholy that is anchored in remembrance.

The narrative takes place in a room. This is a closed, claustrophobic space that was created in a studio. The relationship with the outside is only possible due to a recollection of the projected image of the same window that appears in *Happy Birthday!*. Thus, *As the Flames Rose* is a response to *Happy Birthday!*, as if the films were two halves of a circle and complete each other. The television screens the credits of a TV show of the time, a continuity announcer, a test card, and film excerpts from 1988. The film presents a revision of moments from the 1980s that commenced the further transformation of local urban culture. On the wall, a poster advertising a 30 April 1981 gig by The Clash in Cascais on the outskirts of Lisbon sets the tone. There is a bomber jacket next to it; vinyl records of The B-52's and The The also help to define both the decade and the character.

By the 1980s, the bomber jacket[54] had already become synonymous with counterculture and a revolt against established culture. Ironically, the London gay community would adopt the skinhead style in the 1980s, which in the UK was a decade that marked the struggle for gay rights under Margaret Thatcher's rule. The gay community thus took on the look of their oppressors and imbued it with a new meaning. Pop culture contributed to the spread of the hyper-masculinized image of gay men in skinhead uniforms as an instance of subversion that was reflected in the image of the openly gay, rebel band Bronski Beat, for example.

The London background of the main character in *As the Flames Rose* is highlighted when he states, "I was happy in London, going back to Portugal was so hard"; or when he compares the Pop Dell'Arte concerts at the Rock Rendez-Vous and Aula Magna venues in Lisbon to the Sex Pistols' 1976 gig at the 100 Club in London. The Lisbon concerts coincide with the beginning of their relationship, and thus become a metaphor for a recent shared past, while the London gig represents a life prior to that relationship. The past embodies the memories of Guerra da Mata, who lived in London, and who transfers them to Rodrigues's character. This movement lays bare the merging of reality with fiction, and of lover with beloved.

In the foreground, an Eames House Bird is shown. This is the stylized bird that became famous thanks to the American designer couple, Charles and Ray Eames. As a matter of fact, Charles Perdew was the one who carved the original wooden bird in around 1910 as a decoy for raven hunters. Charles and Ray Eames acquired it on one of their trips and eventually integrated it into many of their works, thus reproducing it as a work of their own. The enigmatic presence of this bird in a film with so few objects acquires a symbolic reading, as it reveals Guerra da Mata's knowledge of and fascination with mid-century modern design. At the same time, it refers to Rodrigues's past ambition to be an ornithologist, a desire that never came to fruition. A more obvious embodiment of this memory is found in the feature film *O Ornitólogo* (*The Ornithologist*, 2016). It is as if the Eames bird presages the later film.

The protagonist recalls his night-time outings in the Bairro Alto. He visits the customary places: Estádio, a café on the Rua da Misericórdia which leads into the neighborhood and where the evenings usually began; Esteves, Gingão, and Arroz Doce, with their juke boxes and cheap drinks; Juke Box, an indie music club; and finally, Frágil. The walk through the nightlife of the Bairro Alto spells out an idea of movement that disrupts the confinement of the narrative space. The projected window in the room is like a freeze-frame device that "tends to freeze the idealized instant,"[55] while also suggesting an idea of transformation: it is the suspending fragment of an ever-changing city. The Chiado fire is the *tabula rasa* of the end of the 1980s, pointing towards the cultural transformations that would come to be reconfigured in the following decade, when a new generation of protagonists instigated by the ghosts of the past and the potential of contemporaneity would arrive in a reconstructed, cosmopolitan Lisbon.

João Pedro Rodrigues and João Rui Guerra da Mata would become vital figures of this new generation. They articulate their individual and common memories in order to redefine the social and historical urban space,[56] and they merge those memories with multiple cinematographic references, from Hollywood to Oriental cinema, and from experimental cinema to B-movies. Without a starry-eyed sense of nostalgia,[57] the echoes of reality in their films are imbued with the artifice of the cinematic gaze, and the urban landscape emerges as the stage on which private desires and obsessions may be represented. Their practice comprises the development of new identities and contexts in order to express a bold space, as opposed to traditional and normative social constructions. As they continue together on this adventurous expedition of experimenting and sharing, in 2020, Rodrigues and Guerra da Mara are developing a new project in which they are filming the contemporary settings of *The Green Years* as a present-day portrait of the city.

PART 3

Artistic Practices

New Frontiers in Art Direction: João Guerra da Mata's Contribution to Portuguese Cinema as a Case Study

Caterina Cucinotta

INTRODUCTION

João Rui Guerra da Mata stands out as a unique case as far as Portuguese cinema is concerned. He made his debut as a costume and set designer in the mid-1990s,[1] working closely with João Pedro Rodrigues as the latter's film career progressed.[2] This partnership motivated Guerra da Mata to start developing his own body of work as a screenwriter, director, and editor, and he is also responsible for introducing the term "art direction" into Portuguese cinema.[3] The aim of this chapter is to introduce Guerra da Mata's work by way of analysis of the shots and scenes that most clearly display his art direction in action.

As I explore the role of the art director, I will focus on the creative processes that materialize in props, décor, and costumes. I will also address the symbolism that is contained in both initial storyboarding and the screenplay, from the very beginning. This is especially important when we consider how objects in cinema can become the carriers of coexisting symbolisms and narrativities. Such an approach is only successful if we focus on the interconnectedness of the films and the narrative threads that develop among moving image sequences. By looking at the historical contextualization of the various meanings of the term "art direction" in contemporary cinema, I will explore the theoretical frameworks that may be used to discuss the various roles played by the film trades in the creative process as a set of signs and developments that propel the materialization of an idea from paper to screen. Hence, the analysis will be informed by a discussion of selected shots and scenes from the feature films *O Fantasma* (*Phantom*, 2000), *Odete* (*Two Drifters*, 2005), *Morrer Como um Homem* (*To Die Like a Man*, 2009), and

O Ornitólogo (*The Ornithologist*, 2016), all of which were directed by João Pedro Rodrigues, with art direction by João Rui Guerra da Mata.

At what point do we start to see the intersection of the selection of artistic material with the stylistic choices that arise from the screenplay and film direction? From what moment does a creative process begin to develop between the film director and the different art departments? Only a few props, sets, and costumes are required to start unveiling the processes of art direction that are activated by contact with the screenplay and the initial selection of the choice of materials. Generally speaking, in Portugal, the role of art director still lacks practical, historical, and methodological scrutiny in terms of film studies research.

A range of methodologies and theoretical frameworks already exist for the study of film. These usually focus on an analysis of the roles played by the screenplay and the director in revealing concepts and complex realities. In this sense, it is important to define art direction. According to Hamburger, the art director is:

> a multidisciplinary artist who outlines the visual relationship between the actor on set, the props, and space, to compose two-dimensional, moving frames endowed with a voice of their own that is intrinsically connected to dramaturgy.[4]

INTERVIEWING JOÃO RUI GUERRA DA MATA: HIS ROLE AS LECTURER

Guerra da Mata's artistic work in and around filmmaking has often extended beyond the role of art director in the strictest sense. This much will become apparent as I elaborate on the artist's approach to the projects under consideration in this chapter. The collaboration between Rodrigues and Guerra da Mata that has been cemented over the years is a perfect example of how the visual materialization of the concepts and symbolisms that are expressed in the screenplay may culminate naturally in a style of art direction that complexifies reality.

In an interview granted to me by Guerra da Mata on 5 March 2018, the art director highlighted the intellectual and conceptual importance of his teaching in the Cinema Department at the Escola Superior de Teatro e Cinema do Instituto Politécnico de Lisboa (Lisbon Theater and Film School) between 2004 and 2011:[5]

> When I give interviews about the various areas in filmmaking, I realize that my thought process is well structured because I taught for many years. I genuinely enjoyed teaching and I believe that my thoughts were organized differently thanks to this.[6]

Guerra da Mata taught Art Direction and Production Design as a vocational subject that is accessible to all career paths (scriptwriting, production, directing, cinematography, editing, and sound). The course was conceived around a combination of costume and set design that is based on an idea of visual creation, the purpose of which would be the consolidation of actions and gestures in filmed sequences: "The only way to learn filmmaking is by watching films. Afterwards, if there is a film that grabs your attention, you'll want to see everything there is to see about that film. In this regard, I consider myself self-taught."[7]

According to Guerra da Mata, the disorderly conflation of the terms "art direction" and "production design" in Portugal arises from the indiscriminate and interchangeable use of these two roles in filmmaking. In his opinion, it is rare in Portuguese film productions to come across the role of "production designer," as it is conceived of in North America. When lecturing, Guerra da Mata would always insist on making a clear distinction between the two roles. For me, the question of how to distinguish between the art director and the production designer is an important one. When I asked "would you call a 'decorator' an art director and a costume designer, a 'wardrobe' [sic]?," Guerra da Mata replied:

On a Portuguese film poster we cannot use the term "Production Design" because this term has a direct linguistic link to another production department which is responsible for handling clerical duties and organization, which in fact does not fall under the artistic scope. What I do is fieldwork, and as such, I have decided to always refer to my film collaboration as "Art Director/Production Design."[8]

Guerra da Mata's comments underline a consciousness both of terminology and of the different roles played by the various film trades, which only someone deeply involved in teaching could have. The production designer, as the role is usually understood in Hollywood, oversees two different teams: costume and set design. The production designer has responsibility for assisting the director and cinematographer, and for establishing and achieving their collective stylistic choices.

From a hierarchical perspective, the art director works for the production designer and manages the art department (set design, décor, props). Equally, the costume designer works with the actors on the visual aspects of their performance in close contact with the production designer, and manages the costume department (costume assistant, wardrobe assistant, seamstress, dresser). During our interview, Guerra da Mata took stock of the situation, almost as though he were teaching a class:

When I taught I often had to look back on history. When does the expression "Production Designer" appear for the first time? In Victor

Fleming's 1939 production of *Gone With the Wind*. William Cameron Menzies is hired to do the film's décor and suddenly, because of the film's immense production complexity, he also starts to oversee the film's set and costume design. The film's director and producer realize that what he is actually doing is crafting the film's global visual identity.[9]

The production of *Gone With the Wind* was indeed complex if we consider how several departmental changes affected both directing and cinematography in the film. Consequently, the role of production designer evolved so that a global vision of the film could be achieved, and continuity and "visual coherence"[10] between costumes and décor was made possible: "[i]n 1939, David O. Selznick has in his hands the colossal production of *Gone With the Wind* and realizes that such a vast team needs a new element, the *production designer*."[11] According to Barreira,[12] it is generally accepted that the term "art director" appeared for the first time in 1916, in reference to Wilfred Buckland, a scenographer who had moved from the theater to cinema thanks to Cecil B. DeMille. He became William Cameron Menzies's tutor.[13]

The way in which Guerra da Mata relays historical fact enables us to learn more about what type of judgment has driven him, be it as a teacher or a "fieldworker" applying his trade in filmmaking. He observes:

> In my classes I taught my students how to make films with a very limited budget. Most of the time this is what happens in Portugal. I showed my students Hitchcock so they could see that the birds hanging from the electrical wires were actually made from black cardboard. I needed to show them these details because during the practical work they would often say that: "We can remove this during postproduction." I wanted to teach them that we cannot conceptualize an entire film through postproduction. In today's great productions there is a CGI [Computer Generated Images] department responsible for fixing these everyday problems. In Portugal, you need to estimate how much the film's postproduction will cost: in a take, if a *perche* [microphone boom] appears, hundreds of euros are needed to erase that *perche*.[14]

PROPS

The idea of engaging both décor and costume as the sensorial continuity of an actor's presence within the frame is central to Guerra da Mata's pedagogy and to his filmic expression:

> The only thing in filmmaking that does not interest me is decoration. I am not, nor have I ever wanted to be, a decorator. Many of the things that

I include in the décor are things that I don't even like. For me, décor, as well as wardrobe, serve exclusively to describe the characters. The visual reaches the brain before words do. This is evident in silent films, which are extraordinary from this point of view because viewers are able to understand everything that is happening through the décor. Jacques Tati was a master at working with décor and sound to develop an entire narrative. Buster Keaton worked in the same manner. Just as with Hitchcock: there is nothing in films that does not serve some purpose.[15]

When Guerra da Mata uses the term "decoration," he does so as an affirmative gesture that encompasses a wider understanding of his trade, and he aligns himself with the North American cinematic tradition of the production designer, in contrast with the *décorateur* that derives from the French terminology. In Portugal, the figure of art director was, for several decades, identified as "decorator," "décor" or "scenery," following the French interpretation. According to Barreira: "The differences between the USA and France, the two cradles of cinema, are clearly evident in the terms *art director* and *décorateur*, respectively."[16] The terminological shift that is proposed by Guerra da Mata and rooted in Hollywood cinema results from the importance that he gives to tracing the creative process, and from his approach, which brings a "global vision" to the "total work."

As well as referring to film history, it is not uncommon for production designers to seek visual references in the field of art history, and particularly in painting. When we speak of inspiration, we immediately make the connection with the type of creativity in filmmaking that could materialize in the form of referencing or general ambience, as Tomasino explains:

Referencing exists when costumes assume the general aspect or a particular feature of a famous painting, print, garment from another film, etc. The reference is made intentionally and to be recognizable, so that those who see it can go back immediately to the element cited, which can elucidate the costume through an absent other, which is present in memory. Thus, a world of relations and reciprocal explanations between the two works results, and both heighten the reality they have in common. Referencing, however, should never fall into the trap of simple imitation; it needs to hold something more, something silly but brilliant, so that we can recognize in it the citation.[17]

On the same topic, Guerra da Mata states:

I see cinema as a painting in movement. With primitive paintings, for a long time, we thought the overlay of the engraved or painted animals was a result of the work of many authors over time. Today, we realize that depending on the variation of light, the animal gains movement as if it were an animation. And this is cinema! I also learn a great deal from classical painting. In Italy for example, in church paintings you can see light hitting the paintings. If you are looking at a painting and its composition, and suddenly a ray of light hits it and you see that there is the hand of an angel that seems to be emerging from the frame. You hadn't noticed it before because when the light hits the painting, it gives it movement. In other words, the painting was conceived in accordance with the location's architecture. This is what I try to do.[18]

This is a deeply material evocation of painting, where the elements represented on the canvas are united with the light that generates movement where it did not exist before. It is also important to underline the intersection of art and film history in the creative work that Guerra da Mata developed while working for several renowned directors.

Several times during the course of the interview cited above, Guerra da Mata mentioned Hitchcock and the particular way that he used used props as a form of presentation or elongation of a character. In the first sequence of *Rear Window* (1954), for instance, while the protagonist sleeps, the sinuous use of the camera in search of objects that are part of his everyday life is paradigmatic. When Jeff wakes up, the viewer already knows a great deal about his life because the camera has performed a visual presentation of him as it glided over the props, the décor, and the surrounding environment.

This visual presentation is preceded by a frame of the character sweating: it is an anticipation of summer. The camera enters Jeff's apartment and shows the protagonist sleeping in a chair; he has a broken leg. The camera slides over some photographic lenses and climbs up to show several pictures of sports competitions. It goes down again and we see the negative, and then the positive, of a portrait of a woman which is also the cover of a magazine.

The information that is given when the camera pans subjectively over the objects creates an indissoluble link between the character, his story, and the narrative of the film. In the words of Guerra da Mata, the subjective shooting creates the impression through the camera that all materials are intimately and primarily connected: environments, props, clothing, and character.

These accessories cannot, in any way, serve as useless ornaments with no function, empty, pleonastic ornaments: the spectators must have the impression that the costume came into being at the same time they did, and that it cannot survive without them, and that ultimately the character cannot survive without them.[19]

The idea of using the props to create a presentation, a continuity, and a profound connection between the actors, the actions, and the environments is, in fact, an important point of this chapter. In his discussion of *To Die Like a Man*, for instance, Guerra da Mata mentions the attention to detail that he invested in Maria Bakker's country house:

> When they are lost in a forest [in Sintra] they discover a typical Portuguese house. Suddenly, upon entering, they realize it resembles a Manhattan apartment with a Corbusier chaise-longue, a photograph taken by us of the transsexual, Jennie Larrue, an exact copy of the image by Leni Riefenstahl. In addition, there is the photograph of Maria Bakker smoking in a pose characteristic of a 1940s diva. From the tea set to the cigarette case with the built-in lighter, even the grand piano, which is straight out of a classical American film, all the props in the house allude to a cliché about the rich bourgeoisie. When I built this set, I had to change everything in the house.[20]

In the transcription of another interview from 2012, in which the same décor is discussed, we read:

> Guerra de Mata recalls that he built the entire house belonging to the character Maria Bakker/Gonçalo Ferreira de Almeida in *To Die Like a Man* so that the actors and the team could *better understand the character* before he destroyed everything and commenced filming.[21]

According to Renira R. Gambarato,[22] Eisenstein and Kracauer are fundamental for an understanding of how the creative process in film is linked to objects, ambiences, and costumes. Eisenstein stresses that the use of props within the frame serves to immerse the viewer in a deeper understanding of the director's narrative intentions. Based upon his own experience as a filmmaker, the Soviet director often commented on how set design was one of his main concerns within the creative process, for the simple reason that it allowed him to represent ideas graphically.

In his discussion of material culture in film, Kracauer argues that "Films tend to explore this texture of everyday life, whose composition varies according to place, people and time."[23] In this sense, materials in films help us to fulfill a timely mission, for they enable us to apprehend and appreciate material objects. As stated by Gambarato, film positions itself between realism and an ontological perception of art. However, cinema retains a profound relationship with reality, and as such it succeeds in unveiling those attributes of experience which are less manifest. For Eisenstein, film possesses the faculty of "redemption of the real" vis-à-vis the penetrating forces of modernity.

In the context of Kracauer's analysis, cinema, along with opera, ballet, and other art forms, represents the ephemeral aspects of society. That is why material objects are able to reveal the darkest secrets of the movie. Only from the changes in the structure of everyday experiences is it possible to provide a detailed description of reality, according to Kracauer. In other words, the material elements of modern society are what reveal its essence.

The common threads that link cultural imports, creative process, and the final product on screen are also one of the chief preoccupations in Cecilia Almeida Salles's writing.[24] She underlines the importance of the *aesthetics of the unfinished* as defined by a *morphology of creation* that is the result of team work.

EMPATHY WHEN COMPLEXIFYING REALITY

In a 2018 interview with Guerra da Mata, the art director reported to me his indispensable exchanges with João Pedro Rodrigues about temporal, cultural, and visual contextualization. He explained that:

> When making a film, the director must ponder a thousand different concerns. If there's someone who's absolutely absorbed in the project and can act as a filter [that shields] the director, that's extraordinarily positive. The problem is if the Production Designer's ego extends beyond the needs of the film. Still, not every director will want a person working with them who has opinions and could pose a challenge.[25]

Albert Rothenberg has stated that empathetic activity when doing team work yields a specific, "generative" creativity, which transcends straightforward imitation and identification. It also allows the possibility of transforming images into symbols. Highlighting the creative value of empathetic activity, Rothenberg has shown the close relationship between empathy and creativity. According to his concept of the *homospatial process*, "[empathetic activity] consists of actively conceiving two or more discrete entities occupying the same mentally represented space or spatial location, a conception leading to the articulation of new identities."[26]

A *homospatial process* generates thought that, in turn, creates new ideas and takes form from the synthesis of two different or opposing elements. It is a conscious process that produces metaphors and symbols during the creative development of a project: a healthy mode of controlling the illogical mental connections that are produced by empathetic activity.

From Guerra da Mata's statements about his work relationship with João Pedro Rodrigues, and bearing in mind my own previous exploration of genetic criticism theories in relation to art direction,[27] this case study reveals one of the most interesting creative processes. Guerra da Mata's distinct position when working on the preparation of a shot gives the resulting footage a quality of unification between cultural and personal elements relating to himself and Rodrigues. These elements materialize concepts or perspectives on life and the world, which become symbols in the process. Art direction, as a "complexification of reality," therefore seeks to incorporate a blending of the ontological value of the artwork with the real. As Margarida Cordeiro puts it:

> Cinema's greatest error is that it oversimplifies reality. There is a clarity in the visual field that must be determined. A rigorous reorganization of reality. Reality captured by us is never simplified; it is made more complex—so much so that the film does not have any one reality, it has many realities. Our image is not dry. [. . . T]herefore, we used reality as a starting point to create another complete reality. It consists in taking what is real and adding what we feel, which has nothing to do with neorealism. And this act of giving something else is what cinema is.[28]

Filmed reality is thus complexified through several "levels" or "surfaces," among which are props and costumes. Together with the landscape, the architecture, and the interiors, these surfaces establish the framing of the shot, thanks to an equally complex creative process that fuses reality and fiction. On this particular point, Guerra da Mata describes a certain "deconstruction of a given wardrobe":

> Patrícia [Dória][29] and I introduced a knitted sweater into the *The Ornithologist*'s two Chinese characters. At first I wasn't entirely convinced with the choice but Patrícia told me to imagine how a knitted sweater was so easy to stash away in a backpack and later use to keep warm. In addition, she added that this piece of clothing could help a great deal in deconstructing the wardrobe. A knitted sweater materializes from nowhere, enters the scene and looks completely out of place! Exactly what happens in real life! The introduction of real life elements, which you do not originally even consider using when you are constructing a character, is why I enjoy working with Patrícia so much.[30]

The introduction of material elements from real life is the kind of deconstructive moment that assists the overall development of a character. It is one of the qualities that propels the "scenographic object" towards convergence with symbolism and complexification within the frame. As another example, Guerra da Mata mentions the following:

> The character of Maria Bakker in "To Die Like a Man" makes an entrance wearing a feather boa and a sequin tunic in a contemporary version of Liza

Minnelli. She is out in the garden wearing slippers and puts on a pair of high heels as she enters the house. She states that she hates slippers because they are comfortable. When she heads out again she is wearing an old worn shawl over her sequin tunic, which she grabs from the sofa, as she hurries out in a rush. I could have chosen a stylish leather jacket for example, for greater coherency but I felt that it made more sense to have the character grab the old shawl on her way out. It is a type of deconstruction of the actual character. It is a practice that pleases me.[31]

SEQUENCE ANALYSIS

It is difficult to pin down Guerra da Mata's exact creative process as he assists the materialization of a queer identity. However, the choice of material elements, such as garments and props, may help us to reach some understanding, if not underpin an explanation of that process. It is important, therefore, to retrace the visual line that unifies all of the elements above: his experience as a lecturer, his specific cultural background when citing or referencing, and the empathy that he invests in the collaborative cinematographic process. As mentioned above, we can draw on a number of sequences to try to understand this method of "global visual planning," which, in the words of Guerra da Mata, somehow condenses the tension between "art director," "production designer," and *décorateur*, that is, the tension between the French and the North American approaches.

Revisiting the films under consideration, we find certain elements that construct narratives parallel to the main plot: specific objects that appear recurrently, as if they were colorful brushstrokes or repetitive gestures that are there to remind us of the existence of another narrative. If we conceive the material editing of a film as a horizontal process, with a beginning and a possible end, then we need to interpret as a vertical process the actions of those who create this kind of ideal preproduction editing. Suggestions on lighting, settings, actors, props, and so on all assemble on a vertical imaginary line and only occasionally will they penetrate the horizontal plane of the final cut. So, what happens to all of the creative lines that did not dovetail with the final version of the film? In the case of Guerra da Mata's work with Rodrigues, these creative lines are semi-camouflaged. As such, visual continuity materializes, generated by cooperative empathetic activity.

In 2013, I wrote an article about *Phantom* by João Pedro Rodrigues (2000), which analyzes Guerra da Mata's performative use of gloves as an item with a specific function:

The scene we will call "Of the Gloves" perfectly re-enacts this type of personality split: on the one hand, Sérgio finds the gloves and together with a friend/colleague imitates a boxer; on the other hand, when he gets to his room, the Phantom strips naked (to his "natural" body) and finalizes the performance as it truly should be done. We switch from miming a boxer to an erotic and fetishistic act, the protagonists of which are the Phantom and the biker's gloves. The gloves, which have been worn by the same body, represent a split between the subject (body) and the object (gloves).[32]

The motorcycle gloves that are reclaimed from the trash can by Sérgio already display the rips and marks of heavy use. A similar exploration of how worn items with holes are reused can be found in *Two Drifters*, when the protagonist is invited to take Pedro's bedroom for the night and, as she is putting on his pajamas, she finds a hole in one of the front pockets of the shirt. Both of these cases involve a split of personality that is triggered by items of clothing that belonged to others. In the case of Sérgio, his performative use of clothing (a similar scene in *Phantom* features a swimsuit) will take him progressively away from his normal life towards a convergence with his perverse fantasies. In Odete's case in *Two Drifters,* the personality split becomes visible during her transition from false pregnancy to reincarnation, which again is enacted through clothing. The change begins with the pajamas, continues through the medical deliberation of her false pregnancy, and ends with the visual (identical clothes and hairstyle) and mental assimilation of Odete into Pedro's body and personality. In this sense, both Pedro and Odete seem to fall victim to their own madness, and this is visually materialized in what they wear, as if these material elements could spark off the assimilation of other personalities.

There is also the case of the anthurium, which appears recurrently in João Pedro Rodrigues's films. In *Two Drifters*, the flower appears in the wake and funeral sequences as the sign of the primordial connection between Pedro and the protagonist. In *To Die Like a Man*, it appears twice, although the first time is a kind of false alarm: in a greenhouse Tónia notices an anthurium that she quickly rejects, declaring that it is "the sort that dies within the week." The anthuriums return with the character Maria Bakker, who plants them in her garden. Finally, they appear again in *The Ornithologist*, where they are linked to two Chinese characters who stop to gaze at them as they walk and take a photograph.

The presence of the anthurium across Rodrigues's filmography once again points to the singular connection between visual planning and empathy within the context of team work. It underlines the importance, stressed by Guerra da Mata, of someone who can accompany the director's creative processes from close up. That person must be a professional who knows, at any given moment, how to translate written creativity and creative thought into visual-material objects.

How, then, do we explain the almost obsessive presence of this flower throughout Rodrigues's filmography? On the one hand, those who grow it will know that this is an indoor plant, as Tónia herself states when she is inside the greenhouse. On the other hand, as we look for a hint of vertical narrativity, we may define the presence of the anthurium as an introduction to the action that will develop with the plot. In the case of *Two Drifters*, for instance, the anthuriums seem to underline that the protagonist's obsession with Pedro will lead to internal transformation. The same happens in *The Ornithologist* when, following Fernando's shipwreck and the appearance of the two Chinese girls, the presence of the anthuriums announces the transformation of the protagonist's life. In *To Die Like A Man*, the anthurium may be seen as a more complex presence, because the flower is used in two completely different ways: Maria Bakker starts growing it as a counterpoint to Tónia's rejection of it. Given that in the other films the anthurium seems to announce change, Tónia's refusal to buy the plant in *To Die Like a Man* appears to suggest that the right path is yet to be discovered. This path is the route taken by Tónia and Rosário, on foot, across the forest and up to Bakker's little cottage, where a bunch of anthuriums awaits. In the "gambozinos" (snipe hunt) musical sequence, the red of the flowers engulfs the screen while the characters remain seated as they listen to "Calvary" by Baby Dee. From that moment, Tónia's life begins to take a turn: sex change surgery does not seem to be the right choice for her. Furthermore, the red of the anthuriums and the moonlight across the forest are connected to Tónia, because they are present in the colors of the sweater that she is wearing as she returns to the patio of her Lisbon house.

CONCLUSION

Filmmakers are constantly confronted with the difficult task of turning abstract concepts into material realities. Responsibility for this transformation lies with the artistic teams—set designers, costume designers, make-up artists, and hairstylists—whose work is supported by an idea of light and shadow that follows the processes that are narrated by the gestures. In the cases considered in this chapter, the narrated processes in question are processes of identity transformation.

The clear artisanal tendency in Portuguese cinema may well serve to explain how the various elements presented above are assimilated: if a team lacks personnel because of a limited budget, the collective creative process between the director and the artistic team will have a significant impact on the final result. In terms of visual matters, the budget determines many of the final decisions. Therefore, the smooth functioning of the relationships between the various departments and the director is highlighted as a fundamental requirement. In many instances, the preproduction choices stand out in a final product that emanates openness and responds to the suggestions put forward by each department.

From a film studies point of view, the analysis of the path of an art director who is also a director requires a methodology that is suitable to analyze the craft itself as well as the films. Such a methodology enables the analysis of films through material culture, the objects and other material elements contained in the film and that have their starting point in the creative process that runs parallel to the direction. For example, implying an analysis of the material elements (props) in the film, Gambarato reads Eisenstein's work in this way:

> Eisenstein was aware of the presence of objects in film sets and their importance in influencing an audience's perception according to the filmmaker's purposes. He comments that: "[a]n advantage of studying the design of film sets is that it can be presented graphically, that is why I always begin with it."[33]

Therefore, the question is not only the study of the objects themselves, but also a means of framing these elements within a broader relationship, of creating a framework that is not only visual and filmic but also mental.

Perhaps we should understand Guerra da Mata's rejection of the term *décorateur* to describe his role as an attempt to accentuate the depth and span of his profession. The rigorous quality of his work is also evident in other films, which clearly display an authorial tendency on his part, whether as production designer or in a different role. His introduction of the term "art director" in Portugal, to denote a fusion between costume and scenography, as well as his classes on this same topic, have made Guerra da Mata an important name in Portuguese cinema.

While I do not wish to belittle any of the other art directors working in Portuguese cinema, Guerra da Mata's position is unequivocally different. From terminological rationalization and change, to his teaching on such topics and the transmission of his experience to his students, to the materialization of ideas and concepts in the films directed by João Pedro Rodrigues, Guerra da Mata's work straddles all of the areas that are directly or indirectly touched by production design. To use Guerra da Mata's own words, his approach reveals a quality of "global visual planning" that is already present in the first stages of scriptwriting. This is a luxury, so to speak, if we consider the working conditions of other *décorateurs*, who are usually hired in the final stages of script adaptation. The flux of ideas within a given creative process must be channeled into the material elements that reflect everyday life. The better the details of the project are known, the better the communication will work between all parties involved. I hope that this critical overview of João Rui Guerra da Mata's work with João Pedro Rodrigues will contribute to a new reading of the role of "art director" in Portuguese contemporary cinema and help to open up dialogue with other new perspectives.

Other Landscapes: On the Expanded Cinema of João Pedro Rodrigues and João Rui Guerra da Mata

Filipa Rosário

INTERMEDIAL BODIES

Identidade Nacional (Príncipe Real) [*National Identity (Príncipe Real)*] is the title of the most recent installation by João Pedro Rodrigues and João Rui Guerra da Mata. The work was created at the invitation of BoCA—Biennial of Contemporary Arts, a Portuguese project focused on visual and performing arts and music that took place in Lisbon, Oporto, and Braga in 2019. The installation was exhibited in the building of the former Reservatório da Patriarcal de Lisboa (Lisbon Patriarchal Reservoir), which was established by the Catholic Diocese of Lisbon and which had been one of the first of its kind in the water distribution network that was established in 1864 to enable the provision of water to the inhabitants of the Portuguese capital. The reservoir ceased operations in the 1940s, and today the building is a site of public interest.[1] Regardless of the processes of gentrification and touristification that Príncipe Real has suffered over recent years, the neighborhood has long since been the center of LGBTQ+ nightlife in Lisbon.

The body is key to any reading of *National Identity (Príncipe Real)*, as it is key to all of the work of Rodrigues and Guerra da Mata,[2] since it is the body that defines the directors' worldview. Equally, the relationship of the body with the surrounding environment leads to the development of the journeys of their heroes, who tend to be socially marginalized and awkward queer characters condemned to a tragic end, which coincides with the unfolding of the plot. *National Identity (Príncipe Real)* operates in the same way: through the mythical figure of D. Afonso Henriques, the first king of Portugal, the installation draws on the theme of the segregation of a non-heteronormative community in relation to the official Portuguese narrative of the formation of the nation. The installation anchors the notion of national identity to a concrete territory, both through its title and through the combined effects of the specificity of the location in which it is exhibited, the elements of which it is composed, and the arrangement of those elements in the exhibition space.

National Identity (Príncipe Real) is composed of the short film by Rodrigues, *O Corpo de Afonso* (*The King's Body*, 2012),[3] which is projected on a loop and juxtaposed with photographs of the transgender woman, Maria Bakker, and the transsexual Jenny Larrue. Bakker and Larrue are characters from the feature-length film, *Morrer Como um Homem* (*To Die Like a Man*, 2009), by the same director. In addition to these elements, props from the two films are on display. One of these is Tónia's silicon death mask, which was created by Guerra da Mata (Tónia is the lead character in *To Die Like a Man*, played by Deborah Krystal, an iconic figure of the Portuguese drag scene). The other prop to be exhibited is a replica of the sword belonging to the first king of Portugal, D. Afonso Henriques, which was used by the men who auditioned for a false casting in *The King's Body*. The sword, a symbol of power and masculinity, hangs over the mask, which is a symbolic object that holds the potential to reveal or hide the wearer's identity.

In fact, *The King's Body* is an experimental short film directed by Rodrigues, which documents a casting for the role of D. Afonso Henriques and analyzes in minute detail the bodies of selected Spanish bodybuilders and go-go dancers who audition. In the film, we hear them speaking about their lives, jobs, unemployment, family histories, and the meanings of their tattoos. They also read historical documents relating to the life and sword of the first king of Portugal, sometimes while wielding a replica of that sword. This all takes place against a chroma key screen, which sometimes displays moving images of the roads and streets of Guimarães,[4] the statue of D. Afonso Henriques, and the king's tomb. The men take off their clothes in response to instructions from João Pedro Rodrigues, who directs the casting, the camera, and the non-actors in a perverse and fetishistic power game,[5] that reinforces in turn the historiographic, cultural, and social critique undertaken by the film.

In the context of *National Identity (Príncipe Real)*, *The King's Body* is projected onto a screen in the center of the Reservatório da Patriarcal. This is an enormous, octagonal space, composed of thirty-one granite pillars with a height of 9.25 meters and of varying widths. The pillars support arches of granite blocks, which in turn hold up the vaulted ceiling of this grand "room": the materials, dimensions, and design of the space construct a heterotopic world and time. Three subterranean galleries extend out from this vast space: in the past, these were used to channel the water from the reservoir to the lower areas of the city. However, the galleries are fenced off from viewers of the installation, who move around the accessible space via iron steps and walkways. The atmosphere is very humid: there are leaks in various parts of the former reservoir, resulting in buckets being placed to collect the water and small puddles appearing on the stone floor. The humidity increases the reverberation of sound in the space, making it difficult to hear the soundtrack to *The King's Body*.

At the lowest level of the room, five rows of chairs are placed in front of the screen onto which the 2012 short film is projected. Below the screen is a rectangular table of the same width, on which a bunch of flowers is placed. In the space between the audience and the screen, in a glass display case, we find the mask that Tónia used in *To Die Like a Man*, with purple feathers around its neck. Above the case hangs the replica of the Portuguese king's mythical sword. The exhibition case is situated between two stone columns, on which large-scale photographs of Maria Bakker and Jenny Larrue are displayed. The photographs confront one another: at the vanishing point between the gazes of the two characters in the photographs hangs the sword, which casts its shadow over the third character (Tónia) who "lived like a woman, but wanted to die like a man," as yet another character in the film explains. The balance between the gazes of the trans women and the centrality of Tónia's condemnation in that stone environment effectively lends a religious and sacrificial dimension to this section of the installation.

Figure 10.1 *Identidade Nacional (Príncipe Real)* [*National Identity (Príncipe Real)*], BoCA— Biennial of Contemporary Arts, 2019

The suspended sword, which reinforces that dimension, is located precisely midway in the field of vision of the spectator, who views *The King's Body* from a seated position. This means that the image projected onto the screen will always to some extent be shattered. The exhibition case also disturbs the viewing experience: Rodrigues and Guerra da Mata's objective is to confront the audience with a game of masks, portraits, and moving images that is both violent and violated. Furthermore, this self-reflexive device, which makes reference to the experience of the cinema and the museum, is located on the lowest level of the Reservatório da Patriarcal and occupies relatively little of the total space available in the "room." From any other point in the exhibition space, the film, photographs, and props become totally or partially imperceptible, meaning that the lines of vision drawn by this game of images/mirrors/identities are blocked. In other words, the conceptual rhetoric of *National Identity (Príncipe Real)* rests on the confrontation of the concept of LGBTQ+ identity with that which is (in)visible and can be represented on the one hand, and with national history and historiography on the other.

The installation materializes a network of symbolic links between metalinguistic narrative elements, and as such, it deepens the politicized discourse that is already inscribed in those items, even before the self-appropriation that is carried out in the piece. In this context, such a discourse comes to claim national identity as a symbolic queer territory. The institutional description of the installation confirms as much:

> The set of these elements questions every code of conduct, perception and appearance and in that process shatters any idea that is more reductive of identity based on self-expression, just like in others' judgment based on gender attribution, that is immediately perceived as being associated with a typified behavior.[6]

Even the image by Bruno Simão that is presented in the institutional publicity for the piece on the BoCA website highlights the forbidden access to this underworld as a space that is considered to be inferior or marginal.[7] The image in question is a nocturnal photograph of the iron railings that delimit the lake in the Príncipe Real Garden that is situated above the underground reservoir, and which blocks the access to the catacombs: the octagonal form of the railings mirrors that of the reservoir.

THE PARACINEMATIC DRIVE

Rodrigues and Guerra da Mata's work for galleries and museums commenced in 2013, at a time when the directors' filmography had already achieved international recognition.[8] In terms of the cosmopolitan, global, Portuguese cinema industry,[9] Pedro Costa is the other internationally acknowledged director[10] who has followed a similar path of producing artistic works, and he also bases his creations on the references that inform his cinematic productions.[11] For instance, between 2018 and 2019, the Serralves Museum (Portugal) presented the exhibition *Pedro Costa: Company*, which brought together works by the director in conjunction with pieces authored by the sculptor Rui Chafes, the photographer Paulo Nozolino, and the filmmakers Danièle Huillet, Jean-Marie Straub, and Chantal Akerman. The exhibition expanded Costa's cinematographic production beyond the movie theater. Addressing installations and moving images in the context of contemporary art, Costa explains: "I don't really like it, I never have [. . .][I] developed my cinephilia in the cinemas of Lisbon and of my neighborhood. That created a type of conviction in me that told me that cinema has, or had, a narrative foundation."[12]

Such a resistance to, and distrust of, this type of artistic practice is shared by João Pedro Rodrigues, who states:

[I] think that the plastic arts [. . .] are more of a serious world. I think that cinema has something in common with popular art, folk art. [. . .] The plastic arts are more erudite. [. . .] The relationship to the other [. . .] is often ignored and forgotten [within plastic art]. [. . .] Even the transitoriness of looking [. . .] These are things that must be seen differently. [. . .] For me, images have to tell a story. Because I like to think that things are stories, things are not a discourse. Usually, I like to think that I don't have a discourse. It is a way of effacing myself. [. . .] Political cinema, at times, gets really dated because it is too closely linked to the time in which it was made. Or else it stagnates. [. . .] And, furthermore, people often forget the excitement. And cinema is an exciting thing.[13]

This essentialist link to filmic narrative remains the structuring force in João Pedro Rodrigues and João Rui Guerra da Mata's installations. Nonetheless, the directors are committed to experimentalism, even if it is always anchored in their filmic universe, as Rodrigues clarifies:

I don't mean for this to happen. [. . .] Things have presented themselves to us. I am a filmmaker, and what I want to make are films. But I have enjoyed doing these things because space is something that interests me. There is something playful in thinking about how it is possible to show films differently. That interests me very much, in spite of me thinking that when I make films, I make them for the cinema.[14]

SANTO ANTÓNIO (SAINT ANTHONY)

The first installation by Rodrigues and Guerra da Mata, *Santo António* (*Saint Anthony*) formed part of the exhibition *Disquiet: Portuguese Modes of Expression*, which brought together works by Portuguese artists that deal with space, movement, and architecture.[15] It was exhibited at the invitation of Paulo Lopes Graça, who at the time was First Secretary to the Embassy of Portugal in South Korea. The exhibition took place at the Mimesis Art Museum (26/11/2013–09/02/2014), which was designed by the Portuguese architect Siza Vieira, and is located in Paju Book City, a new town situated on the outskirts of Seoul.

In one of the museum's spacious galleries, Rodrigues and Guerra da Mata installed a white cube of huge proportions: a monolith that merges with the white space surrounding it, and has no visible entrance. This white cube works both as a passageway and as an exhibition room. On the gallery walls, there is a series of drawings by Guerra da Mata which are portraits of some members of the crew who worked on *Manhã de Santo António* (*Morning of Saint Anthony's Day*, 2012), the fictional short film directed by Rodrigues. The drawings were reproduced on self-adhesive paper, and therefore they did not need any other type of display support.

Morning of Saint Anthony's Day captures the first moments of a municipal holiday—13 June, St. Anthony's Day. St. Anthony is the patron saint of Lisbon and his statue is found in the center of the Praça de Alvalade (Alvalade Square), the main square of a district in the north of the city. On the night of 12 June, all over the city, and especially in the historic quarters, the holiday is celebrated into the early hours of the morning with informal street parties, dancing, live music, and makeshift stalls selling traditional food. The short film documents the return home of young residents of Alvalade—presented in the film as a residential district—as they come out of the metro station in the square after an intense and exhausting night partying. The bodies of the young people are devoid of energy and they move at a slow pace; they are alienated, silent, and their faces are expressionless with a glassy stare. The lines of the roads, the pavements, the crossings, the cobble stones typically used in Portuguese pavements, the separators that divide the streets, and even the air vents on the metro tunnels, together present an urban tessitura made of right angles, in which the inhabitants move numbly, as though they were zombies.

Saint Anthony also addresses the place of the individual in different spaces, the space of the museum, the street, or the cinema. The white cube functions as an obstacle to the free circulation of the viewing public. It is situated at the furthest edge of the gallery and is relatively hidden when regarded from afar. This means that the spectators must go around the cube in order to realize that, actually, there is an entrance to that dark space. Outside it, in the exhibition room itself, the sounds of the street emerge from within the monolith: these are the sounds of the Praça de Alvalade in Lisbon, where the action of *Morning of Saint Anthony's Day* takes place. On the four internal walls of the cube, four different films are projected. These are composed of excerpts and images of the Lisbon neighborhood that were excluded from the final cut of the short film. The architecture of the projection and viewing space ensures continuity between the various videos, and it recreates the configuration of the actual site that is shown in the images, so as to immerse the viewer in a virtual experience of the space they see on screen.

Saint Anthony both portrays and reconfigures the experience of urban space (that of the young passers-by in Lisbon) in order that it can be experienced in the cinema (by the spectator, who is immersed in that world of sound and image). It also represents the medium of cinema itself, through the drawings that invoke the technical team, which is always present in the external space: off-camera, outside the cinema room, and outside the exhibition cube. The physical center of the installation, then, is where looped films are projected, and the perpetual repetition of the films functions as a device that plays with the idea of repetition of movement which, through the reiteration, becomes more choreographed and abstract, without narrative progression.

Part of this installation was shown at the Radcliffe Institute for Advanced Study at Harvard University in 2014, during Rodrigues's artistic residence there. In that showing, only the four channels of video images were projected on a loop onto the walls of a relatively small room, with the projected images occupying the full width and almost the full height of the walls. The drawings by Guerra da Mata were not included in that exhibition. From 25 November 2016 to 2 January 2017, *Saint Anthony* was screened on the lower ground floor of the Centre Pompidou in Paris, as part of a full retrospective of the work of Rodrigues and Guerra da Mata. Once again, it was adapted to the surrounding space: in this case, an enormous cube was used in order to draw the attention of the public to this less frequently visited part of the museum. Furthermore, and as in the Mimesis Art Museum, the cube was positioned out of line with the walls of the exhibition space as a whole, and as such, created an imposing presence within it. Given the size of the monolith, the video was projected onto a higher point in relation to the spectators, just as it was in South Korea. In the Pompidou show of *Saint Anthony*, only the portraits of Rodrigues and Guerra da Mata were exhibited.

WHERE IS CHINA?

In 2014, the short film *Alvorada Vermelha* (*Red Dawn*, Rodrigues and Guerra da Mata, 2011, 20 minutes) was shown simultaneously at the Museu do Oriente

(the Orient Museum) in Lisbon (29 May to 6 July 2014), and at the Beijing
World Art Museum in the People's Republic of China (16 May to 4 June 2014).
It formed part of the collective exhibition, *Where Is China?*, which brought
together the works of Chinese and Portuguese artists.[16]

Red Dawn documents a day in the historic Red Market, a Special Administrative Region of China. At the time of filming in 2011, this was the only market
in Macao to allow the trade of live animals. The film shows the processes and
practices of treatment of live and dead animals, as well as the faces and gestures
of the workers who deal with them. The Chinese censors allowed the film to
be included in the exhibition, but banned it an hour before the projection,
claiming that it was not suitable for a Chinese audience. The museum opted
to exhibit just one still of a female fish seller from the Red Market, who stares
directly into the camera. This "unintentionally confrontational image"[17] was
not chosen by the directors. Explaining the reasons for the censorship, Guerra
da Mata mentions that:

> The images were too shocking for Chinese audiences [. . .] and it's about
> a Chinese market, in a Chinese territory. But I suppose the problem
> was that it's called *Red Dawn*. And *Red Dawn* is such a Maoist, such a
> Cultural Revolution title that they thought we were trying to create a
> metaphor for [. . .] something.[18]

When capturing images of water containers, *Red Dawn* subtly presents
superimposed moving images of small mermaids, who smile at the camera as
they move around as though they were under water. This is an almost imperceptible detail that subverts the documentary form of the film.[19] It is a disrup-
tive element of fantasy that lightens the moment and contrasts with the brutal
reality of the images of the market.

The representations of desperation and death among the animals are
juxtaposed with the surreal lightness of the happy mermaids, who "haunt"
Red Dawn from the moment when they first appear and impose a hypnoti-
cally strange quality on the film. The superimposition of this "queer" element
within the narrative progression of the film reveals its artifice in the way that
this almost Dada-esque collage renders the fabric of the film with an experimental, intermedial, and genre-bending dimension.

Through its presentation of *Red Dawn* with the single still image of
the fish seller who faces us, the Chinese exhibition shows the disquieting
frame of a gaze that contains the film from which it was taken, as well as
the associated experience of censorship, and the disorientation and vertigo
that is provoked by a mythical, supernatural, and threatening being that
stares out at us from the center of cinema itself: it is an installation within
an installation.

Figure 10.2 *Red Dawn* (2011)

FROM THE PEARL RIVER TO THE RIVER AVE

Two years after *Red Dawn*, Rodrigues and Guerra da Mata were invited to create an exhibition at Solar—Gallery of Cinematic Art in Vila do Conde, Portugal.[20] Entitled *Do Rio das Pérolas ao Ave. From the Pearl River to the River Ave*, the collection of works they showed there between 2 July and 25 October all took as their starting point their film productions, invoking different moments in the cinematic trajectory of the pair. They described the exhibition as follows:

> Taking our short films as our main starting point, but also iconic props from the features, we propose a playful journey through the universe of our films, searching for and provoking new dialogues and confrontations that might shed new light on our work.[21]

In total, they presented ten works at Solar:

(1)   a selection of Portuguese and international publicity posters for their films, with designs by Luís Alegre and João Rui Guerra da Mata;

(2)   the video installation *16-05-2014, Esta Obra É Passível de Provocar uma Experiência Desconfortável e Emoções Negativas no Público Chinês (16-05-2014, This Work is Likely to Trigger an Uncomfortable Experience*

and Negative Emotions in Chinese Audiences), which recreates the experience of *Red Dawn* being censored;[22]

(3) *Dream, Oh Dream*—an installation consisting of the original latex suit worn by the actor Ricardo Meneses, who played the protagonist of *Phantom*;

(4) *Hoje É Dia de Festa* (*Today Is a Party Day*), the multi-channel installation made from the rushes of Rodrigues's first short film, *Parabéns!* (*Happy Birthday!*, 1997, 14 minutes);

(5) *Where's Captain Kirk? 14-11-1997*, an installation in which the original slides used at the première of *Happy Birthday!*, which took place in the Captain Kirk Bar in Lisbon, 1997, are projected in the gallery space. The images from the slides are press cuttings of criticism of that same film (Rodrigues's first short), and Guerra da Mata was responsible for the conception and artistic direction of the slides;

(6) Guerra da Mata's video installation, *Casting #1: Telmo Ricardo Meneses, 13-02-1999* (26 minutes, 30 seconds), which shows Ricardo Meneses's full audition interview for the lead role in *Phantom*. The interviewers are Guerra da Mata and Vasco Branquinho, and the interview is played on a loop;

(7) the first version of *Identidade Nacional* (*Portuguese Identity*), the installation that would come to be shown in the Reservatório da Patriarcal in Lisbon in 2019, and which is discussed at the beginning of this chapter;

(8) the video installation, *Praça de Alvalade* (*Alvalade Square*) by João Pedro Rodrigues, in which the short film *Morning of Saint Anthony's Day* is projected on a loop onto a small wooden table;[23]

(9) a projection of the short film *Red Dawn*, by Rodrigues and Guerra da Mata, onto a screen that is placed in front of a small row of chairs originating from the old Cine Clube do Porto (Oporto Cinema Club); and finally

(10) *Duel* (2016), a video installation of 29 minutes, 18 seconds, in which *Happy Birthday!* and *O Que Arde Cura* (*As the Flames Rose*, Guerra da Mata, 2012) are projected onto the same screen from diametrically opposed points in the room. In Rodrigues's first film (*Happy Birthday!*), Guerra da Mata appears as an actor, and equally, in Guerra da Mata's first film (*As the Flames Rose*), Rodrigues appears as an actor. The symmetry and convergence of the projections is mirrored in the synchronicity between the two short films, which share the same backdrop of the same exterior filmed from the same window. The projections start from this shared plane, and result in the looped superimposition of each film on the other.

Figure 10.3 *Happy Birthday!* (1997)

Figure 10.4 *As the Flames Rose* (2012)

In some ways, *Duel* is the materialization of the intricate collaborative dynamic between Rodrigues and Guerra da Mata, for the installation stages the fusion of their individual filmic outlooks on the same platform—the screen—on which their bodies also meet. This romantic, symbolic piece thematizes the meeting of the two through cinema, and relegates to the background the narrative devices and narrative progression of the films that make up the installation. *Duel* also subverts the cinematic experience, thus ensuring the autonomy of the spectator, whose body moves in and out of this space as s/he sees fit.[24]

CONCLUSIONS: EXPANDED CINEMA AS PARACINEMA

When cinema is expanded beyond conventional time and space, the spectator is free to determine the durations, intervals, and meanings of the medium, which in turn becomes metacinematographic too, offering a more objective key to understanding the collaboration between Rodrigues and Guerra da Mata. Their works for galleries and museums open up a territory for freer experimentation for both of them. In this sense, the installations give continuity and breathe new life into the artistic production of the two, and this is tested in their short films.

However, in their work for galleries and museums, the experimentalism of Rodrigues and Guerra da Mata rests exclusively on the idea of filmic self-appropriation. They deterritorialize diegetic and extra-diegetic components: their films, props, memorabilia, and even preproduction elements of their films are appropriated in order to construct intertextual and intermedial pieces in which those components are configured within the exhibition space, and simultaneously to open up for them the possibility of an alternative viewing rhythm and time.

By definition, the installation is the result of differentiated elements that are placed in dialogue with one another in the exhibition space. As such, the meaning that is produced relies on the structural arrangement; in other words, significance hinges on the way in which the objects and bodies are distributed in the space, and the questions that emerge from that arrangement.[25] Ultimately, it is the movement of the spectator's body when viewing the work that constructs the meaning of the conceptual piece and the ambience that it creates. The artistic direction of the filmic universe in the work of both filmmakers becomes central to their artistic practice. Consequently, the thought and craft of Guerra da Mata in particular gains agency, as he takes responsibility for artistic direction both in his own films, and in those of Rodrigues. It is Guerra da Mata who, in a certain way, is responsible for the visual identity of their films. The works produced by the pair for galleries and museums reconfigure that identity in an exercise of "paracinematic" self-remembering,[26] and of shifting social and political engagement, as we see in the selection of film posters which pose a counterpoint to *National Identity (Príncipe Real)*, for example.

From the point of view of the reception of their works, these pieces and installations provide new contexts and intended uses for the directors' films and the material items associated with them. Rodrigues and Guerra da Mata's installations work through (and from the starting point of) these other elements being out-of-place, yet without removing the original connection of those elements to the films from which they are taken; as such, the installations become archival documents.[27] Collectively, and although they may not have been conceived for this purpose, they constitute a powerful archive that is both reflexive and self-questioning, and that works with and gives new meaning to the (self-) remembrance of (the work of) Rodrigues and Guerra da Mata.

PART 4

Interview

CHAPTER 11

Interview with João Pedro Rodrigues and João Rui Guerra da Mata

Julián Daniel Gutiérrez Albilla

I had the honor and pleasure of conducting this interview with the Portuguese filmmakers João Pedro Rodrigues (JPR) and João Rui Guerra da Mata (JRGdM) in Lisbon in June 2019. The text below evolved from a series of productive encounters that I had with João Pedro Rodrigues and João Rui Guerra da Mata in Lisbon and Los Angeles over the preceding two years. I believe that these encounters have been transformative and galvanizing. Rather than offering clear-cut answers, they enabled me to explore several important questions with them, with regard to the aesthetic, ethical, or political significance and distinctiveness of their cinema.

Cinema could be considered a dying medium, or one that metamorphoses into other media. I wonder whether you conceive of filmmaking as a heroic act of resistance to the death of cinema, as, perhaps, a disavowal of the obsolescence of the film medium, or as a tragic act that makes us conscious of our inevitable confrontation with the death of cinema.

JPR—I do think that I make films in an "ancient way." New cameras, for instance, make everything easier, so people think less about what they are doing. Making films on film is very expensive, as cinema is, indeed, a very expensive medium. This is why I think very carefully about the way that I am shooting. I believe that having filmed my three first feature films on film made me more precise. I always make films the way I know how to make them. For each film I direct, I always try to find the best way, or at least the only way I think that it is possible and plausible to tell the story, so each film for me embraces this uniqueness. Even when I am writing the script, I am also thinking about how

I am going to shoot a particular scene. I am thinking in a visual manner, and I am also writing in a visual (and of course aural) way. For instance, I pay a lot of attention to sound descriptions. When I am thinking about the music included in my films, this is written on the script.

So, do you think that your cinema has a productive anachronistic quality? For instance, _Odete_ (_Two Drifters_, 2005), whose English title explicitly refers to the main song in _Breakfast at Tiffany's_ (Blake Edwards, 1961), seems to establish a productive dialogue with classical Hollywood cinema.

JPR—Yes. _Two Drifters_ establishes a parallel with old-style films, even if the story is completely contemporary. To go back to the question of the use of music in films, in many films, music is omnipresent. We are too used to listening to music. It seems as though there is always a soundtrack in our lives. I find this superfluous. I do not think that music used in this way adds something to the film. For me, music cannot function just as ambience. I think that the use of music in cinema, or in life, is symptomatic of the fact that people are afraid of silence. Yet, I am very concerned with the sense of rhythm in my films. A film can have a lot of rhythm (even when a film is made of fewer shots as opposed to relying on fast editing). I do not mean that my films are always composed in the same way. Sometimes, I also resort to a fast rhythm (even at the level of editing), so it is always a question of finding the right balance. I conceived of _Morrer Como um Homem_ (_To Die Like a Man_, 2009) as a musical, but only in order to undo the conventions of the musical genre. For instance, most of the main character's (Tónia) musical performances in the film are off-screen, or they take place when the characters are rehearsing, thereby problematizing the spectacular quality of musical numbers in mainstream films. The only musical number which follows in some ways those generic conventions is the final scene, which shows Tónia on a roof singing a fado song by Paulo Bragança. Tónia is contemplating her own burial from the top and yet she is also performing a song, so she could be considered the spectacle of death. I used a crane to film this sequence. The film ends with a panoramic view of Lisbon and the 25th of April Bridge. Tónia has now become a ghost. Dressed in blue and red (like a Renaissance or Baroque virgin), she is also the Madonna of the transgender community. I show the bridge that connects Lisbon to Almada to suggest that Tónia is here and there. She has now gone to the other side, to another place. But, I want to think of cinema as if it were a symphony. As I told you, I try to avoid the use of fast editing, but I like thinking about the musicality of the film structure, which entails the shift from slow to fast movement and vice versa (again even at the level of the editing). I associate cinema with the movement of a symphony, which has to do less with fast rhythm than with the use of different movements. But what is important is the fact that classical music also tells a story; so do plays. When a play is divided into three or five acts, this also relates to the fact that plays are concerned with the articulation of different rhythms, and each act conveys a different pace. I think that, since cinema came after theater and classical music or opera, cinema inherits or shares with theater and classical music a concern with musicality.

I understand that you try to find a balance between resorting to fast editing and to fewer shots. As is well known, resorting to long takes seems to be an obvious way of succumbing to the conventions of art-house cinema (we can think of Antonioni as a paradigmatic example). Yet, I think that your cinema resists the features of the so-called slow cinema. In other words, I do not think that your cinema could strictly fall under the category of art-house cinema, even if, to me, your cinema is certainly a *cinéma d'auteur*.

JPR—American cinema was deeply formative for me, as well as for many European filmmakers. I think that American classical films are the matrix of cinema, and this is why many of these films are considered cult movies. I do not think that these films were intentionally made to become cults. These films were just telling stories. Since I was very young, I have often gone to the Cinemateca Portuguesa to watch films from all over the world, including American classical films, so this is the way that I was cinematically educated. But I also learned about life there, so this formative experience was part of my sentimental education. I think that this inevitably permeates in my films. So, making films cannot be reduced to thinking about what has to be used. Writing is also a crucial aspect of making films and, when I am writing, I do think about what I am inventing, but I am not so worried about being the first to do something. Yet writing is a very complicated process. I struggle when I am in the process of writing. This is why I like writing with someone else. This means that I am forced to work when I am collaborating with another writer. But, to return to the question of the category that my cinema falls under, when we are writing, we are not thinking about these references. These references are inside me, so I conceive them as words or languages to which I resort. Whether genre cinema or art-house cinema, this is a vocabulary to which I resort in order to find the right word. I do not mind if this language comes from art-house, from Hollywood, or from avant-garde cinema. I do not think about these references but about finding the right words for my films.

Indeed, you wrote your first feature film, *O Fantasma* (*Phantom*, 2000), with the late Paulo Rebelo, among others. If we want to focus on the question of references in your films, whether cinematic, literary, or artistic, I am not sure if you were actually inspired by the dissident Surrealist writer, Georges Bataille. When I first saw *Phantom*, which was

deeply transformative, I was very much thinking about Bataille's 1929 article on "Le gros orteil" ("The Big Toe").[1] In the final scene, the main character "falls" into the horizontal space, thus losing his verticality, which is what distinguishes us from animals. The latter are situated along the horizontal axis, even if they try to raise themselves up to the vertical position. Bataille argues that humanity is defined by the basest of human features, the toe, which is what subjects us to the vertical axis. The toe distinguishes us from other primates, as it enables us to stand up. For Bataille, the toe conditions the hierarchies of the body and society, which partake of clear-cut distinctions between the "high" and the "low." Therefore, the main character of this film fulfills the condition of what Rosalind Krauss refers to as "man-as-animal,"[2] thus foregrounding the animal violence that lies below our civilized human behavior. I think that this has huge political implications, as your film undercuts the hierarchical distinctions established between humans and non-humans, thereby moving beyond the anthropocentrism that still dominates our way of thinking about our "being-in-the-world" with humans and non-humans. By obsessively immersing himself in the bodily, which is associated with the horizontal axis, the main character points to the lines of flight or ruptures within our dominant culture. The film intervenes in human life as a way of overcoming the repression associated with the hegemony of the vertical axis. Such an immanent intervention potentially transforms perceptible and imperceptible reality, thereby producing resistant forces of creation and differentiation for the possibility of becoming. So, it seems to me that the film's political potential, or that of your cinema as a whole, is the way it provides us with what the Brazilian Deleuzean psychoanalyst Suely Rolnik identifies as a mobile and complex cartography of the forces operating in the production of subjectivation within the field of the social.[3] This enables us to think about the potentially transformative effects of one's physical and symbolic resistance.

JPR—If we are thinking about literary references, or the horizontal axis for that matter, I could refer to Proust, who wrote *In Search of Lost Time* [*À la recherche du temps perdu*, 1913–27] while lying on a bed. Therefore, it seems to me that Proust proved that one can contribute to our human civilization (the fact that he wrote such a literary masterpiece) while situated along the horizontal axis. But what I find fascinating about Proust is the fact that the novel is based on recollections, and this relates somehow to my film. As you can see, there is a tree outside my apartment window, so I could not see the trash collectors very well when they were collecting the trash at night. I was very intrigued by their lives, so I approached them directly and asked permission to follow them. I decided to go to the place from which they leave every night. I went there once or twice a week. I wanted the film to have a documentary quality about trash collectors. My film describes their work routine, and I learned a great deal about their work. For instance, I found out that each trash collector is part of a team, and each team is responsible for collecting the trash in a specific area of Lisbon. I was trying to map or trace a cartography, so I think that the film very much focuses on the geography of my neighborhood, which, to return to Proust, is a place for me that is full of personal recollections. In fact, this apartment belonged to my grandmother. The film enabled me to film my own street. It attests to my perception of this area, so the film functions as a documentary of my neighborhood, but it may also be considered a portrait of their lives.

Yet, although you are emphasizing this documentary quality, I do not think that this film, or your cinema as a whole, falls under the category of social realism.

JPR—Filmmakers often come from a privileged social background, so I think that representing socially marginalized people runs the risk of looking down on the underprivileged. In fact, I think that it is very easy to fall into this trap. If we think about TV today, it is full of programs where we see people who want to become stars, so, without being too moralistic about it, I think that there is an element of cynicism, and I think that one should be clear about the extent to which your film can speak for others who are different from you and the extent to which you are representing other people to fulfill your own interests, such as making your own film. It seems to me that we need to be aware of the asymmetrical relation that takes place between the filmmaker and the subjects you are trying to represent. In fact, I think that it is more difficult to talk about your own social stratum. Of course, I was interested in these trash collectors, who are often uneducated, but I found out that some of them did have an education and this was their way of earning a living. But, if we need to talk about the relationship between the collective and the individual, my film very much focuses on one individual. I invented this character and put him in this specific environment. In real life, I did not find anyone like the main character, so this character has, if you like, a kind of iconographic quality. *Phantom* [*O Fantasma*] means *The Ghost* and the film has this title because these subjects who deal with the trash of a city operate at night. They are the ghosts of the city. One does not pay attention to them because they work at night. Like phantoms, they are invisible and yet, their actions affect us on a deeply tangible level.

But it seems to me that this film foregrounds the relationship between trauma and fantasy, between pleasure and pain, between Eros and Thanatos. In other words, the main character's violent tendencies toward the pursuit of pleasure to the point of killing others

is paradoxically associated with his own tendencies towards self-destruction and self-shattering, and this inevitably leads him to a social and symbolic death.

JPR—The main character is coping with his job, and I think that there is some kind of dignity in what he does, so, again, I was not trying to look down on someone who belongs to a lower social stratum than my own. I was not trying to differentiate between the main character and the other guys he meets in his sexual encounters. You do not know what they do, because they are objects of his sexual lust. I was interested in conveying the fact that he does not know how to cope with his solitude. He does not know how to socialize, so violence is the only language he understands. Therefore, to go back to the question of animality, I think that the main character also embodies the kind of innocence that children have. He is not conscious of his actions. He does not know how to deal with his own feelings. In some ways, he is just playing. For instance, he does not know how to reach his object of desire. Of course, in real life, he may be considered a psychopath, but I do not judge my characters in the realm of fiction. I wanted to foreground the fact that, for him, he has a good job. He has the privilege to work by himself most of the time. It is true that he does not seem to have a social life, as his only friend is a dog. I think that we see this in Disney films. So the film also focuses on the relation between a kind of child and an animal and on how he builds this affective relationship with an animal. He takes care of this living creature, so he could also be seen as a caring and compassionate person.

I want to insist on the question of desire in your films. What I find fascinating about *To Die Like a Man* is the fact that you provide us with a plethora of representations of the male and transgendered body, and this ranges, for instance, from the beautiful and sexualized bodies of the soldiers having sex at the beginning of the film, to the vulnerable and dying body of Tónia, so we are exposed to a wide range of conceptions of the naked body. I find deeply moving the scene which shows Tónia lying on the hospital bed, and the camera lingers on her body as we listen to a love song sung by her lover, who is washing her body as if Tónia were Christ before his entombment. In the light of the obsessive cult of the perfect, young, and cosmetic body in contemporary society in general, and within gay culture in particular, I find your attention to different conceptions of the male nude deeply enriching, as you enable us to be exposed to the vulnerability of the irreducible other. We thus become aware that vulnerability and precariousness are constitutive elements of our own subjectivity as well. Yet I also think that your films do focus on the eroticization of male bodies, thus eliciting in the spectator (I can only speak from my subject position as a queer spectator) physical and visual pleasure, or even a sexual, corporeal response to the desired male bodies. I wonder whether you conceive of filmmaking as a creative process of sublimation of desire, or, to the contrary, as the condition of possibility for the release of physical and psychical pleasure on the part of the filmmaker and the spectator. From this perspective, filmmaking can be associated with an instinctive liberation of libidinal impulses, rather than with a formal process of sublimation, thus conceiving cinematic representation as a violent and obsessive, yet productive process of liberating unconscious desires.

JPR—I do think that filmmaking enables me to have a physical connection (I am speaking in a figurative manner) with the bodies I film. For instance, we can see this very clearly in my short, *O Corpo de Afonso* (*The King's Body*, 2012). The film was commissioned for the Guimarães European Capital of Culture. The film is based on a casting call, and it alludes to the first king of Portugal when it was founded as a country. I wanted to problematize the mythology around the birth of Portugal as one of the kingdoms of the Iberian Peninsula. It is rather paradoxical that our first king came from northern Spain (Galicia), so our first king was Spanish. As is well known, there are so many linguistic and cultural connections between Galicia and Portugal, as the Galician language is a sort of mixture of Portuguese and Spanish. Indeed, Galician-Portuguese evolved from Vulgar Latin, in the same way as Spanish and Catalan did. So, I wanted to play, to the point of being subversive, with this mythology around our first king by foregrounding his Spanish nationality. It was interesting to note that, when the film was shown, there were no reactions on the part of the audience. The film touched delicate spots at the core of the cultural imaginary of Guimarães. Since the film is about a casting call, I interviewed several men from Galicia as a way of looking for the image of our first king. Incidentally, when I was shooting this short, there was a huge economic crisis in both Spain and Portugal, so most of the men appearing in the film were trying to find a job. Most of them talked about their challenging economic situation and the difficulties they were facing in life. As I said earlier, it was not my intention to film the underprivileged, but, in a rather incalculable manner, their personal predicaments permeated into the film. Although I tend to be in control of everything I do when I film, I let these surprises be imprinted on the film. So, the film also functions as a documentary of the unemployed condition of these Spanish guys, and I appreciated the way they openly and truthfully talked about their particular situations. It is interesting to note that there is a still a monarchy in Spain, but, while I was trying to look for the Spanish king, the lives of these Spanish guys were completely removed from anything related to the monarchy. In many ways, my film is about looking for the impossible. In other words, it was impossible to find this impossibility.

Indeed, the film productively juxtaposes the beauty of these male bodies with the pathos of their material existence. I like the way you talk about letting these incalculable elements permeate into the film, thus taking you and the viewer to unexpected places. If you allow me to make an analogy, I am fascinated by the way Roland Barthes[4] engages with the erotic in a photograph by Robert Mapplethorpe. He comes to the conclusion that the erotic is less associated with the naked body of the male model than with the haptic effects created by the texture of the model's underwear on the spectator. In a similar way, I would suggest, a film that focuses on the beautiful and on pleasure unexpectedly takes us to a space inhabited by pain and pathos.

JPR—By all means, my focus on these male bodies emphasized their scars and their tattoos, and this is a way of tracing one's personal and shared history. If we return to the story of the first king of Portugal, in the twelfth century there was no material evidence of his life, so the emissary of the Pope came to Portugal to confirm that he was the king. When the emissary met with the king, the latter undressed and showed him his body's scars, as these indicated all the battles that he had fought, so the body tells your own history, and such an inscription of your private history becomes the story of the entire country. I wanted to pay attention to their scars, not only the visible scars but also the scars that result from shaping their bodies, from building their bodies, as if these actions left their traces on the body. In a similar way, although tattoos are nowadays more visible, some of these guys told me about the association of their tattoos with their private lives. One of them told me that his tattoos indicated his experience of having been in jail due to drug-dealing, so, even if they are hidden, tattoos are part of your body and they carry your private history.

Even if your cinema pays attention to the eroticization of the desired body or to the physicality of the male body, it seems to me that your cinema cannot be reduced to the category of gay cinema, even if some of your films, especially in the United States, are shown in gay film festivals.

JPR—Yes! Although these categories may be enabling, I think that the use of these categories (gay cinema, women's cinema, African cinema) are a very reductive way of engaging with the complexity of films. For me, making films is about the story I want to tell, and this is not incompatible with having gay characters in my films. The fact that some of them happen to be gay is secondary. In fact, Odete, the main female protagonist, is not gay. She may be a "fag hag," but she is not gay. The main character in *O Ornitólogo* (*The Ornithologist*, 2016) has a gay sexual experience, but my main interest was to portray an actualization of the life of St. Anthony when he became a monk.

I think that we could, indeed, engage in a queer interpretation of the story of this holy figure, but I want to return to the question of finitude and the possibility of resurrection and your concern with one's possibility of becoming someone or something else in life or after death.

JPR—As we get older, we become more conscious of our own mortality. So I think that films are a way of overcoming death. I will die, but my films will always remain alive, and the film characters will remain. I was always attracted by stories about love after death. Film materializes this idea. This does not happen, I believe, when filming on digital. The latter has a shorter life than film, so digital technology is corrupted from the outset on a stylistic level, as it will not last forever. Film has a longer life. Digital technology is ephemeral and immaterial. By contrast, film carries the idea that something material is inscribed on the technology itself.

I understand that you are inspired by literature, painting, and cinema and that you do not conceive your cinema as an illustration or instantiation of theoretical concepts. Having said that, when I listen to you talking about film as a process of confronting or transcending the perishability of our existence, I think again about Barthes's text, *Camera Lucida*.[5] This is, perhaps, a foundational book on the theory of photography. Yet I think that this book functions as the way in which Barthes tries to work through his mother's death. When Barthes describes a picture of his mother when she was young (and we never see this picture) after her death, he tells us that, when this picture was taken, his mother will die and she is now dead. Hence, it is very interesting that Barthes comes to the conclusion that the temporality of the photographic medium is the future anterior by writing an elegy to his dead mother. I think that this attests to the inextricable relationship between theory and practice, and I do think that your films lend themselves to wonderful theoretical speculation.

JPR—I am interested in these paradoxes. My grandmother was both very religious and a Communist. As a Portuguese filmmaker, I am inevitably shaped by Catholicism, but I was always more interested in learning about religion through religious paintings. It is interesting that you talk about photography, because film is a very realistic medium. In other words, it embodies a photographic reality and yet it can become very unreal. Film enables you to recreate phantasies, ghosts, apparitions. Indeed, cinema has often dealt with spectral apparitions, giving a photographic reality to scenes that are unreal. I am fascinated by the fact that film can make ghosts real, and this takes place at the level of the *mise en scène*. Therefore, the *mise en scène* functions at the same level as a real actor. Film enables you to deal with the impossibility of the supernatural or afterlife, but, through emotion, you can believe in it. In *To Die Like a Man*, I was concerned with this impossibility. Tónia is dead, but she is singing. This is totally constructed, but film gives you the freedom to present a character who is dead in a very glorious manner. As we said earlier, Tónia is performing her own death. This is materialized by means of the iconography. She is portrayed as the Notre Dame of the transsexuals. She is Our Lady dressed in the colors of the Virgin going up to heaven. There is a certain romanticism in this scene, so the film alludes to older mythologies, when people believed that they would be reunited after death. My films deal with the juxtaposition of the natural with the supernatural, the transcendental with the physical, so film is a process of materializing the supernatural, of making it physical because you see it thanks to the *mise en scène*. Of course, this is artificial, but this artificiality becomes believable. By contrast, when you resort to digital technology, it is hard to imagine that the supernatural can be rendered physical. This is why I would love to continue filming on film. There are always financial reasons that prevent you from filming on film, but I am glad to be able to shoot my next documentary on film. I regret not having shot *The Ornithologist* on film, but, even though I shot it on digital, my process of working remained the same.

I am very grateful to you for insisting on screening *To Die Like a Man* in 35 mm when we showed this film at the Downtown Independent in Los Angeles in April 2019. In effect, for me, I had a completely different cinematic experience (on a phenomenological level) from previous screenings of this film. So, what comes out of our intensive conversations throughout these two years is your passion for cinema and filmmaking as a possible act of love. But I would like to ask you both about the films you shot in Portugal's former colony, Macao, both *A Última Vez Que Vi Macau* (The *Last Time I Saw Macao*, 2012) and its precursor. *Alvorada Vermelha* (*Red Dawn*, 2011). How did Macao come to interest you?

JRGdM—My father was in the navy, stationed in Mozambique and then in Macao (both of them are former colonies of Portugal). Macao is very much part of my formative years, so I often talked about Macao with João Pedro. I lived in Macao in the 1970s, while it was still a Portuguese colony. Almost five centuries ago, Macao was offered by China, which is now a Communist country, to Portugal, but the latter had to pay a tribute to China, first to the monarchy and then to the republic. Macao was the way in which you could come in and out of China, and its colonial story is very different to that of Hong Kong, which was taken by force. I was fascinated by the transition Macao experienced, from being a small fishermen's village to being considered the Las Vegas of the East.

***The Last Time I Saw Macao* is a documentary (it could also be considered a travelogue), but it could also be seen as a thriller. We never see**

the main characters. We see the traces of their actions, but I under-stand that both of you are the voice-over narrators, especially you, João Rui.

JRGdM—I agree, the film can be considered a documentary or a fiction. Or both. Actually, it was presented as either one, depending on the festival for which it was selected, and it won prizes for both categories. We like to think of this film, shot in Macao, China, and Portugal over six months, as a cross between film noir and science fiction, in between personal memories and visions of the apocalypse. I lived in Macao during my formative years and I had never been back. When we decided to make a documentary about returning to Macao thirty years later, the project was supported by the Portuguese Film Institute (ICA) and the Macao Cultural Institute. Based on my recollections of the city, the film explores the contrast between my personal memories of Macao and the changes that have taken place there since I left. Cities are living organisms in constant mutation but Macao is a city that has been radically transformed in the last ten years. When we arrived there, we encountered a different city from the one I remembered. As a result, our project focused on documenting what had changed in Macao, using a fictional narrative to develop this investigation. The main character, who carries my family name (Guerra da Mata), arrives in Macao for the first time and gets lost in the city, the same way as I also got lost, not recognizing the "new" Macao. Also, it was João Pedro's first time in Macao, so he was guided by me on my journey of re-discovering the city. That said, it made sense that we used our voices as narrators in this remapping of Macao, an emotional mapping. In other words, filming is a way of paying attention to the feeling of remapping spaces. If a map is something rational, film enables us to connect places under the logic of the film, letting the irrational come forward.

It seems to me that, by focusing on the morphological transforma-tions of Macao, your cinema also engages with the postcolonial condi-tion of Portugal. I am deeply interested in the way in which you talk about the significance of memory in your cinema and the way in which film is the condition of possibility for the inscription and transmission of our emotional attachment to actual and imaginary spaces, to past and present places.

JRGdM—The working title of our next documentary is *Where is this Street?* This documentary departs from a film made in our Lisbon neighborhood in the 1960s: *Os Verdes Anos* (*The Green Years*, 1963), directed by Paulo Rocha, who was João Pedro's teacher in Film School. At the end of the Avenida Esta-dos Unidos da América in Lisbon, one of the locations where we will be shoot-ing, you can still see the hills of what, back in the 1960s, was the countryside. There were farms and until relatively recently there was a herd of sheep that usually went up that avenue. This area was considered the borderline between the city and the countryside, the city limits. In this new project, we are deeply committed to filming the area where we live and the transformations that this neighborhood has experienced. We have always been very interested in the ambivalent tension between the natural (associated with the countryside) and the artificial (associated with the city). If one thinks about João Pedro's features, their plots reflect precisely the idea of the borderline between the city and the countryside, between the human and the animal, or the rational and the irrational. In *Phantom*, there are scenes that focus on locations which are neither the city nor the countryside. In *To Die Like a Man*, the main characters need to escape from the city to the countryside, but once there, they are intimidated and return to the city, if only to die. *The Ornithologist*, finally, takes place entirely in nature, as if that border were crossed.

Is there a connection with the way Pasolini's early cinema focused on this border between the city and the countryside to explore the extent to which modernity inscribes the traces of the rural?

JPR and JRGdM—Pasolini focused on the poor areas of the city. The buildings of this neighborhood where we usually shoot, the Alvalade neighborhood, never functioned as social housing or public housing. Its architecture is defined as International Style from the 1960s, Mid-Century Modern architecture that was despised by our dictator, Salazar. This area was the main entrance to Lisbon for tourists arriving by plane, and this modern architectural style was designed for them not to think of Portugal as an economically backward, politically authoritarian, and isolated nation. The upper middle classes from the Portuguese colonies in Africa had their second homes here. Like Spain, our dictatorship was one of the last fascist regimes in Western Europe. Such an anachronistic political system contrasted with the modern image of Portugal that many wanted to convey, and this architectural style encapsulated that modern image. Yet, such a contrast attests to the fact that our modernity was quite peculiar. Our political regime was, indeed, quite peculiar. Our colonies played an essential role in the design of this part of the city, as this modernist style mostly developed in our colonies in Africa.

I am very interested in this political question, however we understand the concept of the political. I do not think that your cinema has a political agenda, or that it can be defined as political cinema, but it certainly functions on a political level.

JPR and JRGdM—We could talk of how cinema articulates metaphors for particular political situations. Even *X-Men* (Bryan Singer, 2000) can be considered a political film, as it deals with growing up differently in a society that tries to normalize you.

By all means, it is a question of thinking about the concept of the political, whether the political is inscribed in the film or the film lends itself to a political reading. Yet it seems to me that we need to think about both form and content. In other words, I think that close attention to the poetics of cinema enables us to ask whether the films re-inscribe the means of representation and vision that underpin the dominant ideological structures they attempt to criticize, or whether the films subvert these dominant economies of representation and vision at the level of cinematic form. I think that if a film changes your aesthetic perception and the way you relate to others, this can have political implications in the sense that it may potentially transform your consciousness of reality.

JPR—Some filmmakers, for instance Fassbinder, are more obviously or explicitly political than others, but we agree that something embodied in a film can be political in many ways. Yet we resist the obsolete and rigid categories used traditionally to define cinema (i.e. entertainment versus political cinema in the 1970s, or entertainment versus art-house cinema in the 1960s). We think that blaxploitation films could be seen as political films, as they portrayed powerful women as an antidote to the representation of mostly white women as housewives in mainstream cinema. But we do not think that our cinema has *a priori* a political agenda. In fact, in *To Die Like a Man*, a film with no biological women except the dog Agustina, the character Maria Bakker is actually quite politically incorrect, but, of course, their political incorrectness has nothing to do with the political incorrectness advocated by today's right-wing political leaders. Their sentences in the film, including their citations of Célan's poetry, give them an esoteric quality and an edge that today could run the risk of being censored by our move toward sanitized and decaffeinated representations of queer characters or gay sex in the cinema. If one compares *Call Me by Your Name* (Luca Guadagnino, 2017) with my first film, *Phantom*, the latter is like a punch in your stomach. Yet when I screened the film in San Francisco, a member of the audience asked us about what had happened to the rabbit. I answered that we had eaten him [. . .] But, to go back to the question of what is political, we are now preparing a fiction film that is set in a particular political moment, the revolutionary period in Portugal. At the end of the day, it is up to the audience or the film critic to read a film politically or not. We think, for instance, that *The Last Time I Saw Macao* and especially *Red Dawn* are very political. In fact, *Red Dawn* was censored in China. The film is about a typical Chinese market. It attests to all the images that one can encounter in a market. It emphasizes the rituals that take place in this market and the repetitive gestures performed by these Chinese workers, so in the film the violence of killing animals coexists with the beauty of the choreographic movements of these workers. It was important for us not to focus too much on the violence but on showing the process involved in those products we choose to eat. In other words, unlike American or Western European supermarkets, we wanted to show the origin of the products we eat, and this took us to moments when these animals were still alive. We never understood why the Chinese government decided to censor this film on the grounds that it represented a violent image of the country and that it was too violent for the Chinese audience. When the film was censored in an exhibition in Beijing, the censor chose a shot of the film, a woman looking at the camera, so our film was reduced to a freeze-frame that, of course, could not be held there for much time. On the occasion of a full retrospective of our work here in Portugal, we made an installation based on the censorship we experienced with *Red Dawn*. As you went down a red-lit staircase, you entered a room, which felt like a dungeon, and you could read the fax (in Chinese) that the Chinese government sent to inform us of the censorship and you could listen to the Chinese national anthem. In the room, it was not the film, but only the freeze-frame the censor had chosen for the Beijing exhibition that was projected. We did not translate the fax, as we wanted to foreground the impossibility of a total translation of one culture to another, so this installation was overtly political. So, it is a question of thinking about your disposition to be exposed, to expose things, the need to expose things. We think this is much more effective than engaging in political propaganda or having a political agenda.

My final question has to do with how you feel about your contribution to a global interest in Portuguese cinema and about the current condition of cinema in Portugal.

JPR and JRGdM—We do not have nationalist feelings, and we do not believe in the category of world cinema, but in a cinematic world. Indeed, most of our films focus on Lisbon, and we did not make films outside Portugal until we made the films in Macao. We can use fado music, which is the Portuguese music *par excellence*, in our films, such as in *To Die Like a Man*, and mix it with American music, such as "Calvary" by Baby Dee.

I find sublime the scene showing all the characters listening to the entire song by Baby Dee in the forest. I find fascinating the way that they stand still, as if they were part of a *tableau vivant*, listening to this song and looking at us listening to the song.

JPR—So, we have different generations of Portuguese filmmakers and different cinemas in Portugal. But this is a reductive way of conceiving our film practices. What constitutes Portuguese cinema? Is it the nationality of the filmmakers? Is it the subject matter? Perhaps the common denominator is the lack of funding for our films and the long time it takes to make a film, especially for art-house cinema. In our case, we have to rely on the Portuguese Institute of Cinema, as we don't receive money from public TV any more, as was the case in the past. We also have commercial cinema in Portugal, but we need to emphasize that there is a lack of support for cinema that is not overtly commercial. This is unfortunate, as cinema brings international prestige to the country. In Portugal, we do not care much about our artists, only about those who are easier to understand, more accessible, or who know how to reach consensus. Even regarding our most famous filmmaker, Manoel de Oliveira, his films were only seen by very few people, and he became famous because he was the oldest director making films, according to Guinness World Records. We are a very schizophrenic country. This also happened to Fernando Pessoa, one of our best poets. During the dictatorship, there was a competition and he ended up being number two. Nobody knows who the number one was. Pessoa died working in an office, so he was only recognized after his death.

I want to finish this interview by expressing my deepest thanks to both of you for engaging in these productive conversations with me. This has been a wonderful experience for me to work so closely with filmmakers. Since we come from different enunciative positions, I found it deeply enriching to establish these productive tensions in relation to how we experience and understand your cinema.[6]

Notes

INTRODUCTION

1. The short film was premiered and still streams on the website of the Cinemateca Portuguesa—Museu do Cinema, accessed 5 July 2021 <https://saladeprojecao.cinemateca.pt/turdus-merula-linnaeus-1758/>.
2. Álvarez López and Martin, "Drifting."
3. Rodrigues also directed *Nude Descending a Staircase, 2020* (2020); *Potemkin Steps* (2019), which premiered at MoMA NYC; *Où En Êtes-Vous, João Pedro Rodrigues?* (*Where Do You Stand Now, João Pedro Rodrigues?*, 2017); *O Corpo de Afonso* (*The King's Body*, 2012); *Allegoria della Prudenza* (2013); *Manhã de Santo António* (*Morning of Saint Anthony's Day*, 2012); *Viagem à Expo* (*Journey to Expo*, 1998); *Esta É a Minha Casa* (*This Is My Home*, 1997); *Parabéns!* (*Happy Birthday!*,1997); and *O Pastor* (*The Shepherd*, 1988). Guerra da Mata directed *O Que Arde Cura* (*As the Flames Rose*, 2012). Together, they have co-directed *Iec Long* (2015), *Mahjong* (2013), *The Last Time I Saw Macao, Alvorada Vermelha* (*Red Dawn*, 2011), and *China, China* (2007).
4. João Pedro Rodrigues was a visiting artist at Le Fresnoy—Studio National des Arts Contemporains in France during 2010–11. He was a Radcliffe-Harvard Film Study Center Fellow/Carl and Lily Pforzheimer Foundation Fellow in 2014–15. In 2017, he lived in Berlin with Guerra da Mata as a DAAD Fellow, researching and writing their new Asian feature: SAN MA LO 270, MACAU. The project won one of the Crouching Tigers Project Lab Awards at the First International Film Festival & Awards Macao in December 2016.
5. Liz, "Introduction: Framing the Global Appeal of Contemporary Portuguese Cinema," 2–4.
6. The effects on film funding of the economic crisis caused by the current COVID-19 pandemic are yet to be known and measured. In 2012, the Portuguese Institute of Cinema and Audiovisual (ICA)—which supports, represents, and distributes national film productions—did not open any calls for funding artistic projects. This was an effect of the financial crisis that commenced in 2008. Moreover, the 2000s had already been a period of erratic film policies which generated controversy and tension between film directors,

producers, and the state, and contributed to the shifting landscape of national film production. (Filipa Rosário, "Portugal's Year Zero," 212–4.)

7. Liz, "Introduction: Framing the Global Appeal of Contemporary Portuguese Cinema," 5.

8. Dennis Lim argues that "incubated on the literal and figurative margins of Europe, Portuguese cinema can often seem a world unto itself, a semiautonomous territory that evolved at its own pace and at a productive remove from the rest of the continent. The lost years of the Salazar dictatorship and the pent-up energies from decades of repression and dormancy; the deep-seated agrarian tradition and the delayed arrival of industrialization; the vast storehouse of local history and myth and the vibrant cinematheque scene of the post-Salazar years—all have conspired to create in Portugal one of the richest and most distinctive film cultures in the world." (Lim, "António Reis and Margarida Cordeiro.")

9. Rosário, "Portugal's Year Zero," 214.

10. Silva, "The Portuguese Queer Screen," 70.

11. Silva, "The Portuguese Queer Screen," 70.

12. Schoonover and Galt, "Introduction: Queer, World, Cinema," 8.

13. Sedeño Valdellós, "Imaginarios del Cuerpo y la Memoria en el Cine Portugués Contemporáneo," 278.

14. Haaf, "Exploring the Neither," 462.

15. Rodrigues, *Le jardin des fauves*, 52.

16. In 2010, *The Guardian* published online *My City: João Pedro Rodrigues's Lisbon*, as part of the *My City: video guides* series. The film presents places in the city which have been selected according to Rodrigues's personal and filmic affinities. Notably, the account predates the touristification and gentrification of Lisbon in recent years <https://www.theguardian.com/travel/video/2010/sep/30/lisbon-portugal-my-city-guide> (accessed 5 July 2021).

17. Père, "Locarno 2012 Day 6: João Pedro Rodrigues."

18. Villarmea Álvarez, "Mudar de Perspetiva," 111.

19. Guest, "The Road to Macao."

20. Solomon, "Self-Portrait of an Exquisite Corpus."

21. Baptista, "Nationally Correct," 12–13.

22. Liz, "Introduction: Framing the Global Appeal of Contemporary Portuguese Cinema," 8.

23. Cutler, "He and 'I'," 6.

24. Solomon, "Self-Portrait."

CHAPTER 1

1. BoCa "National Identity (Príncipe Real)."

2. For further exploration of this idea, see Salvadó-Corretger and Benavente, "The Statuary Condition in Contemporary Portuguese Cinema," 131–42.

3. The global economic crisis, which began to manifest itself visibly in 2008, particularly affected Portugal, where the economy had already been showing signs of weakness since 2006. Successive center-left governments followed the recommendations and adjustment policies that the European Union demanded of its members. In 2011, a new conservative government led by Pedro Passos Coelho came to power and promoted deregulation and flexibility in the economic sector. His government was also in charge of applying the severe new austerity measures that were promoted by the European Union to reduce deficit through the containment of public spending. These measures led the country into deep recession and social conflict. This is the context of the film in question.

4. On 25 April 1974, a military uprising led mainly by junior military officers (who came to be known as the *Capitães de Abril* [April Captains]) took place in Portugal. Most of them were in the *Movimento das Forças Armadas*—MFA (Armed Forces Movement), a military movement that opposed the dictatorial regime and its colonial policy. The military uprising put an end to the dictatorship, which had endured since 1926. The markedly anti-authoritarian revolutionary process was carried out suddenly and without violence, and the officers quickly gathered popular support. As a sign of their intention not to fire, the rebel military put carnations in their weapons. The event hence came to be known as the "Carnation Revolution."

5. "No baile em que dançam todos/Alguém fica sem dançar./Melhor é não ir ao baile/Do que estar lá sem lá estar." (Pessoa, *Quadras ao Gosto Popular*.)

6. Brenez, *De la figure en général et du corps en particulier*, 4.

7. Del Don, "João Pedro Rodrigues."

8. Bhabha, *The Location of Culture*, 1.

9. Bhabha, *The Location of Culture*, 1.

10. Leutrat, *Vida de fantasmas*, 17–18.

11. Proust, *L'histoire à contretemps*, 48.

12. Leutrat, *Vida de fantasmas*, 20.

13. "When I was eighteen, I went to Venice for the first time and spent two weeks there by myself. I wanted to see every painting there, so I mapped all the paintings that existed in the churches, palaces and museums. In Italy, the hours change all the time, so I sometimes had to go back many times before I was able to see a painting. I think looking at painting taught me a lot about narrative. It's a frame. There are these Titian paintings at the National Gallery that depict scenes from Ovid's Metamorphoses, which are important for my new film." Dallas, "Lisbon: João Pedro Rodrigues on Birds, Maps, Saints, and Kings.".

14. Deleuze, *Francis Bacon: The Logic of Sensation*, 6–9.

15. Malabou, *El porvenir de Hegel*, 25.

16. Malabou, *Ontología del accidente*, 11.

17. Malabou, *Ontología del accidente*, 13.

18. Bhabha, *The Location of Culture*, 1.

CHAPTER 2

1. I refer to my interview with João Pedro Rodrigues: "La Vierge des travelos," interview by Olivier Cheval.

2. Bourcier, *Queer Zones*, 30.

3. A Christian anthropology of the flesh conceived from the Adamic and Christic models, as exploited by Irenaeus and Tertullian, is outlined by Falque, *Dieu, la chair et l'autre*, 138–76.

4. Didi-Huberman, *L'image Ouverte*, 336–7.

5. Author's translation from: "la propagation du peuplement animal de l'homme." Deleuze and Guattari, *Mille Plateaux*, 296.

6. Author's translation from: "A travers le corps à corps de l'imitation et de l'incarnation, quelque chose passe, chez Tertullien, sans jamais être théorisé, sans jamais être rendu tout à fait clair; quelque chose qui nous raconterait comment le visuel s'arrache du visible. Le visible, c'est le monde de l'idolâtrie, monde où l'image s'exhibe, se met en représentations, en spectacles ignobles, en concupiscences satisfaites. Le visuel, au contraire, c'est ce qui se voit au-delà, dans l'au-delà. Le visuel caractérise un monde où l'image est en présence

et en promesse tout à la fois—bref, en aura, matière de l'âme." Didi-Huberman, *L'image Ouverte*, 119.

7. Didi-Huberman, *L'image Ouverte*, 134. Author's translation from: "le sang qui jaillit [. . .] dénote exactement ce qu'on pourrait nommer l'incursion du visuel dans le visible: soit, ici, l'irruption du dedans—l'irruption de la couleur viscérale, de la couleur d'âme, dans un monde visible d'où âme et viscère sont normalement retranchés, repliés dans les fonds de la chair."

8. Author's translation from: "Pour cette pensée d'un regard toujours en extase et d'une voix toujours en exode dans leurs inséparables réponses à l'appel, la chair même qu'ils élèvent en gloire semble toutefois faire difficulté. Le regard et l'écoute la mettent toute entière en jeu, mais s'épuise-t-elle pour autant en eux? En quoi l'obscure intériorité de la chair en sa souffrance ou sa jouissance serait-elle extatique? En quoi s'offrirait-elle à un appel qui d'emblée l'excéderait?" (Chrétien, *L'Appel et la Réponse*, 101.)

9. During a conversation in 2014, João Pedro Rodrigues told me that if he had not thought of Caravaggio's painting for this sequence, he knew that it would have a central place in the film he was about to shoot at the time, *The Ornithologist*.

10. *The Bible*, John, 25.

11. *The Bible*, John, 27.

12. *The Bible*, John, 29.

13. Derrida, *Jean-Luc Nancy, Le Toucher*, 179–82.

14. Author's translation from: "Le fond noir est beaucoup plus qu'un 'fond' d'espace scénique. Le fond est à la limite la surface même du tableau. Par suite la projection du faisceau lumineux dans le plan du tableau ne laisse à la disposition des figures que l'extrême bord de la surface, la première ligne du tableau: le sol de la scène est une avant-scène et les figures sont continûment poussées vers l'avant, à peu près comme si nous avions affaire à des figures en relief sur une paroi solide, la paroi du tombeau arcanien." (Marin, *Détruire La Peinture*, 204–5.)

15. Careri, "Heureux ceux qui, sans avoir vu, ont cru!," 71.

16. Careri, "Heureux ceux qui, sans avoir vu, ont cru!," 83.

17. Agamben, *L'uso dei Corpi. Homo Sacer IV, 2*, 269–341.

18. Author's translation from: "Cette pensée implique une 'entrée' de chacun des élus dans le corps glorieux du ressuscité et si l'on doit imaginer par quelle ouverture on pourra pénétrer dans le corps du Christ, on ne peut penser qu'à la plaie." (Careri, "Heureux ceux qui, sans avoir vu, ont cru!," 78.)

CHAPTER 3

1. Boileau and Narcejac, *D'entre les morts* (*The Living and the Dead*)—the book that inspired Hitchcock's *Vertigo*.

2. Except where otherwise indicated, all translations are mine.

3. Rodrigues, *Le jardin des fauves*, 195.

4. Schefer, *Images Mobiles*, 206.

5. Todorov, *The Fantastic*, 1975.

6. Rodrigues, *Le jardin des fauves*, 195.

7. Chessel, "Raccord sexuel," 208.

8. Álvarez López and Martin, "Drifting."

9. In a way, both films center on interdimensional love stories. In addition, the topic of the metamorphosis is central both in Hitchcock's film, where Scottie tries to shape Judy

according to the image of Madeleine, and in Rodrigues's film, where Odete imitates the physical appearance of the dead man, Pedro.

10. Vernet, *Figures de l'absence*.
11. Bértolo, "Galeria de Retratos," 190–7.
12. In Portuguese, the morphological difference between "son" and "daughter" is marginal: "filho/filha."
13. Guerreiro, *Cinema El Dorado*, 379.
14. Bourgois, *Angélica!*, 55–7.
15. Morin, *Le Cinéma ou l'Homme Imaginaire*.
16. The "Asian Trilogy" corresponds to a group of five films directed by João Pedro Rodrigues and João Rui Guerra da Mata. Among them are four short films—*China, China* (2007), *Alvorada Vermelha* (*Red Dawn*, 2011), *Mahjong* (2013), and *Iec Long* (2015)—and one feature film, *A Última Vez Que Vi Macau* (*The Last Time I Saw Macao*, 2012). Some relationship to Asia is common to all of these films: three of them take place in Macao, and two of them were shot in Portuguese Chinatowns. For further discussion of the reflexive nature of this set of films, see Bértolo, "'Um lugar indeciso'," 51–67.
17. Johnson, *Manoel de Oliveira*, 28.

CHAPTER 4

1. For further discussion of this subject, see Silva, "The Portuguese Queer Screen," 69–78.
2. Haaf, "Exploring the Neither," 461–70.
3. Heidegger, "The Age of the World Picture,", 115–54.
4. Ibid., 129.
5. Ibid., 149.
6. Ibid., 132.
7. Ibid., 132.
8. Agamben, *The Omnibus Homo Sacer*, 1,107.
9. Ibid., 1,108.
10. For more detailed discussion, see Schalow, *The Incarnality of Being*, 91–115.
11. Agamben, *The Omnibus Homo Sacer*, 1,109.
12. Agamben, *The Omnibus Homo Sacer*, 1,108.
13. Agamben, *The Omnibus Homo Sacer*, 1,110.
14. Agamben, *The Omnibus Homo Sacer*, 1,110.
15. Redner, *Deleuze and Film Music*.
16. Deleuze and Guattari, *A Thousand Plateaus*, 191.
17. Ibid., 186.
18. Ibid., 189.
19. Ibid., 191.
20. Ibid., 191.
21. Turner, "A Lonely Geography."
22. Deleuze and Guattari, *What is Philosophy?*, 185–6.
23. Turner, "A Lonely Geography," 2018.
24. Guillen, "TO DIE LIKE A MAN—Interview."
25. Deleuze and Guattari, *Anti-Oedipus*, 2.
26. Deleuze and Guattari, *Anti-Oedipus*, 45.
27. Elphick, "*O Ornitólogo*—An Interview with João Pedro Rodrigues."
28. Aguilar, "'I Am All My Characters'."

29. Deleuze and Guattari, *Kafka: Toward a Minor Literature*.
30. Aguilar, "'I Am All My Characters'."
31. Deleuze and Guattari, *Anti-Oedipus*, 2.

CHAPTER 5

1. Cascais, "Metamorphosis of *O Fantasma* by João Pedro Rodrigues," 170–7.
2. Pacinotti, "Spider Rose's Metamorphosis," 71–9.
3. Clarke, *Allegories of Writing*, 3.
4. Clarke, *Allegories of Writing*, 4.
5. Pacinotti, "Spider Rose's Metamorphosis," 71.
6. Canevacci, "Hybridentities," 64–9.
7. Canevacci, "Hybridentities," 66.
8. Canevacci, "Hybridentities," 69.
9. Canevacci, "Hybridentities," 65.
10. Puff, "Acting in the Interstices," 57.
11. Rimbaud, *Œuvres complètes*, 343–4.
12. Puff, "Acting in the Interstices," 56.
13. Puff, "Acting in the Interstices", 57.
14. Clarke, *Allegories of Writing*, x.
15. Clarke, *Allegories of Writing*, 46.
16. Patanè, *L'altra metà dell'amore: dieci anni di cinema omosessuale* (Roma: DeriveApprodi, 2005), 145.
17. Ferreira, "The Politics of Desire in Portuguese Cinema," 243–4.
18. Armone, "I luoghi oscuri dell'anima," 248–9.
19. Kramer, *Independent Queer Cinema*, 26.
20. Armone, "I luoghi oscuri dell'anima," 249.
21. Gide, *Les nourritures terrestres*, 72.
22. Cucinotta, "Origens possíveis," 116–20.
23. Ibid., 124.
24. Baptista, *A Invenção do Cinema Português*, 198.
25. Bértolo, *Sobreimpressões*, 253.
26. Ibid.
27. Ibid., 257.
28. Curopos, *Queer(s) périphériques*, 50.
29. Ibid., 51.
30. Ibid., 52.
31. Sedgwick, *Touching Feeling*, 61–3.
32. Foucault, "Des espaces autres," 752–62.
33. Curopos, *Queer(s) périphériques*, 56.
34. Roth-Bettoni, *Les années sida à l'écran*, 110–1.

CHAPTER 6

1. Deleuze, *The Fold*, 5.
2. Serrão, "Environment, Nature, and Landscape," 36.
3. Lim, "António Reis and Margarida Cordeiro."

4. Vieira, "The Nature of Portuguese Cinema," 112–33.
5. The distinction of the Baroque and the Neo-Baroque within the frame of art history is beyond the thematic frame of this chapter, especially when Deleuze (who offers the theoretical perspective for this project) did not distinguish the Neo-Baroque from the Baroque even in his reading of Borges. When it comes to the history of culture, however, one should point out that the term "Baroque" is tied to the specific ideology, characteristics, and styles of Spanish Baroque literature during the seventeenth century, whereas the term "Neo-Baroque" emerged in the transcultural "Latin American" literature and art of 1960s and 1970s. The latter was "closely concerned with reclaiming history in an effort to understand the present; the illusory nature of identity and existence, related to cultural transformation and, in particular, to the increased impact of technology and foreign interests on Latin American culture, which are reflections of the new age of globalization." See Ndalianis, *Neo-Baroque Aesthetics and Contemporary Entertainment*, 261. Even while the term "Neo-Baroque" is appropriate for this paper, which is situated in the transcultural discussion of the Baroque, due to Deleuze's insistence on the usage of "Baroque" that is rooted in his conceptual reading of Leibniz, I will not delve in detail into the distinctions between the terms in this chapter. However, I believe that demarcation is important in order to locate the Neo-Baroque in a historically and culturally open, layered, and deterritorializing context.
6. Irby, "Introduction,", 18.
7. Deleuze, *The Fold*, 62–3.
8. The director chose to shoot in this location, with its reference to the medieval story of St. Anthony, and attempted to revive the medieval mood of the region in the film.
9. Rodrigues mythologizes the false images of "the reserve" through the interview as much as he did with the film itself. In his interview for *Village Voice* with Ren Jender, the filmmaker states: "the types of birds we filmed were there when St. Anthony was alive in the thirteenth century." See Jender, "*The Ornithologist* Director João Pedro Rodrigues."
10. Deleuze discusses Caravaggio's paintings with respect to the Baroque power of the colors covering the figures, which is reminiscent of the throat-slit scene towards the end of *The Ornithologist*. "Tintoretto and Caravaggio use a dark, red-brown background on which they place the thickest shadows, and paint directly by shading toward the shadows. The painting is transformed. Things jump out of the background, colors spring from the common base that attests to their obscure nature, figures are defined by their covering more than their contour." (Deleuze, *The Fold: Leibniz and the Baroque*, 31–2.)
11. Lim, "António Reis and Margarida Cordeiro," 101.
12. Daney and Oudart, "*Trás-os-Montes*: An Interview with António Reis."
13. In this sense, Reis and Cordeiro even rejected the notion of "ethnography" because it implies the pre-objectification of the subject to be filmed.
14. Daney, "In the midst of the end of the world" ("Au milieu du bout du monde").
15. Borges, *The Book of Sand* and *Shakespeare's Memory*, 3–11.
16. Borges, "The Simurgh and the Eagle," 294–7.
17. Heron, "A Voyage in Space and Time."
18. Deleuze, *The Fold*, 22.
19. Thain, "A Bird's-Eye View of *Leviathan*," 46.
20. Deleuze, *The Fold*, 20.
21. Sutton, *Photography, Cinema, Memory*, 108.
22. Thain, "A Bird's-Eye View of *Leviathan*," 41–8.
23. The author's conversation with the director over Skype on 8 May 2019.
24. Thain, "A Bird's-Eye View of *Leviathan*," 42.
25. Thain, "A Bird's-Eye View of *Leviathan*," 43–4.

26. Lucien Castaing-Taylor, "Iconophobia," 64–88.
27. Castaing-Taylor, "Iconophobia," 87.
28. Ibid., 86.
29. Ibid., 75.
30. Ibid., 76.

CHAPTER 7

1. Cutler, "He and 'I'," 8.
2. Miñano and Núñez, "João Pedro Rodrigues y la Desinhibición del Gesto Cinematográfico," 123.
3. Hoeij, *The Last Time I Saw Macao.*"
4. Weaver, "Ghosts of Macau," 78–86; Elsaesser, "World Cinema: Realism, Evidence, Presence," 3–19.
5. Haaf, "Exploring the Neither," 461–70.
6. Halberstam, *The Queer Art of Failure*, 96–8, 120–1.
7. Rabinowitz, *Black & White & Noir*, 18 and passim.
8. Ibid.
9. Fay and Nieland, *Film Noir*, 105 and passim.
10. This is one of the recurring arguments in the classic collection edited by E. Ann Kaplan, *Women in Film Noir*. See, for example, Pam Cook, "Duplicity in *Mildred Pierce*," 79, 81.
11. Hybridity and duplicity are dominant tropes in the literature on Macao. Some good overviews of Portuguese–Chinese interaction in Macao are: Hao, *Macau: History and Society*, 103–17; Simas, "Macau: A Plural Literature?," 55–67; Wong and Wei (eds), *Macao—Cultural Interactions, Literary Representations*; and Sadlier, *The Portuguese-Speaking Diaspora*, 93–116 and 217–21. Sadlier's volume contains a pithy commentary of *The Last Time I Saw Macao*, see pages 218–20.
12. There is a fictional license in this allusion: the Congress usually takes place in the spring, and da Mata's arrival is supposed to take place around Christmas, to judge from the ever-present Christmas and New Year decorations. The Eleventh People's Congress took place in 2008.
13. 2010 was the previous Year of the Tiger, which indicates that some of the film's scenes were shot in late December to mid-February. The 2010 Year of the Tiger started on 14 February. Candy claims in her farewell letter that the tiger is the animal that rules her destiny.
14. Rodrigues and Guerra da Mata, "Entretien et avant-premiére," interview; Miñano and Núñez, "João Pedro Rodrigues y la Desinhibición del Gesto Cinematográfico," 122–3.
15. Cutler, "He and 'I'," 10.
16. Pina-Cabral, "New-Age Warriors," 9–22; Simpson, "Macau Noir."
17. Tieben, "Urban Image Construction in Macau," 55.
18. Simpson, "Macau Noir".
19. Chu, "Spectacular Macau," 450–60.
20. Cited in Lam, "Promoting Hybridity: The Politics of the New Macau Identity," 699.
21. Chu, "Spectacular Macau," 441–2.
22. Pons, *Macao*, 109–20.
23. Sheng and Gu, "Economic Growth and Development in Macau (1999–2016)," 74–5.
24. Simpson, "Macau Noir."
25. Rodrigues himself has pointed out the connection. See Miñano and Núñez, "João Pedro Rodrigues y la Desinhibición del Gesto Cinematográfico," 115.

26. Benjamin, "On Some Motifs in Baudelaire," 198.
27. Benjamin, "On Some Motifs in Baudelaire," 179.
28. Cutler, "He and 'I'"; Quandt, "The Dragon Has Spoken"; Haaf, "Exploring the Neither," 465.

CHAPTER 8

1. Baudrillard, "Cool Memories II, 1987–1990," 67. Jean Baudrillard, a key figure in French postmodernism, owned an apartment in the historic district of Alfama in Lisbon. Portugal emerged as one of his favourite destinations. "'He liked Portugal very much and knew Lisbon very well', has said [philosopher José] Gil . . ." (Gomes, "Jean Baudrillard, o filósofo diferente."

2. For the purposes of this chapter, their body of work is understood as the set of films on which they have collaborated, whether by directing together or by assuming other specific artistic roles, in particular films that are directed by only one of them.

3. This chapter derives from several conversations with Rodrigues and Guerra da Mata that took place in Lisbon between May and October 2019.

4. Gaudin, L'espace cinématographique: esthétique et dramaturgie, 5.

5. Barber, Projected Cities, 13.

6. Barber, Projected Cities, 31.

7. Mennel, Cities & Cinema, 32.

8. Guerin, A Culture of Light, 155.

9. Mennel, Cities & Cinema, 37.

10. Barber, Projected Cities, 32–3.

11. Barber, Projected Cities, 55–6.

12. Ramos, Dicionário do Cinema Português 1895–1961, 134. When a translator is not mentioned in the References, the translation is our own.

13. Matos-Cruz, Panorama do Cinema Português, 50.

14. Costa, Stories of the Cinema, 45.

15. Costa, Stories of the Cinema, 70.

16. Areal, Cinema Português, 373.

17. Soromenho, "A geração Vává," 34.

18. Paulo Rocha in Sales, Em Busca de Um Novo Cinema Português, 194.

19. Areal, Cinema Português, 392.

20. Nunes, "Portugal: sociedade dualista em evolução," 407.

21. Nunes, "Portugal: sociedade dualista em evolução," 407. Paulo Cunha expands on Nunes's essay to frame the aesthetic transformations of Portuguese cinema after 1960. (Cunha, "Um buraco chamado Portugal," 185.)

22. Rocha, Os Verdes Anos.

23. Ibid.

24. José de Almada Negreiros (1893–1970) was a pioneering and charismatic figure of Portuguese Modernism. He produced an extensive oeuvre of paintings, drawings, ballets, poetry and prose, essays, and theoretical and critical reflection that conferred on him, according to Ana Filipa Candeias, "a degree of recognition that remains unique amongst the artists of his era" (Candeias, "José de Almada Negreiros," 15).

25. Menez (1926–95) was a self-taught artist who collaborated in several modern architectural projects. "The uniqueness of her painting is generally recognized by the way in which she worked on space and the quality of the light effects" (Mendes, "Menez," 166).

26. In addition to painting, drawing, engraving, and tapestry, Querubim Lapa (1925–2016) was one of the most important Portuguese ceramicists and "one of the artists who best understood the principles of the integration of the arts in architecture." Ferrão, *Querubim Lapa*, 5.

27. Although this was their first autonomous collaborative work, their joint experiences had started with Joaquim Sapinho's *Corte de Cabelo* (*Haircut*, 1995), where the duo were responsible for the costume design.

28. The music theorist, composer, engineer, and architect Iánnis Xenákis was of Greek origin. He collaborated with Le Corbusier on the projects *Sainte Marie de La Tourette* and *Philips Pavilion* at Expo 58 (Brussels). He is considered to be one of the most influential composers of the twentieth century. In his work, Xenákis explores a spatial conception of musical composition.

29. The atmosphere and figures of the Príncipe Real neighborhood inspired Rodrigues and Guerra da Mata's work in *To Die Like a Man*.

30. As in Édouard Manet's painting *Olympia* (1863), the cat reflects the reaction of those who stare at him.

31. Teixeira and Valla, *O Urbanismo Português*, 90.

32. Oliveira, "Bairro Alto."

33. Soromenho, "Quando a noite explodiu na cidade."

34. Ibid.

35. Seabra, "E no início houve o Manuel Reis."

36. Both film theaters were run by the producer and distributor Paulo Branco and they specialized in screening *cinéma d'auteur*.

37. Cunha, "O Novo Cinema Português," 208.

38. Cunha, "António Reis e Margarida Cordeiro," 96.

39. Margarida Cordeiro, quoted in an interview by Anabela Moutinho, in Moutinho and Lobo (eds), *António Reis e Margarida Cordeiro*, 7, 25.

40. Costa, *Stories of the Cinema*, 165.

41. Monteiro, "The Burden of a Nation," 26–7.

42. Rosmaninho, "Montagem e Cidade," 317, 323.

43. According to Jacques Lemière, "from the end of the '70s and especially in the '80s, a particularly Portuguese mode is established on the international scene," which obeys three criteria: "(1) the formal invention and inscription of cinema on a new stage of cinematographic modernity; (2) the affirmation of the filmmaker's freedom and the constant search for the means of that freedom against all norms of the industry; (3) the primacy of reflection on national issues." Lemiére, "Um centro na margem," 736. In addition to the directors Manoel de Oliveira, António Reis and Margarida Cordeiro, Paulo Rocha, João Botelho, João César Monteiro, José Álvaro Morais, Alberto Seixas Santos, Fernando Lopes, Jorge Silva Melo, and João Mário Grilo, he adds Teresa Villaverde, Pedro Costa and João Pedro Rodrigues with regard to the 1990s.

44. Mozos, *Lisboa no Cinema*.

45. Cipriano, "O mistério das origens."

46. Rodrigues, *Le jardin des fauves*, 125.

47. Delmer Daves used the same device in *Dark Passage* (1947) to portray the first impressions of a fugitive (Humphrey Bogart) after his escape from the prison.

48. Sarris, *The Films of Josef von Sternberg*, 8, 52.

49. But also other films by Sternberg such as *The Shanghai Gesture* (1941) or *Anatahan* (1953).

50. Schweinitz, *Film and Stereotype*, 11.

51. Sarris, *The Films of Josef von Sternberg*, 53.

52. Rodrigues and Guerra da Mata, "Entretien et avant-premiére," 3.

53. The 25 April 1974 revolution symbolically used carnations in the barrels of guns, and brought an end to Salazar's authoritarian regime.
54. Bomber jackets were originally designed as military jackets for airmen during World War II. They were adopted in the late 1960s by British skinheads, as they called themselves. Subsequently, the "mod" subculture began to divide as the so-called hard mods emerged from the poorer working classes, who were too cash-strapped to buy more sophisticated apparel. This trend arose in poor immigrant neighborhoods, where the fusion of black and white cultures gave rise to musical movements such as ska. Hard mods worked in factories or offices, where long hair was not permitted and workwear was given preference, for example jeans, work boots such as Monkey Boots or Dr. Martens, and reused military apparel. These early skinheads cultivated multicultural experiences. In the 1970s, as the skinhead groups split and began to lean towards the racist far-right, the bomber jacket started to be used by the punk movement and revival rockers.
55. Campany, *Photography and Cinema*, 55.
56. Even in *The Ornithologist* the depiction of the natural world is imbued with memories of the city, which is slowly abandoned by the protagonist before his return to his urban condition, when he embraces a path of transfiguration that is inspired in the mythology of St. Anthony.
57. Rodrigues and Guerra da Mata, "Entretien et avant-premiére," 8.

CHAPTER 9

1. Guerra da Mata's film debut as a costume designer was in *Corte de Cabelo* (*Haircut*, Joaquim Sapinho, 1995), in collaboration with João Pedro Rodrigues.
2. In 2000, Guerra da Mata took the roles of set and costume designer, and make-up artist, in *Phantom*, João Pedro Rodrigues's first feature film.
3. In 2017, as part of a collaborative effort between myself and Nívea Faria de Souza, from the Universidade Estatal do Rio de Janeiro (State University of Rio de Janeiro), a series of interviews were conducted with several Portuguese film costume design professionals. According to interviewees, the change that took place in Portuguese film credit terminology from "décor" to "art direction" was first suggested by Guerra da Mata. The conclusions resulting from this set of interviews will be published in a forthcoming article.
4. Hamburger, *Arte em Cena*, 52.
5. Guerra da Mata has a command of technical language and a natural theoretical approach to art direction that derives, in part, from his practice of granting interviews about his work.
6. Caterina Cucinotta (2018), interview with João Rui Guerra da Mata.
7. Ibid.
8. Ibid.
9. Ibid.
10. Barreira. "A Direcção de Arte," 226.
11. Ibid.
12. Ibid., 224.
13. It is obvious that, in smaller productions, the art director also takes the role of production designer.
14. Caterina Cucinotta (2018), interview with João Rui Guerra da Mata.
15. Ibid.
16. Barreira, "A Direcção de Arte," 237.

17. Tomasino, *Il Costume Cinematográfico*, 38.
18. Caterina Cucinotta (2018), interview with João Rui Guerra da Mata.
19. Tomasino, *Il Costume Cinematográfico*, 36.
20. Caterina Cucinotta (2018), interview with João Rui Guerra da Mata.
21. Câmara, "João Guerra da Mata. Põe a Mão no Fogo."
22. Gambarato "Methodology for Film Analysis," 105–15.
23. Kracauer, *Theory of Film*, 60.
24. Salles, *Gesto Inacabado*, 61–71.
25. Caterina Cucinotta (2018), interview with João Rui Guerra da Mata.
26. Rothenberg and Sobel, "A Creative Process in the Art of Costume Design," 27.
27. Among others, I would like to mention two papers that I have presented on the theme of the creative process in art direction: "*Mysteries of Lisbon*: Literature Materialization in Images, Bodies and Atmosphere" (presented at the conference *From Text to Screen and Back to Text. Film and Literature, the Portuguese Context*, in 2017), and "Materialidades e Oficios no Cinema Português. Estilistas, Figurinistas e Diretores de Arte ao Longo da História" (which addresses the topic of Rosário Moreira's costume design in Flora Gomes' film *Nha Fala* (2002) and was presented at the *Annual Congress of AIM* in 2019).
28. Moutinho and Lobo (eds), *António Reis e Margarida Cordeiro*, 15.
29. The costume designer Patrícia Dória was also interviewed in 2017. She is an important figure in João Pedro Rodrigues's films because of her creative role in the process of costume design.
30. Caterina Cucinotta (2018), interview with João Rui Guerra da Mata.
31. Ibid.
32. Cucinotta, "Origens Possíveis," 116.
33. Eisenstein, *Selected Works. Vol. II*, 448.

CHAPTER 10

1. The Reservatório da Patriarcal de Lisboa is located underground, beneath the Jardim do Príncipe Real, a public garden in a sophisticated and cosmopolitan neighbourhood of the city, close to the Tagus River. In Príncipe Real, nineteenth-century mansions stand alongside small, picturesque apartment blocks and houses, with the vast majority currently being used as tourist accommodation and commercial establishments. Príncipe Real is adjacent to the Bairro Alto, a center for nightlife in the city. This historic area is one of the few that survived the earthquake of 1755 that partially destroyed Lisbon.
2. Miñano and Núñez, "João Pedro Rodrigues y la desinhibición del gesto cinematográfico," 107–8.
3. *The King's Body* was commissioned by Guimarães for the European Capital of Culture. This initiative that was launched by the European Economic Community in 1985 with the objective of promoting the diversity of European cultures and celebrating their different characteristics, increasing citizens' sense of belonging to a common European cultural space, and contributing to the development of European cities. To date, Portugal has hosted this event three times: Lisbon in 1994, Oporto in 2001, and Guimarães in 2012.
4. Guimarães is a historic city located in the north of Portugal. It has its origins in the tenth century and is considered the "cradle of the nation" because it was there that the Battle of São Mamede took place in 1128, in which Afonso Henriques liberated the country from a Galician attempt to conquer it.
5. Lisboa, "Doc's Kingdom 2018–2019."

6. BoCa, "National Identity (Príncipe Real)."

7. Ibid.

8. By 2013, *Phantom* had entered the official Venice Film Festival competition, and it had won the prize for Best Film at the Entrevues Belfort Cinema Festival in France, and at NewFest: the New York LGBT Film Festival. By the same date, *Odete* (*Two Drifters*) had been selected for the Directors' Fortnight, which runs in parallel to the Cannes Film Festival, and *To Die Like a Man* had been part of the official selection for the Cannes Film Festival in the Un Certain Regard section, for the Toronto International Film Festival, and for the New York Film Festival, and it had also been awarded the Cinema of the Future Award at the Buenos Aires International Festival of Independent Cinema (BAFICI) in the same year. *A Última Vez Que Vi Macau* (*The Last Time I Saw Macao*, Rodrigues and Guerra da Mata, 2012,) won the Prize of the City of Torino at the Torino Film Festival, having also been nominated for the Golden Leopard. It also received a Special Mention at the Locarno Film Festival and had been part of the official selection of both the Toronto International Film Festival and the New York Film Festival.

9. Liz, "Introduction: Framing the Global Appeal of Contemporary Portuguese Cinema," 2–8.

10. Jorge, *ReFocus: The Films of Pedro Costa*.

11. Nisa, "Do Filme à Exposição: As Instalações Vídeo de Pedro Costa," 301.

12. Marmeleira, "Nas salas escuras de Pedro Costa com Chantal Akerman, filmes e vídeos."

13. Rodrigues in an interview with Filipa Rosário (2019).

14. Ibid.

15. The collective exhibition also showed pieces by the sculptor Mário Lopes, as well as photographs of projected works by the contemporary architects João Luís Carrilho da Graça, Eduardo Souto de Moura, Manuel Aires Mateus, Nuno Brandão Costa, Inês Vieira da Silva and Miguel Vieira, Ricardo Bak Gordon, Ricardo Carvalho and Joana Vihen, and João Ventura Trindade.

16. The curators of the exhibition were José Drummond, Luís Alegre, and Nuno Figueiredo. In total, works by twenty-eight artists were shown: Alice Kok, Ana Pérez-Quiroga, António Julio Duarte, Bianca Lei, Carlos Lobo, Chen Shaoxiong, Cui Xiuwen, Fortes Pakeong Sequeira, James Chu, João Pedro Rodrigues & João Rui Guerra da Mata, José Drummond, José Maçãs de Carvalho, Liao Chi-Yu, Luís Alegre, Maria Condado, Miguel Palma, Paulo Mendes, Pedro Loureiro, Peng Yun, Rui Calçada Bastos, Song Dong, Tereza Carneiro, Tiago Baptista, Wang Qingsong, Xing Danwen, Yin Xiuzhen, and Zhang Huan.

17. Lawson, "João Pedro Rodrigues & João Rui Guerra da Mata."

18. Ibid.

19. Bértolo, "'Um lugar indeciso'," 59–60.

20. Solar—Galeria de Arte Cinemática (Gallery of Cinematic Art) specializes in cinematic art, and exhibits experimental audiovisual media, cinema, and video. The gallery was created by the cinema festival, Curtas Vila do Conde (Vila do Conde Shorts), which since 1993 has promoted, celebrated, and awarded prizes to Portuguese and international short films. It has become one of the most highly regarded festivals in Portugal, and the programming at the Solar Gallery is closely linked to that of the festival. Indeed, Rodrigues is from the so-called Portuguese "short films generation," which is composed of directors who followed this path in their cinematic practice in the 1990s, producing numerous short films.

21. Guerra da Mata and Rodrigues, *Do Rio das Pérolas ao Ave*.

22. The space in which the installation was shown in the Solar Gallery is located on the lowest floor of the building, in a dark, damp room, in its catacombs, effectively. On the stairs leading down to the room, visitors could hear the Chinese national anthem being

played. A Chinese Revolution light fitting illuminated the corridor with a red light, and hanging on the wall at the entrance to the room was the original fax that communicated to the directors the exclusion of their film from the collective exhibition. The fax was displayed in a golden frame, acquired from a Chinese shop selling cheap goods (such shops are common in Portugal). Also displayed, but not framed, were the Portuguese and English translations of the fax. Inside the dark room, the still image that was displayed in the Beijing World Art Museum was projected: the female fish seller who confronts the camera.

23. The angle of vision of the spectators of this installation is the same as that of the camera, and thus prolongs it. The scale of the projection invokes *City Square* (Piazza, 1948), a sculpture by Alberto Giacometti, in which five copper figures—four men and a woman— are placed on a copper flagstone (21 × 62.5 × 42.8 cm). By means of the miniaturization of the figures in proportion to the surrounding space, the vastness of the empty square and the anonymity of the figures are revealed, as Elisabeth C. Childs states. João Pedro Rodrigues works in the same way in this installation in order to engage with similar topics, which are present throughout his work.

24. Dressler, "Specters of Douglas," 10.
25. Kabakov, Tupitsyn, and Tupitsyn, "About Installation," 62.
26. Rees, "Expanded Cinema and Narrative," 12.
27. Baron, *The Archive Effect*, 19.

CHAPTER II

1. Bataille, "Le gros orteil," 75–82.
2. Krauss, "Corpus Delicti," 58.
3. Rolnik, "The Geopolitics of Pimping," and "The Body's Contagious Memory: Lygia Clark's Return to the Museum."
4. Barthes, *Camera Lucida*.
5. Ibid.
6. I would like to express my deepest thanks to João Pedro Rodrigues and João Rui Guerra da Mata for their generosity and excellent revision of earlier drafts of this text.

References

Adachi, Masao, *Ryakushô: Renzoku Shasatsuma (A.K.A. Serial Killer)*, film. Japan, 1969.
Agamben, Giorgio, *L'uso dei Corpi. Homo sacer IV, 2* (Vicenza: Neri Pozza, 2014).
—— *The Omnibus Homo Sacer: The Use of Bodies*, trans. Adam Kotsko (Stanford: Stanford University Press, 2017).
Aguilar, Carlos, "'I Am All My Characters': Director João Pedro Rodrigues on the Transformative Delights of *The Ornithologist*," *MovieMaker*, 30 June 2017, <https://www.moviemaker.com/archives/interviews/i-am-all-my-characters-joao-pedro-rodrigues-the-ornithologist/> (last accessed 22 July 2019).
Akerman, Chantal, *Là-bas (Down There)*, film. Belgium and France: Audiovisuel Multimedia International Production (AMIP), Paradise Films, Le Fresnoy, Studio National des Arts Contemporains.
—— *News from Home*, film. Belgium and France: Institut National de l'Audiovisuel (INA), Paradise Films, Unité Trois, Zweites Deutsches Fernsehen (ZDF), 1976.
Almodóvar, Pedro, *La Piel que Habito (The Skin I Live In)*, film. Paris: Pathé Films, 2011.
Álvarez López, Cristina and Adrian Martin, "Drifting" (video essay), Mubi Notebook, 2016, <https://mubi.com/notebook/posts/video-essay-drifting> (last accessed 18 August 2020).
Areal, Leonor, *Cinema Português: Um País Imaginado. Vol. I—Antes de 1974* (Lisbon: Edições 70, 2011).
Armone, Flavio, "I luoghi oscuri dell'anima," *Da Sodoma a Hollywood* (23rd Torino GLBT Film Festival, 2008), 248–9.
Baptista, Tiago, "Nationally Correct: The Invention of Portuguese Cinema," *P: Portuguese Cultural Studies*, Vol. 3, Issue 1 (2010): 12–13.
—— *A Invenção do Cinema Português* (Lisbon: Tinta-da-china, 2008).
Barber, Stephen, *Projected Cities: Cinema and Urban Space* (London: Reaktion Books, 2002).
Baron, Jaimie, *The Archive Effect: Found Footage and the Audiovisual Experience of History* (Oxford and New York: Routledge, 2014).
Barreira, Hugo, "A Direcção de Arte," in Pedro Alves and Francisco García (eds), *Ofícios del Cine: Manual de Prácticas Cinematográficas* (Madrid: CITCEM/Icono14, 2017), 203–45.
Barros, José Leitão de, *Maria Papoila*, film. Lisbon: Lusomundo Filmes, 1937.
—— *Lisboa, Crónica Anedótica (Lisbon, Anecdotal Chronicle)*, film, produced by Salm Levy Jr. Lisbon: Cinemateca/Museu do Cinema, 1930.

Barthes, Roland. *Camera Lucida: Reflections on Photography*, trans. Richard Howard (New York: Hill and Wang, 1984).

Baudrillard, Jean, "Cool Memories II, 1987–1990," trans. Chris Turner, in David Campany (ed.), *The Cinematic* (*Whitechapel: Documents of Contemporary Art*) (Cambridge, MA: MIT Press, 2007), 67.

Bauer, Yevgeni. *Gryozy* (*Daydreams*), film. Moscow: Khanzhonkov Company, 1915. Available at <https://www.youtube.com/watch?v=XXvP9VtQsnk> (last accessed 11 November 2020).

Bataille, Georges, "Le gros orteil," in Bernard Noël (ed.), *Documents* (Paris: Mercure de France and Éditions Gallimard, [1929] 1968), 75–82.

Benjamin, Walter, "On Some Motifs in Baudelaire," *Illuminations: Essays and Reflections*, trans. Harry Zohn (New York: Schocken, 1968), 155–200.

Bértolo, José, *Espectros do Cinema: Manoel de Oliveira e João Pedro Rodrigues* (Lisbon: Documenta, 2020).

—— "Galeria de Retratos: Figuras da Espectralidade em Manoel de Oliveira e João Pedro Rodrigues," PhD diss., University of Lisbon (2019).

—— *Sobreimpressões: Leituras de Filmes* (Lisbon: Documenta, 2019).

—— "'Um lugar indeciso': geografias do imaginário no ciclo asiático de João Pedro Rodrigues e João Rui Guerra da Mata," in Catarina Nunes Almeida and Marta Pacheco Pinto (eds), *O Oriente em Tradução: Línguas, Literaturas e Culturas Asiáticas no Espaço Luso* (V. N. Famalicão: Húmus, 2017), 51–67.

Bhabha, Homi K., *The Location of Culture* (London: Routledge, 2004).

BoCA (Biennial of Contemporary Arts), "Identidade Nacional (Príncipe Real): João Pedro Rodrigues & João Rui Guerra da Mata. 15 March 2019–07 April 2019." Available at <http://bocabienal.org/en/evento/national-identity/> (last accessed 19 May 2019).

Boileau, Pierre and Thomas Narcejac, *D'entre les morts* (*The Living and the Dead*) (Paris: Éditions DeNoël, 1954).

Borges, Jorge Luis, *The Book of Sand* and *Shakespeare's Memory*, trans. Andrew Hurley (London: Penguin Books, 2007).

—— "The Simurgh and the Eagle," *Selected Non-fictions*, Eliot Weinberger (ed.), trans. Esther Allen, Suzanne Jill Levine, and Eliot Weinberger (New York: Viking, 1999).

Bourcier, Marie-Hélene, *Queer Zones. Politique des identités sexuelles et des savoirs* (Paris: Éditions Amsterdam, 2006).

Bourgois, Guillaume, *Angélica!* (Paris: De l'incidence éditeur, 2013).

Brenez, Nicole, *De la figure en général et du corps en particulier: L'invention figurative au cinéma* (Louvain-la-Neuve: De Boeck Supérieur, 1998).

Câmara, Vasco, "João Rui Guerra da Mata. Põe a Mão no Fogo," *Ípsilon*, 6 July 2012, <https://www.publico.pt/2012/07/06/jornal/joao-rui-guerra-da-mata-poe-a-mao-no-fogo-24820562> (last accessed 25 July 2019).

Campany, David, *Photography and Cinema* (London: Reaktion Books, 2008).

Candeias, Ana Filipa, "José de Almada Negreiros," in Leonor Nazaré (ed.), *Centro de Arte Moderna José de Azeredo Perdigão—Guide to the Collection* (Lisbon: Fundação Calouste Gulbenkian, 2004), 14–17.

Canevacci, Massimo, "Hybridentities," in Gerfried Stocker and Christine Schöpf (eds) *Hybrid—Living in Paradox: Catalog Ars Electronica 2005. Festival für Kunst, Technologie und Gesellschaft* (Ostfildern-Ruit: Hatje Cantz Verlag, 2005), 64–9.

Careri, Giovanni, "Heureux ceux qui, sans avoir vu, ont cru! L'Incrédulité de Saint Thomas du Caravage," *Les Carnets du Bal, Que peut une image?* No. 4 (2014): 66–87.

Cascais, António Fernando, "Metamorfoses de 'O Fantasma' de João Pedro Rodrigues," in C. António and F. João (eds), *Cinema e Cultura Queer/Queer Film and Culture* (Lisbon: Associação Cultural Janela Indiscreta, 2014), 162–77.

Castaing-Taylor, Lucien, "Iconophobia," *Transition*, No. 69 (1996): 64–88.

Castaing-Taylor, Lucien and Ilisa Barbash, *Sweetgrass*, film. London: Dogwoof, 2011.

Castaing-Taylor, Lucien and Véréna Paravel, *Leviathan*, film. New York and elsewhere: Arrête ton Cinéma, Cinereach, Creative Capital et al, 2012.

Chessel, Luc, "Raccord sexuel: Les noms de João Pedro Rodrigues," in João Pedro Rodrigues, *Le jardin des fauves: conversations avec Antoine Barraud* (Paris: Post-éditions, 2016), 203–23.

Cheval, Olivier, "La Vierge des travelos," interview with João Pedro Rodrigues, *Débordements*, 30 November 2016, <http://www.debordements.fr/spip.php?article550> (last accessed 19 May 2019).

Childs, Elisabeth C., *Alberto Giacometti. Piazza*. Guggenheim.org, <https://www.guggenheim.org/artwork/1426> (last accessed 12 December 2019).

Chrétien, Jean-Louis, *L'Appel et la Réponse* (Paris: Les Éditions de Minuit, 1992).

Chu, Cecilia L., "Spectacular Macau: Visioning Futures for a World-Heritage City," *Geoforum*, Vol. 65 (2015): 450–60.

Cipriano, Miguel, "O mistério das origens ou o cinema português no tempo da pós-ruralidade," (Lisbon: Escola Superior de Teatro e Cinema/CIAC, 2011). Available at <https://repositorio.ipl.pt/bitstream/10400.21/257/1/Cipriano.pdf> (last accessed 9 July 2021).

Clarke, Bruce, *Allegories of Writing. The Subject of Metamorphosis* (Albany: State University of New York Press, 1995).

Coppola, Francis Ford, *The Godfather III*, film. Los Angeles: Paramount, 1990.

Cook, Pam, "Duplicity in Mildred Pierce," in E. Ann Kaplan (ed.), *Women in Film Noir* (London: British Film Institute, 1978), 68–82.

Costa, João Bénard da, *Stories of the cinema* (Lisbon: Europália, Imprensa Nacional/Casa da Moeda, 1991).

Costa, Pedro, "Company," exhibition at Serralves Museum of Contemporary Art, 19 October 2018 to 29 January 2019.

Cucinotta, Caterina, "Origens possíveis e consequentes desenvolvimentos contemporâneos da longa-metragem *O Fantasma*, de João Pedro Rodrigues," in Ana Catarina Pereira and T. C. Cunha (eds), *Geração Invisível: Os novos cineastas portugueses* (Covilhã: LabCom Books, 2013), 105–28.

Cunha, Paulo, "O Novo Cinema Português. Políticas Públicas e Modos de Produção (1949–1980)," (PhD diss., Universidade de Coimbra 2014).

——— "António Reis e Margarida Cordeiro: Cinema do Vivido e do Pensado," in Câmara Municipal de Lisboa, Videoteca and Animação Cultural Apordoc (ed.), *Panorama 2010, Catálogo da 4º Mostra de Documentário Português* (Lisbon: Videoteca/CML, 2010), 96–9.

——— "Um buraco chamado Portugal: a «europeização» da geração do novo cinema português (1962–74)," *Revista Estudos do Século XX*, no. 10 (2010): 185–203. Available at: <http://dx.doi.org/10.14195/1647-8622_10_11> (last accessed 9 August 2020).

Curopos, Fernando, *Queer(s) périphériques: Représentations de l'homosexualité au Portugal (1974–2014)* (Paris: L'Harmattan, 2016).

Cutler, Aaron, "He and 'I': João Pedro Rodrigues and João Rui Guerra da Mata on *The Last Time I Saw Macao*," *Cinema-Scope*, No. 53 (2012): 6–11.

Dallas, Paul, "Lisbon: João Pedro Rodrigues on Birds, Maps, Saints, and Kings," *Extra Extra* 4, <https://www.extraextramagazine.com/talk/joao-pedro-rodrigues-on-birds-maps-saints-and-kings/> (last accessed 12 May 2019).

Daney, Serge, "In the midst of the end of the world" ("Au milieu du bout du monde"), *Libération*, June 1983. Trans. Stoffel Debuysere, available at <https://www.diagonalthoughts.com/?p=1921> (last accessed 7 July 2021).

Daney, Serge and Oudart, Jean-Pierre, "*Trás-os-Montes*: An Interview with António Reis," trans. Kelsey Brain, Ted Fendt, and Bill Krohn. *Cahiers du Cinéma*, No. 276 (May 1977):

337–41, <https://kinoslang.blogspot.com/2012/07/antonio-reis-and-margarida-cordeiro. html> (last accessed 15 June 2019).

Daves, Delmer, *Dark Passage*, film. Los Angeles: Warner Bros., 1947.

Del Don, Muriel, "João Pedro Rodrigues—Director: 'Para mí, es imposible filmar a los actores sin desearlos'," *Cineuropa 10*, 10 August 2016, <https://cineuropa.org/es/ interview/314091/> (last accessed 12 May 2019).

Deleuze, Gilles, *Francis Bacon: The Logic of Sensation* (London: Continuum, 2003).

—— *The Fold: Leibniz and the Baroque*, trans. Tom Conley (Minneapolis: University of Minnesota Press, 1993).

Deleuze, Giles and Guattari, Félix, *Mille Plateaux* (Paris: Les Éditions de Minuit, 1980).

—— *What is Philosophy?*, trans. Hugh Tomlinson and Graham Burchell (New York: Columbia University Press, 1994).

—— *Kafka: Toward a Minor Literature*, trans. Dana Polan (Minneapolis: University of Minnesota Press, 2003).

—— *Anti-Oedipus: Capitalism and Schizophrenia*, trans. Robert Hurley, Mark Seem and Helen R. Lane (London and New York: Continuum, 2004).

—— *A Thousand Plateaus*, trans. Brian Massumi (London and New York: Continuum, 2004).

Derrida, Jacques, *Jean-Luc Nancy, Le Toucher* (Paris: Galilée, 2000).

Didi-Huberman, Georges, *L'image Ouverte, Motifs de l'incarnation dans les Arts Visuels* (Paris: Gallimard, 2007).

Dressler, Iris, "Specters of Douglas," in Hans D. Christ and Iris Dressler (eds), *Stan Douglas: Past Imperfect. Works 1986–2007* (Ostfildern: Hatje Cantz, 2008), 8–24.

Edwards, Blake, *Switch*, film. New York: HBO Studios, 1991.

—— *Breakfast at Tiffany's*, film. Los Angeles: Paramount, 1961.

Eisenstein, S. M., *Selected Works. Vol. II: Towards a Theory of Montage* (London: British Film Institute, 1991).

Elphick, Jeremy, "*O Ornitólogo*—An Interview with João Pedro Rodrigues," *4:3*, 11 August 2016, <https://fourthreefilm.com/2016/08/o-ornitologo-an-interview-with-joao-pedro-rodrigues/> (last accessed 20 July 2019).

Elsaesser, Thomas, "World Cinema: Realism, Evidence, Presence," in Lucia Nagib and Cecilia Mello (eds), *Realism and Audiovisual Media* (New York: Palgrave Macmillan, 2009), 3–19.

Falque, Emmanuel, *Dieu, la chair et l'autre* (Paris: Presses Universitaires de France, 2001).

Fay, Jennifer and Nieland, Justus, *Film Noir: Hard-Boiled Modernity and the Cultures of Globalization* (New York: Routledge, 2009).

Fassbinder, Rainer Werner, *Die bitteren Tränen der Petra von Kant* (*The Bitter Tears of Petra von Kant*), film. Frankfurt: Filmverlag der Autoren, Tango Film, 1972.

Ferrão, Rita Gomes, *Querubim Lapa: Primeira Obra Cerâmica 1954–1974* (Lisbon: Objectismo, 2015).

Ferreira, João, "The Politics of Desire in Portuguese Cinema," *Da Sodoma a Hollywood* (23rd Torino GLBT Film Festival, 2008), 243–4.

Fleming, Victor, *The Wizard of Oz*, film. Los Angeles: MGM, 1939.

Ford, John. *Mogambo*, film. Los Angeles: MGM, 1953.

Foucault, Michel, "Des espaces autres," in Daniel Defert and François Ewald (eds), *Dits et écrits*, Vol. IV—1980–8 (Paris: Éditions Gallimard, 1994), 752–62.

Franju, Georges, *Le Sang des Bêtes* (*Blood of the Beasts*), film. Paris, 1949.

Gambarato, Renira R, "Methodology for Film Analysis: The Role of Objects in Films," *Revista Fronteiras—Estudos Midiáticos*, Vol. 12, No. 2 (2010): 105–15.

Gaudin, Antonin, *L'espace cinématographique: esthétique et dramaturgie* (Paris: Armand Colin, 2014).

Gide, André, *Les nourritures terrestres* (Paris: Gallimard, 1927).

Gomes, Kathleen, "Jean Baudrillard, o filósofo diferente," *Público*, 8 March 2007, <https://www.publico.pt/2007/03/08/jornal/jean-baudrillard--o-filosofo-diferente-179239> (last accessed 20 July 2019).

Guadagnino, Luca, *Call Me by Your Name*, film. Milan, Paris, and São Paulo: Frenesy Film Company, La Cinéfacture, and RT Features, 2017.

Guerin, Frances, *A Culture of Light: Cinema and Technology in 1920s Germany* (Minneapolis: Minnesota University Press, 2005).

Guerra da Mata, João Rui, *O Que Arde Cura (As the Flames Rose)*, film. Lisbon: Blackmaria, 2012. Available at <https://vimeo.com/groups/642954/videos/398049418> (last accessed 18 August 2020).

Guerra da Mata, João Rui and João Pedro Rodrigues, *Do Rio das Pérolas ao Ave. From the Pearl River to the River Ave*, exhibition at Vila do Conde, 2016.

——— *Alvorada Vermelha (Red Dawn)*, film. Lisbon: Blackmaria, 2011.

Guerreiro, Fernando, *Cinema El Dorado—Cinema e Modernidade* (Lisbon: Colibri, 2015).

Guest, Haden, "The Road to Macao. The Floating Worlds of João Pedro Rodrigues and João Rui Guerra da Mata," Harvard Film Archive, <https://harvardfilmarchive.org/programs/the-road-to-macao-the-floating-worlds-of-joao-pedro-rodrigue> (last accessed 18 August 2020).

Gilbert, Lewis, *Ferry to Hong Kong*, film. London: Pinewood Productions, The Rank Organisation, 1959.

Guillen, Michael, "TO DIE LIKE A MAN—Interview with João Pedro Rodrigues & Alexander David," *Screen Anarchy*, 22 September 2009, <https://screenanarchy.com/2009/09/tiff09-to-die-like-a-man--interview-with-joao-pedro-rodrigues-alexander-david > (last accessed 20 July 2019).

Haaf, Rachel ten, "Exploring the Neither in João Pedro Rodrigues and João Rui Guerra da Mata's *A última vez que vi Macau*," *Hispania*, Vol. 100, No. 3 (September 2017): 461–70.

Halberstam, Judith, *The Queer Art of Failure* (Durham, NC: Duke University Press, 2011).

Hamburger, Vera, *Arte em Cena—A Direção de Arte no Cinema Brasileiro* (São Paulo: Edições SESC/Senac São Paulo, 2014).

Hamilton, Guy, *The Man with the Golden Gun*, film. London: Eon Productions, 1974.

Heidegger, Martin, "The Age of the World Picture," in *The Question Concerning Technology and Other Essays*, trans. William Lovitt (New York and London: Garland Publishing, 1977), 115–54.

Hernández Miñano, Pablo and Violeta Martín Núñez, "João Pedro Rodrigues y la desinhibición del gesto cinematográfico," *L'Atalante. Revista de Estudios Cinematográficos*, Vol. 28 (2019): 105–29.

Heron, Christopher, "A Voyage in Space and Time: João Pedro Rodrigues Interview (*The Ornithologist*)," *The Seventh Art*, 15 October 2016, <http://theseventhart.org/joao-pedro-rodrigues-interview-the-ornithologist/> (last accessed 20 July 2019).

Hitchcock, Alfred, *Vertigo*, film. Los Angeles: Alfred J. Hitchcock Productions, 1958.

Hoeij, Boyd van, "*The Last Time I Saw Macao*," *Variety*, 23 August 2012, <https://variety.com/2012/film/reviews/the-last-time-i-saw-macao-1117948105/> (last accessed 21 December 2020).

Huston, John, *The Maltese Falcon*, film. Los Angeles: Warner Bros., 1941.

Irby, James E., "Introduction," in Jorge Luis Borges, *Labyrinths*, ed. Donald A. Yates and James E. Irby (Ringwood: Penguin Australia, 1970), 15–23.

Jender, Ren, "*The Ornithologist* Director João Pedro Rodrigues: 'You Have to Choose the Moment'," *Village Voice*, 21 June 2017, <https://www.villagevoice.com/2017/06/21/the-ornithologist-director-joao-pedro-rodrigues-you-have-to-choose-the-moment/> (last accessed 20 July 2019).

Johnson, Randal, *Manoel de Oliveira* (Urbana and Chicago: University of Illinois Press, 2007).

Jorge, Nuno Barradas, *ReFocus: The Films of Pedro Costa. Producing and Consuming Contemporary Art Cinema* (Edinburgh: Edinburgh University Press, 2020).

Kabakov, Ilya, Margarita Tupitsyn, and Victor Tupitsyn, "About Installation," *Art Journal 58*, No. 4, Winter (1999): 62–73.

Kaplan, E. Ann (ed.), *Women in Film Noir* (London: British Film Institute, 1978).

Ki-duk, Kim, *Pietà*, film. South Korea: Good Film, Finecut, Kim Ki-Duk Film, 2012.

Ki-duk, Kim, *Shi gan* (*Time*), film. South Korea: Happinet/Kim Ki-duk Film, 2006.

Kracauer, Siegfried, *Theory of Film—The Redemption of Physical Reality* (New York: Oxford University Press, 1960).

Kramer, Gary M., *Independent Queer Cinema. Reviews and Interviews* (New York: The Haworth Press, 2006).

Krauss, Rosalind, "Corpus Delicti," in Rosalind Krauss and Jane Livingston (eds), *L'Amour Fou: Photography and Surrealism* (New York: Abbeville Press, 1985), 56–112.

Lam, Wai-man, "Promoting Hybridity: The Politics of the New Macau Identity," *The China Quarterly*, Vol. 203 (2010): 656–74.

Lawson, David Gregory, "João Pedro Rodrigues & João Rui Guerra da Mata," *Film Comment*, 17 June 2015, <https://www.filmcomment.com/blog/interview-joao-pedro-rodrigues-joao-rui-guerra-da-mata/> (last accessed 12 December 2019).

Lemière, Jacques, "Um centro na margem: o caso do cinema português," *Análise Social*, No. *XLI 180* (2006): 731–65.

Leutrat, Jean-Louis, *Vida de fantasmas: lo fantástico en el cine* (Valencia: Ediciones de La Mirada, 1999).

Lim, Dennis, "António Reis and Margarida Cordeiro," *Artforum*, Vol. 50, No. 10, Summer (2012). Available at <https://www.artforum.com/print/201206/antonio-reis-and-margarida-cordeiro-31085> (last accessed 18 August 2020).

Lisboa, Ricardo Vieira, "Doc's Kingdom 2018–2019: 'Ficar desconfortável, numa sala de cinema, é um privilégio!'," *À Pala de Walsh*, 5 August 2019, <http://www.apaladewalsh.com/2019/08/docs-kingdom-2018-2019-ficar-desconfortavel-numa-sala-de-cinema-e-um-privilegio/> (last accessed 12 December 2019).

Liz, Mariana, "Introduction: Framing the Global Appeal of Contemporary Portuguese Cinema," in Mariana Liz (ed.), *Portugal's Global Cinema: Industry, History and Culture* (London: I. B. Tauris, 2018), 1–14.

Lopes, Fernando, *Belarmino*, film. Lisbon: produced by António da Cunha Telles, 1964.

Malabou, Catherine, *El porvenir de Hegel: plasticidad, temporalidad, dialéctica* (Buenos Aires: Palinodia/La cebra, 2013).

—— *Ontología del accidente. Ensayo sobre la plasticidad destructiva* (Santiago de Chile: Pólvora Editorial, 2018).

Mankiewicz, Joseph L., *The Ghost and Mrs. Muir*, film. Los Angeles: 20th Century Fox, 1947.

Marin, Louis, *Détruire la Peinture* (Paris: Galilée, 1977).

Marker, Chris, *Sans Soleil* (*Sunless*), film. Paris: Argos Films, 1983.

—— *Le fond de l'air est rouge* (*A Grin Without a Cat*), film. Paris: Dovidis, Institut National de l'Audiovisuel (INA), Iskra, 1977.

Marmeleira, José, "Nas salas escuras de Pedro Costa com Chantal Akerman, filmes e vídeos," *Público*, 17 November 2012, <https://www.publico.pt/2012/11/17/jornal/nas-salas-escuras-de-pedro-costa-com-chantal-akerman-filmes-e-videos-25603227> (last accessed 15 December 2019).

Matos-Cruz, José de, *Panorama do Cinema Português* (Lisbon: Cinemateca Portuguesa/Museu do Cinema, 1980).

Maurois, André, "Preface," in Jorge Luis Borges, *Labyrinths*, ed. Donald A. Yates and James E. Irby (Ringwood: Penguin Australia, 1970), 18.

Mendes, Carla, "Menez," in Leonor Nazaré (ed.), *Centro de Arte Moderna José de Azeredo Perdigão—Guide to the Collection* (Lisbon: Fundação Calouste Gulbenkian, 2004), 166–7.

Mennel, Barbara, *Cities & Cinema* (London: Routledge, 2008).

Mercer, John, "The Love That Dare Not Speak Its Name: *O Fantasma* and Erotomania," in Darren Kerr and Donna Peberdy (eds), *Tainted Love: Screening Sexual Perversion* (London: I. B. Tauris, 2017), 32–46.

Miñano, Pablo Hernández and Violeta Martín Núñez, "João Pedro Rodrigues: The Naturalness of Desire," *L'Atalante. Revista de Estudios Cinematográficos*, No. 28 (2019): 105–28.

Morin, Edgar, *Le Cinéma ou l'Homme Imaginaire* (Paris: Minuit, 1956).

Monteiro, Paulo Filipe, "The Burden of a Nation," in Nuno Figueiredo and Dinis Guarda (eds), *Portugal: Um Retrato Cinematográfico* (Lisbon: Número—Arte e Cultura, 2004), 23–69.

Montgomery, Robert, *The Lady in the Lake*, film. Los Angeles: MGM, 1947.

Moutinho, Anabela and Lobo, Maria Graça (eds), *António Reis e Margarida Cordeiro: a poesia da terra* (Faro: Cineclube de Faro, 1997).

Mozos, Manuel, *Lisboa no Cinema, um Ponto de Vista* (*Lisbon in Cinema, a Point of View*), film. Lisbon: Rosa Filmes, 1994.

Ndalianis, Angela, *Neo-Baroque Aesthetics and Contemporary Entertainment* (Cambridge, MA: MIT Press, 2004).

Nisa, João, "Do Filme à Exposição: As Instalações Vídeo de Pedro Costa," in Ricardo Matos Cabo (ed.), *Cem Mil Cigarros* (Lisbon: Orfeu Negro & Midas Filmes, 2009), 301–13.

Nunes, Adérito Sedas, "Portugal: sociedade dualista em evolução," *Análise Social II*, No. 7–8 (1964): 407–62.

Oliveira, Catarina, "Bairro Alto," *Património Cultural*, June 2005. Available at: <http://www.patrimoniocultural.gov.pt/pt/patrimonio/patrimonio-imovel/pesquisa-do-patrimonio/classificado-ou-em-vias-de-classificacao/geral/view/71979> (last accessed 20 July 2019).

Oliveira, Manoel, *O Estranho Caso de Angélica* (*The Strange Case of Angélica*), film. Paris: Les Films de l'Après-Midi et al., 2010.

—— *Benilde ou a Virgem Mãe* (*Benilde or the Virgin Mother*), film. Lisbon: Centro Português de Cinema (CPC), Tobis Portuguesa, 1975.

—— *O Passado e o Presente* (*The Past and the Present*), film. Lisbon: Centro Português de Cinema (CPC), Tobis Portuguesa 1972.

—— *Douro, Faina Fluvial* (*Labor on the Douro River*), short film, produced by Manoel de Oliveira. Lisbon: 1931.

Pacinotti, Lia, "Spider Rose's Metamorphosis: A Consolatory Nihilism," in Carla Dente, George Ferzoco, Miriam Gill, and Marina Spunta (eds), *Proteus: The Language of Metamorphosis* (Aldershot: Ashgate, 2005), 71–9.

Parajanov, Sergei, *Tini zabutykh predkiv* (*Shadows of Forgotten Ancestors*), film. London: Artificial Eye, 2010.

Patanè, Vincenzo, *L'altra metà dell'amore: dieci anni di cinema omosessuale* (Rome: DeriveApprodi, 2005).

Père, Olivier, "Locarno 2012 Day 6: João Pedro Rodrigues," Olivier Père blog, 6 August 2012, <https://olivierpere.wordpress.com/2012/08/06/locarno-2012-day-6-joao-pedro-rodrigues-2/> (last accessed 18 August 2020).

Pessoa, Fernando, *Quadras ao Gosto Popular* (Lisbon: Ática, 1965).

Petzold, Christian, *Phoenix*, film. Berlin: Indigo, 2014.

Pina-Cabral, João, "New-Age Warriors: Negotiating the Handover on the Streets of Macao," *Journal of Romance Studies*, Vol. 5, No. 1 (2005): 9–22.

Pons, Philippe, *Macao*, trans. Sarah Adams (London: Reaktion, 2002).

Proust, Françoise, *L'histoire à contretemps* (Paris: Éditions du Cerf, 1994).

Proust, Marcel, *À la recherche du temps perdu* (Paris: Bernard Grasset and Gallimard, 1913–1927).

Pudovkin, Alexander, *Mat* (*The Mother*), film. Los Angeles: Image Entertainment, 1999.

Puff, Melanie, "Acting in the Interstices: Thoughts on an Ethic of Hybrid Identity," in Gerfried Stocker and Christine Schöpf (eds), *Hybrid—Living in Paradox: Catalog Ars Electronica 2005. Festival für Kunst, Technologie und Gesellschaft* (Ostfildern-Ruit: Hatje Cantz Verlag, 2005), 56–9.

Quandt, James, "The Dragon Has Spoken," *Cinema Guild Home Video* (2013), <http://cinemaguild.com/homevideo/ess_macao.htm> (last accessed 25 October 2019).

Rabinowitz, Paula, *Black & White & Noir: America's Pulp Modernism* (New York: Columbia University Press, 2002).

Ramos, Jorge Leitão, *Dicionário do Cinema Português 1895–1961* (Lisbon: Editorial Caminho, 2012).

Redner, Gregg, *Deleuze and Film Music: Building a Methodological Bridge Between Film Theory and Music* (Bristol and Chicago: Intellect, 2011).

Rees, A. L., "Expanded Cinema and Narrative: A Troubled History," in A. L. Rees, Duncan White, Stephen Ball, and David Curtis (eds), *Expanded Cinema: Art, Performance, Film* (London: Tate Publishing, 2011), 12–23.

Reis, António and Cordeiro, Margarida, *Ana*, film. Lisbon: Nacional Filmes/Studios Bilancourt/Tobis Portugusa/Fundação Calouste Gulbenkian, 1982.

—— *Trás-os-Montes*, film. Lisbon: CPC, 1976.

Reygadas, Carlos, *Batalla en el Cielo* (*Battle in Heaven*), film. Barcelona: Cameo Media, 2005.

Ribeiro, António Lopes, *A Revolução de Maio* (*May Revolution*), film. Lisbon: Secretariado da Propaganda Nacional (SPN), 1937).

Rimbaud, Jean Arthur, *Œuvres complètes* (Paris: La Pléiade, 2009).

Rocha, Paulo, *Mudar de Vida* (*Change of Life*), film. Lisbon: Produções Cunha Telles, 1966.

—— *Os Verdes Anos* (*The Green Years*), film. Lisbon: Produções Cunha Telles, 1963.

Rodrigues, João Pedro, *Nude Descending a Staircase, 2020*, film. Lisbon: Filmes Fantasma, 2020.

—— *Turdus merula Linnaeus, 1758*, film. Lisbon: Filmes Fantasma, 2020.

—— *Potemkin Steps*, film. Lisbon: Filmes Fantasma, 2019.

—— *Où En Êtes-Vous, João Pedro Rodrigues?* (*Where Do You Stand Now, João Pedro Rodrigues?*), film. Tourcoing: João Pedro Rodrigues, Filmes Fantasma, Le Fresnoy, 2017.

—— *Le jardin des fauves: conversations avec Antoine Barraud* (Paris: Post-éditions, 2016).

—— *O Ornitólogo* (*The Ornithologist*), film. Lisbon: Blackmaria, 2016.

—— *Allegoria della prudenza*, film. Venice: Veneza 70, 2013.

—— *Manhã de Santo António* (*Morning of Saint Anthony's Day*), film. Lisbon: Blackmaria, 2012.

—— *O Corpo de Afonso* (*The King's Body*), film. Lisbon: Blackmaria, 2012.

—— *Morrer Como um Homem* (*To Die Like a Man*), film. Lisbon: Rosa Filmes, 2009.

—— *Odete* (*Two Drifters*), film. Lisbon: Rosa Filmes, 2005.

—— *O Fantasma* (*The Phantom*), film. Lisbon: Rosa Filmes, 2000.

—— *Esta É a Minha Casa* (*This Is My House*), film. Lisbon: Rosa Filmes, 1997.

—— *Viagem à Expo* (*Journey to Expo*), film. Lisbon: Rosa Filmes, 1999.

—— *Parabéns!* (*Happy Birthday!*), film. Lisbon: Rosa Filmes, 1997.

—— *O Pastor* (*The Shepherd*), short film. Portugal, 1988.

Rodrigues, João Pedro and João Rui Guerra da Mata, *Iec Long*, short film. Lisbon: Blackmaria, 2015.

—— *Mahjong*, short film. Vila do Conde: Curtas Metragens C.R.L., 2013.

—— *A Última Vez Que Vi Macau* (*The Last Time I Saw Macao*), film. Lisbon: Blackmaria, 2012.

—— "Entretien et avant-premiére," interview in DVD collection extras, press kit, *L'Integrale*. *João Pedro Rodrigues*, DVD 4: *La dernière fois que j'ai vu Macao*. Lisbon: Blackmaria 2012.

Available at <https://medias.unifrance.org/medias/238/68/83182/presse/la-derniere-fois-que-j-ai-vu-macao-dossier-de-presse-francais.pdf> (last accessed 8 July 2021).
—— *China, China*, film. Lisbon: Blackmaria, 2007.
Romero, George, *Dawn of the Dead*, film. Pittsburgh: Laurel Group, Dawn Associates, 1978.
—— *Night of the Living Dead*, film. Pittsburgh: Image Ten, 1968.
Rolnik, Suely, "The Geopolitics of Pimping," *Transversal* (2006), <http://eipcp.net/transversal/1106/rolnik/en> (last accessed 24 June 2019).
—— "The Body's Contagious Memory: Lygia Clark's Return to the Museum," *Transversal* (2007), <http://eipcp.net/transversal/0507/rolnik/en> (last accessed 24 June 2019).
Rosário, Filipa, "Interview with João Pedro Rodrigues." File recording (Lisbon, 16 June 2019).
—— "Portugal's Year Zero: Emergent Women Directors, 2013–2017," in Mariana Liz and Hilary Owen (eds), *Women's Cinema in Contemporary Portugal* (London: Bloomsbury, 2020), 212–30.
Rosmaninho, João, "Montagem e Cidade: Lisboa no Cinema" (PhD diss., Escola de Arquitectura— Universidade do Minho, 2017).
Rossellini, Roberto, *Paisà (Paisan)*, film. Italy: Organizzazione Film Internazionali (OFI), 1946.
—— *Roma, città aperta (Rome, Open City)*, film. Rome: Excelsa Film, 1945.
Rothenberg, Albert and Sobel, Robert S., "A Creative Process in the Art of Costume Design," *Clothing and Textile Research Journal*, Vol. 1, No. 9 (1990): 27–36.
Roth-Bettoni, Didier, *Les années sida à l'écran* (Cassaniouze: ÉrosOnyx Éditions, 2017).
Ruttmann, Walter, *Berlin – Die Symphonie der Großstadt (Berlin: Symphony of a Great City)*, film, produced by Walter Ruttmann. Paris: Fox Europa Film, 1927. Available at <https://www.youtube.com/watch?v=wY5GdeqOkfc> (last accessed 25 July 2021).
Sadlier, Darlene, *The Portuguese-Speaking Diaspora: Seven Centuries of Literature and the Arts* (Austin: University of Texas Press, 2016).
Sales, Michelle, *Em Busca de um Novo Cinema Português* (Covilhã: Livros LabCom, 2011).
Salles, Cecilia Almeida, "Comunicação em Processo," *Galáxia. Artigos, Análises e Extensões*, No. 3 (2002): 61–71.
—— "Imagens em Construção," *Revista Olhar*, Vol. 2, No. 4 (2000): 1–8.
—— *Gesto Inacabado: Processo de Criação Artística* (São Paulo: FAPESP, Anablume, 1998).
Salvadó-Corretger, Glòria, and Fran Benavente, "The Statuary Condition in Contemporary Portuguese Cinema," *L'Atalante*, No. 22 (2016): 131–42.
Santos, Alberto Seixas, *Mal (Mercy)*, film. Lisbon: Costa do Castelo, 1999.
Sapinho, Joaquim, *Corte de Cabelo (Haircut)*, film. Lisbon: Rosa Filmes, 1995.
Sarris, Andrew, *The Films of Josef von Sternberg* (New York: Museum of Modern Art, 1966).
Schalow, Frank, *The Incarnality of Being: The Earth, Animals, and the Body in Heidegger's Thought* (Albany: State University of New York Press, 2006).
Schefer, Jean-Louis, *Images Mobiles: Récits, visages, flocons* (Paris: P.O.L.,1999).
Schoonover, Karl and Rosalind Galt, "Introduction: Queer, World, Cinema," in Karl Schoonover and Rosalind Galt (eds), *Queer Cinema in the World* (Durham, NC: Duke University Press).
Schweinitz, Jörg, *Film and Stereotype: A Challenge for Cinema and Theory* (New York: Columbia University Press, 2011).
Scorsese, Martin, *Bringing Out the Dead*, film. Los Angeles: De Fina-Cappa, Paramount Pictures, Touchstone Pictures, 1999.
Seabra, Augusto M, "E no início houve o Manuel Reis," *Público*, 26 March 2018, <https://www.publico.pt/2018/03/26/culturaipsilon/cronica/o-homem-que-inventou-uma-lisboa-cosmopolita-1808085> (last accessed 19 June 2019).

Sedeño Valdellós, Ana María, "Imaginarios del Cuerpo y la Memoria en el Cine Portugués Contemporáneo: Reflexiones sobre El Cine de Miguel Gomes y João Pedro Rodrigues," *Revista Científica de Cine y Fotografía*, No. 13 (2016): 267–80.

Sedgwick, Eve Kosofsky, *Touching Feeling: Affect, Pedagogy, Performativity* (Durham, NC and London: Duke University Press, 2003).

Serrão, Adriana Veríssimo, "Environment, Nature, and Landscape: Conceptual Affinities and Distinctions in the Portuguese Context," in Victor K. Mendes and Patrícia Vieira (eds), *Portuguese Literature and the Environment* (Lanham: Rowman & Littlefield, 2019), 31–48.

Sheng, Mingjie and Gu, Chaolin, "Economic growth and development in Macau (1999–2016): The Role of the Booming Gaming Industry," *Cities*, Vol. 75 (2018): 72–80.

Silva, Antônio M. da, "The Portuguese Queer Screen: Gender Possibilities in João Pedro Rodrigues's Cinematic Production," *Rupkatha Journal on Interdisciplinary Studies in Humanities. Special Issue on LGBT & Queer Studies*, Vol. 6, No. 1 (2014): 69–78.

Silvano, Filomena, *De Casa em Casa—Sobre um Encontro entre Etnografia e Cinema* (Caldas da Rainha: Palavrão, 2011).

Simas, Monica, "Macau: A Plural Literature?," *Asian Diasporic Visual Cultures and the Americas* 2 (2016): 55–67.

Simpson, Tim, "Macau Noir: Chinese Brotherhoods, Casino Capitalism, and the Case of the Post-Socialist Consumer," *Fast Capitalism*, Vol. 8, No. 1 (2011), <https://www.uta.edu/huma/agger/fastcapitalism/8_1/simpson8_1.html> (last accessed 25 October 2019).

Singer, Bryan. *X-Men*, film. Los Angeles: 20th Century Fox, 2000.

Solomon, Stefan, "Self-Portrait of an Exquisite Corpus: An Interview with João Pedro Rodrigues (Part Two)," *Kinoscope*, 15 July 2018, <https://read.kinoscope.org/2018/07/15/self-portrait-exquisite-corpus-interview-joao-pedro-rodrigues-part-two/> (last accessed 18 August 2020).

Sokurov, Alexander, *Mat i syn* (*Mother and Son*), film. London: Artificial Eye, 2007.

Soromenho, Ana, "Quando a noite explodiu na cidade," *Expresso,* 25 March 2018, <https://expresso.pt/cultura/2018-03-25-Quando-a-noite-explodiu-na-cidade> (last accessed 18 July 2019).

—— "A geração Vává," *Expresso, Revista Actual,* 24 April 2004, <http://hemerotecadigital.cm-lisboa.pt/ExposicoesVirtuais/Alvalade/Paineis/CAFEVAVA.pdf> (last accessed 18 July 2019).

Sternberg, Josef von, *Macao*, film. Los Angeles: RKO Radio Pictures, 1952.

—— *Anatahan*, film. Tokyo: Daiwa Production, 1953.

—— *The Shanghai Gesture*, film. Hamburg: Arnold Pressburger Films, 1941.

Sutton, Damian, *Photography, Cinema, Memory: The Crystal Image of Time* (Minneapolis: University of Minnesota Press, 2009).

Tang, Billy, *Ho kong fung wan* (*Casino*), film. Hong Kong: Skylark Production, 1998.

Tat-Chi, Yau, *Am Faa* (*The Longest Nite*), film. Hong Kong: Milky Way Image Company et al, 1998.

Teixeira, Manuel and Margarida Valla, *O Urbanismo Português: Séculos XIII–XVIII: Portugal–Brasil* (Lisbon: Livros Horizonte, 1999).

Thain, Alanna, "A Bird's-Eye View of *Leviathan*," *Visual Anthropology Review*, Vol. 31, No. 1 (Spring 2015): 41–8.

Tieben, Hendrick, "Urban Image Construction in Macau in the First Decade after the 'Handover,' 1999–2008," *Journal of Current Chinese Affairs*, Vol. 38, No. 1 (2009): 49–72.

To, Johnnie, *Fuk sau* (*Vengeance*), film. Hong Kong: Milky Way Image et al, 2009.

—— *Fong juk* (*Exiled*), film. Hong Kong: Milky Way Image et al, 2006.

—— *Joi gin a long* (*Where a Good Man Goes*), film. Hong Kong: Milky Way Image, 1999.

Todorov, Tzvetan, *The Fantastic: A Structural Approach to a Literary Genre*, trans. Richard Howard (Ithaca, NY: Cornell University Press, 1975).

Tomasino, Renato, *Il Costume Cinematográfico* (Rome: Accademia, 1977).

Turner, Kyle, "A Lonely Geography: João Pedro Rodrigues on *O Fantasma*," *Paste Magazine*, 2 August 2018, <https://www.pastemagazine.com/articles/2018/08/a-lonely-geography-joao-pedro-rodrigues-on-o-fanta.html> (last accessed 20 July 2019).

Vernet, Marc, *Figures de l'absence: de l'invisible au cinéma* (Paris: Editions de l'étoile, 1988).

Vieira, Patrícia, "The Nature of Portuguese Cinema: Environment on the Silver Screen," *Journal of Lusophone Studies*, Vol. 2, No. 1 (2017): 112–33.

Villarmea Álvarez, Iván, "Mudar de Perspetiva: A Dimensão Transnacional do Cinema Português Contemporâneo," *Aniki: Revista Portuguesa da Imagem em Movimento*, Vol. 3, No. 1 (2016): 101–20. Available at: <https://aim.org.pt/ojs/index.php/revista/article/view/212> (last accessed 3 November 2020).

Weaver, Jimmy, "Sirens and Flames: The Short Films of João Pedro Rodrigues & João Rui Guerra da Mata," in *Framework: The Journal of Cinema and Media*, Vol. 60, Iss. 2 (2019): 227–34.

—— "Ghosts of Macau: *The Last Time I Saw Macao*'s haunting transnational performance," *Studies in European Cinema*, Vol. 13, No. 1 (2016): 78–86.

Welles, Orson, *Touch of Evil*, film. London: Universal International Pictures, 1958.

Wong, Katrine K. and Wei, C. X. George (eds), *Macao—Cultural Interactions, Literary Representations* (London: Routledge, 2014).

Zhidong, Hao *Macau: History and Society* (Hong Kong: Hong Kong University Press/University of Macau, 2010).

Zucker, Jerry, *Ghost*, film. Los Angeles: Paramount, 1990.

Index